SAVING ALEX

SAVING ALEX

When I Was Fifteen I Told My
Mormon Parents I Was Gay, and
That's When My Nightmare Began

Alex Cooper

with *Joanna Brooks*

HarperOne
An Imprint of HarperCollins*Publishers*

HarperOne

This is a work of nonfiction. The events and experiences detailed herein are all true and have been faithfully rendered as remembered by the author, to the best of her ability. Some names have been changed in order to protect the privacy of individuals involved.

SAVING ALEX. Copyright © 2016 by Alexandra Cooper with Joanna Brooks. All rights reserved. Printed in the United States of America. No part of this book may be used or reproduced in any manner whatsoever without written permission except in the case of brief quotations embodied in critical articles and reviews. For information address HarperCollins Publishers, 195 Broadway, New York, NY 10007.

HarperCollins books may be purchased for educational, business, or sales promotional use. For information please e-mail the Special Markets Department at SPsales@harpercollins.com.
HarperCollins website: http://www.harpercollins.com
HarperCollins®, 🏢 ®, and HarperOne™ are trademarks of HarperCollins Publishers.

FIRST EDITION

Library of Congress Cataloging-in-Publication Data
Cooper, Alex.
Saving Alex : when I was fifteen I told my Mormon parents I was gay, and that's when my nightmare began / Alex Cooper with Joanna Brooks.
    pages cm
ISBN 978–0–06–237460–8 (hardcover)—ISBN 978–0–06–237462–2 (e-book)—ISBN 978–0–06–245529–1 (audio) 1. Cooper, Alex, 1994– 2. Mormon gays—United States—Biography. I. Brooks, Joanna, 1971– author. II. Title.
 BX8695.C57A3 2016
 289.3092—dc23
 [B]

16 17 18 19 20   OV/RRD   10 9 8 7 6 5 4 3 2 1

This book is dedicated to anyone who believes deep inside that they are not broken, no matter what other people say.

CONTENTS

Dead End

"LOOK AT THAT DYKE," came the voice from the dark of the living room as I stood facing the wall, weight from my heavy backpack biting down into my shoulders, pain arcing down my spine.

"You're at a dead end, dyke."

I did not know how many hours I had been standing there, quietly trying to manage the pain by shifting my weight from foot to foot.

"Your family doesn't want you. God has no place for people like you in His plan."

Only the lengthening dark of the afternoon measured the time passing. Only the light and the changing stream of people who came and went from the house hour after hour, day after day— good people who believed that I deserved whatever I was getting and God wanted it that way.

God has a plan for all of us—that's what my parents had raised me to believe. If we followed the plan, God would keep us safe and together as a family, forever.

My parents wanted that most of all. They wanted it so badly that they were willing to send me away, into the hands of strangers who promised they could change me, cure me, whatever it took.

But standing at that wall, the word "dyke" slapping the side of my face, pain biting into my back, I realized that what made me different also made me strong.

I would need that strength to get out and get my family back together again. And to embrace who I really was.

CHAPTER I

Families Are Forever

THEY JUST WANTED ME to be safe.

Why else would my parents have moved to Apple Valley, a little town tucked behind a big ridge of mountains east of Los Angeles and surrounded by miles and miles of sand, yucca, and Joshua trees? The main road that ran through town was named Happy Trails Highway because Roy Rogers and Dale Evans had lived just on the edge of town for many years. That's how it was, once upon a time, when movie stars came to build ranches, ride horses, and get away from the stresses of city life.

Now it was families like mine who were looking to get away— families who wanted their kids to be safe and happy, and they weren't sure they could pull it off, or could afford to pull it off, even in the suburbs. My mom had already had more than her share of stress. Her first husband had died from early onset heart disease, leaving her with my five older brothers and sisters to raise by herself on a nurse's salary. She was a pretty and sensitive redhead, and she was strong in her own way, but I wouldn't call her a fighter. She just wanted to keep everything comfortable for herself and the people she loved—the kind of person who, no matter what was happening around her, made sure that her nails were perfectly manicured.

My mom came from a big Mormon family with eight children and deep roots in the faith. Her father had been a convert but her mother's side of the family had been in the church since its beginnings in the early nineteenth century. Her great-great-great-grandparents had been Mormon pioneers who crossed the plains to Utah, sacrificing everything to live the way they believed. Mom went to church pretty much every Sunday.

Dad wasn't even Mormon yet when he met Mom on a blind date, but eventually he decided to join the church. He never explained why, really, and he was never the type to stand up in Sunday meetings and talk about his conversion or any of his private feelings. Once he did tell me privately that it took him a few months of soul-searching to decide that Mormonism was what he wanted. Maybe it was because Mom would only marry another Mormon. Maybe it was because as a former military man he liked the orderliness of Mormonism, with its strict rules for living and the church's tight top-down organization. Maybe he just wanted a fresh start.

Dad also never really explained what it was about Mom that he fell in love with, or why after just six months he asked her to marry him. It was always clear to me, watching them, that they needed each other. I'm sure he loved the ways she looked after him— cooking, cleaning, keeping the household together—ways in which I'm not sure he could look after himself. As for my mom, it was simple: she always said she married my dad because he was the first person who didn't care that she already had five children. I think they had a silent agreement to look after each other, no matter what, and they stuck to it.

The home my parents made together was surrounded by apricot, pear, and plum trees, which flowered in the springtime and grew heavy with fruit in the summer. There were chickens, roosters, and rabbits in the yard, a reminder of my mom's childhood in a farmhouse in a little California ranch town called Ojai. Our street was the kind where a bunch of kids were always out, riding bikes or scooters until the sun went down. Inside the house, pictures of Jesus hung on the walls, and on the entry table was a little wooden tree with Mom's and Dad's names painted on the trunk, and my name and the names of all my brothers and sisters painted on the branches.

My dad had a job selling mortgages that took him all over Southern California, driving from place to place with a thick briefcase of paperwork, helping other families get into the houses they wanted for their kids. Early in the morning he would get into his big, loud pickup truck, and by the time he got home, I was often asleep. My mom really loved being a stay-at-home mother, even after raising five kids from her first marriage, so she quit her job as a nurse and stayed home with me. After school, she would pick me up, and I would sit at the kitchen table and do my homework. She would make dinner for the two of us, and then we would lie on the couch and watch television, snuggling under our favorite blue-and-white afghan with yarn fringe and tassels on the corners. I'd lie there with my mom and run my fingers through the fringe, untangling the knots as the sun went down and the house got darker, until there was just the light from the television screen.

I was baptized at eight years old, just like all Mormon kids. And just like in most traditional Mormon families, my father performed the baptism. Every night my father was home we had family prayer before I went to bed. My parents would come into my bedroom, and we would all kneel at the side of my bed and fold our hands on the purple-and-green-flowered bedspread. Usually it was my dad who said the prayer for all of us, out loud. He would ask Heavenly Father to watch over us and keep us safe.

I especially loved Monday nights because my parents would sit down and teach me lessons from a church manual, and we'd have homemade treats. Mormon families the world over did the same thing on Monday nights; we called it Family Home Evening.

But there were signs even when I was young that I was the kind of person who couldn't stay in a place like Apple Valley for long. School I found dreadfully boring, and even in elementary school I fought my mom about going. When I got there, I goofed off to kill the boredom. I also fought her over piano, karate, and ballet lessons. Looking back, I remember arguing with my parents a lot and always getting into trouble. I was a bit of a handful at times—rowdy and independent.

But being strong willed and spirited also had its benefits. One time I organized all the kids on the block to build a tree house for me. I had asked my dad to build me one, but he hadn't gotten around to it, so when he got home from work and found me directing a group of five or six neighborhood kids cutting up the wood, I think that's when he realized it would be better for everyone if he finished the project. When he'd completed it, a ladder went up to the tree house, and built-in seating benches were inside. It even had a basket you could raise and lower. I loved it. I would stay up in that tree house all day when I could, reading *Little House on the Prairie* books—the whole set, over and over again.

My big dream was to grow up and become a lawyer in New York City. Not that I knew any lawyers, especially women lawyers. But one of the shows Mom and I loved to watch was *Law & Order*. I felt outraged watching bad things happen to good people, especially watching good people go to jail. I loved watching the gray-haired prosecutor put a case together and try to get things to turn out right. I wanted to help. And the fact that I was really good at arguing— with my parents, for example—could only be an asset.

But all that seemed so far away. Even when I was goofing off or talking back or riding my purple go-cart a little too fast down the street, I could not imagine a life apart from my parents. I can see now that when I was testing them it was because I wanted to know they loved me. I wanted to belong to them as badly as they wanted to keep me safe.

When I was about ten, my oldest brother came home for a visit. He was in his twenties then—tall, with big muscles, not married, but going to community college and feeling newly serious about his life. He made a special point of sitting me down in my bedroom for a talk. We sat side by side on my flowered bedspread.

"Alex," he said, "do you have a testimony? Do you know the church is true?"

He wanted to know if I felt as strongly as he did about being Mormon, if I believed in everything I learned on Sundays, if I believed as he did that our religion had the answers we needed to get us safely back to heaven.

I wanted to make him happy. I looked at my brother and I nodded my head. He smiled.

"I just have this really good feeling," he continued, "that Jesus is going to come back before we die."

In church sometimes my Sunday school teachers would show us a picture of Jesus coming down through the clouds, surrounded by hundreds of angels. We talked about the Second Coming and how it would solve so many problems.

"I think we're the generation," my brother told me, smiling. We would be the ones to see it happen in our lifetimes, to make it happen even.

I remember looking at my brother and a warm feeling washed over me. I felt excited by the idea that we would be the ones to see Jesus come back. I wanted to have a testimony. I wanted to believe, I really did.

We all wanted to believe that everything would work out, that our home and our faith could save us. If we just kept to all the rules, if we held it all together, our family would be safe and together forever. We'd be protected against the stresses and dangers of the outside world—that's what our religion promised, and my parents worked for it every day.

Who can blame them for feeling this way, really?

I don't blame them still.

CHAPTER 2

Cracks in the Plan

W HEN I WAS ABOUT ten years old we moved from the big house in Apple Valley to a smaller place in Victorville, another desert town just a few miles down the highway. Our new house was a tile-roofed, beige stucco two-story at the end of a cul-de-sac, on a street full of tile-roofed, beige stucco two-story houses.

Our very first Sunday morning in the new house, I stood in the kitchen in my pajamas, begging my mom to let me stay home from church. "Mom," I pleaded, "I'm not going to know anyone!"

But my begging did not work. Church was one of the things that held our world together.

Sunday mornings would start early, with the sound of my dad getting into the shower. He'd shave, put on a white shirt and a tie, get into his truck, and drive down to the church building for early administrative meetings with the men of the ward, the Mormon term for a local congregation. He was as serious about it as his job—maybe even more so. It wasn't that he talked a lot around the house about God or Mormon doctrine or what it was that made him believe. It was more like he was a responsible man who had been given a serious responsibility, and he meant to fulfill it.

An hour after my dad left, my mom would get up, shower, and do her hair and makeup in the bedroom mirror. She put extra care into her long red hair on Sundays, blowing it dry and curling it with a fat curling iron. I loved to sit and watch her. To me, she was never more beautiful than when she got ready on Sunday mornings.

The church building in Victorville looked pretty much like all the other LDS Church buildings. It was built to last on the standard Salt Lake City plan, designed to hold hundreds of Mormons and their big families, with thick beige brick walls, scratchy standard-issue grass-cloth wallpaper lining the hallways, floral-print uphol-stered couches in the foyers, wooden pews in the chapel, and metal folding chairs, chalkboards, and tables in all the classrooms. A green lawn stretched out around it, then abruptly stopped, its neat edges marking the boundary against the desert all around us.

Church lasted three hours every Sunday. We'd sit on wooden pews for the first hour to sing hymns, hear talks from other members of the congregation, and take a bread-and-water sacrament, then we'd move into little classrooms for the next two hours, where we'd sit in a circle of metal folding chairs while our teachers bal-anced poster-board-backed pictures of Jesus on their knees as they read from the manuals church leaders wrote in Salt Lake City.

Three hours. I was never the kind of kid who made it through church patiently. But the older I got, the longer those hours seemed and the more I resisted going to church, the same way I had resisted going to karate, soccer, and even school. I realize now I was some-what of a handful, but in many ways, I was just trying to figure out who I was and how I fit into the plan set out for me.

Meeting Ashley and Brianna changed all that.

Just a few days after our first Sunday in Victorville, there came a knock on our front door. My mom answered, with me on her heels.

Cathy Flores—blond, with a round face and twinkly eyes—stood on the doorstep, smiling and holding a paper plate of homemade snickerdoodle cookies in her hands. Next to her were her three daughters, Angela, Pamela, and Brianna, all three of them dark haired, big boned, and bursting with mischief.

Before Sister Flores—we called all the adults at church "Brother" and "Sister"—could so much as introduce herself, Angela, Pamela, and Brianna just stepped past my mom and over the threshold.

"Girls!" Sister Flores yelled, horrified. "Get back outside."

"No way," said Angela, the oldest. She wore big square dark sunglasses, and her black hair was cut in a cute shag that framed her face.

"Come on in, everyone," said Pamela, who elbowed her way in, then planted her feet in the entryway and did a dramatic bow. She wore her hair in a short bob.

I made eye contact with Brianna, the youngest daughter, who looked to be about my age. Her smile revealed a mouth full of braces. Her hair was streaked with blond.

I knew right away that the Flores sisters and I would become fast friends.

They showed up unannounced again the next week, Tuesday night, when an activity for girls was scheduled down at the church. I looked out my bedroom window to see Sister Flores's big white passenger van rattle into our driveway, kicking up a bit of dust. Out piled Pamela, Angela, and Brianna. Their laughter penetrated the walls of the house. And they didn't even knock on the front door this time. They walked right through the door, down the hall, and into my bedroom, picked me up by my shoulders and ankles, and carried me back to the van.

"We're kidnapping you," Angela said. "You have no choice."

There were about three hundred people in our congregation. Brother Flores—Angela, Pamela, and Brianna's dad—was the bishop, the man in charge of taking care of us all. Not that being a religious leader was his job; he was a welder, and he had been asked to take on the job of bishop as a volunteer, just as everyone else in the church volunteered for their jobs. Bishop Flores was born in El Salvador and had moved to California when he was a teenager. He converted and married Sister Flores, and together they had four children: the three girls and their older brother, Sergio. Bishop Flores loved his family and loved to have his fun. Every summer he'd take them on long camping trips down at the beach in San Diego, to ride boogie boards all day and roast marshmallows over the fire at night. At home, he always joked around with his kids, and soon, as we settled into Victorville and I began spending long hours with the Flores girls, that came to include me too.

"Alex! Those shorts! They are too short!"

Bishop Flores would greet me with mock outrage every time I came over to the house. He was right, of course. The church put a lot of emphasis on modest dress, including requiring that shorts and dresses reach the top of the kneecap. But long shorts fit neither the hot desert weather nor our sense of fashion. Angela, Pamela, Brianna, and I wore the same low-waisted, bottom-skimming shorts every other girl in the desert did. Bishop Flores accepted his powerlessness with a sense of humor.

Sister Flores stood about five feet four. She was a stay-at-home mom, the kind who always seemed preoccupied with taking care of everyone and everything. Her job in the ward was to lead, teach, and look after all the girls. That job fit right in with Sister Flores's natural inclination to worry, and frankly, we were a lot to look after.

Along with Angela, Pamela, Brianna, and me, our ward had about fifteen girls my age in it. Among them, our friend Ashley Lopez was like Brianna and me: she was funny, spirited, and a bit mischievous. Her dad was a child welfare agent who worked for the next county over, so just like my dad, he'd get up early every morning and commute long distances from the desert through the mountain passes just to get to work. Ashley was the youngest of five. She had long dark hair, china-doll skin, and lips always painted bright red, and despite the fact that she was a big girl—about five feet seven inches tall and two hundred and fifty pounds—she had this squeaky, high-pitched voice that sounded really obnoxious until you got used to it.

Ashley, Brianna, and I found ways to make those long Sunday hours more entertaining. We would stuff our scripture cases with fruit snacks and granola bars and snack our way through sacrament meeting. We would find reasons to leave the chapel: a bathroom break, a drinking fountain break—anything to get up and take a lap of the building, to meet in one of the empty classrooms, draw on the chalkboard, and have a laugh, before returning to the chapel to take our places next to our parents so we wouldn't get in too much trouble.

But deep down I did want to have a testimony, like everyone else who got up during testimony meeting. I knew my parents both had a testimony. I wanted to share their certainty. I wanted to feel what my older brother felt when he'd sat me down on my bed to tell me about Jesus coming back to earth. I wanted to be able to stand up at the pulpit and say that I knew the church was true and that I knew it beyond a shadow of a doubt.

It did take hold in me, what I learned sitting in those wooden pews and on those metal folding chairs, Sunday after Sunday. Mormonism taught that our spirits, our souls, lived with God in heaven before this life. Earth had been created as a place where we could gain experience, make choices, and learn from them. We all chose to come here, to exercise what my teachers called "free agency"— the power to choose and be accountable for our choices. Even when we chose poorly or made mistakes, there was a way to return to be with God again, through repentance, through forgiveness, through Jesus Christ. No matter what happened here in this confusing world, we could be together someday, as families. If we followed the plan, families could be together in heaven. This was the core of my Mormonism. This was what my parents, my Sunday school teachers, Bishop and Sister Flores, all the people in the ward who stood at the microphone to bear their testimonies on Sunday, taught me, week after week.

I found it comforting. Even at ten or eleven years old, I wanted to know what would happen to me after I died. As much as I wanted to makes jokes in the back pew or sneak out of church with Brianna and Ashley, I also wanted to know that life made sense, that there was a purpose, that there was some meaning to it all, that if I followed the plan, everything would be okay. That families would be together forever, laughing and joking as we did then. As much as I wanted to get out of Apple Valley, and then Victorville, out of these small desert towns, I also wanted to roast marshmallows around the fire with the Flores family or stay on the couch with my mom under that blue-and-white afghan. Forever. I wanted to be with my family forever.

But one day I realized there were some gaps in the plan my teachers so carefully laid out for me. The plan might not keep me safe after all.

I was sitting in my Sunday school class, and the lesson was about families. My teacher, Sister Chapman, sat with a poster-board-backed picture of a Mormon temple balanced on her knees. "When a husband and a wife are married in the temple," she said, "they are sealed for eternity."

Sister Chapman wore pink lipstick. Her voice was calm and sweet.

"All of the children born to parents who are sealed in the temple get to be together with them as a family for eternity too."

I thought of the "Families Are Forever" wooden tree on the entryway table back at home, with the names of all my older brothers and sisters—all the children from my mom's first marriage. I looked at the picture of the Salt Lake City temple balanced on Sister Chapman's knees, with its great spires and gray granite walls and the golden angel Moroni perched proudly on top. My own parents, I realized, had not been sealed in the temple. My mom had been sealed to her first husband, but church policy prohibited her from being sealed to her second husband, my dad. When it came time to get married, they had just driven across the desert to Las Vegas. The rules said that no matter how much they loved each other, theirs would be a marriage for time only.

That's when it struck me: my older brothers and sisters were sealed to Mom and their dad. But Mom and my dad had not been married in the temple. Was I sealed to anyone?

I raised my hand.

"Sister Chapman," I asked, "can families be sealed twice?"

She looked at me, starting to put the pieces behind my question together. A pitying look came over her face. "No."

I sat quietly in my seat, absorbing the implications of the idea. Sun came through the frosted glass of the classroom windows. I felt a hotness in my chest. Who would I be with in heaven? Was my family not forever?

A few weeks later, one Saturday afternoon over at Ashley's house, I told Brother Lopez about the Sunday school lesson. "Who will I be with in heaven?" I asked.

He paused, then looked at me kindly. "Alex," he said, "I don't know, but don't you think Heavenly Father will work it out for us?"

That's what everyone told me: my teachers, the bishop, my parents. If I made it to heaven, would I not have a family? Who would I be with? Who would I spend eternity with? Would I get to be with my parents? They couldn't answer my questions, but they felt certain that God would work something out. And they assured me I could feel the same way if I just prayed about it.

AT NIGHT, I LAY in my bed under the purple-and-green covers and prayed out all my questions. I looked at the ceiling and talked out loud to God. I waited. I listened. I heard my mother finishing the dishes in the kitchen. I heard the sound of cars on the highway far away. But that feeling of certainty did not come. On Sundays, I found myself looking at the families in the pews all around me.

Everyone seemed to be happily sitting together, singing the hymns, content in feeling they had all the answers. For them, it seemed everything was safe, as long as they followed the plan. But my little family—my dad, my mom, and me—if there was a crack in the plan, I had found it, and my family seemed to fall right through it.

Seeing the cracks in the plan didn't stop me from wanting it to work. It didn't stop me from wanting to belong just like everyone else. Even if we were rebels, for Brianna and Ashley and me, church was like a home. Being Mormon was a huge part of our lives, and even when we misbehaved, we never imagined leaving it.

I remember sitting around a campfire at church camp one night when I was twelve, watching all these girls my age—there must have been two hundred Mormon girls from all over Southern California up there at camp together—stand up, walk down to the campfire, and bear their testimonies. One after another, each one said how grateful they were for God, how much they loved the church and their families.

Even Brianna went down and stood by the campfire. "I want to be with my family forever," she said, tears rolling down her cheeks. "Someday, I want to have a family of my own."

I felt the warm, pine-scented air close around me and listened to the sound of hundreds of teenage girls crying softly in the dark and leaning into one another. All around me, I could feel a deep yearning for belonging and safety.

That's when I realized how it would go. We would make our trouble, Brianna, Ashley, Pamela, and me. We would have our doubts. Maybe I would take a break from it all for a few years and strike out on my own. But someday we would end up back in the church and get married. We would sit with our families in the pews, and we would be the leaders then and drive our girls to girls' camp.

It would all come around in the end. The idea was so comforting.

Even when I had no answers about who I would be with in heaven, I couldn't imagine my life on earth going any other way.

CHAPTER 3

Just This One Girl

SOMETHING ELSE WAS GNAWING at me—something I could not even find words for yet but that I sensed might stand in the way of my fitting into the plan my parents and church teachers had so carefully taught me.

It started in seventh grade. With a girl named Samantha.

Samantha was tall, really tall, and had red hair. Ginger-colored freckles spiraled across her cheekbones. She was in orchestra with me at University Preparatory School. There was a seventh-grade orchestra, an eighth-grade orchestra, and a high school orchestra for the most advanced musicians. I was only a seventh grader, and Samantha was in eighth, but we both played in the high school orchestra, and we both played cello.

For as much as I fought against many of the things my parents tried to get me to do—school and church, for one, but also other activities—I loved playing cello. I loved bending into my bow and moving my fingers over the strings, loved shutting myself up in my room and confronting the challenge of the music. Whenever I was bored or angry, I would go into my room and play my cello, and it felt like a kind of traveling—like leaving Victorville, leaving all the identical beige two-story stucco houses and the growing tensions in my relationship with my parents—leaving all of it far, far behind me.

For a while, Samantha was first-chair cello, and I was second. But she never talked to me. We would sit side by side in orchestra, holding our cellos between our knees, bent over our bows, while Mr. O'Rane, the orchestra teacher, stood in front of the class and barked directions.

I barely heard the directions. I was too busy looking at Samantha's shoes. The school dress code specified black shoes only. But Samantha broke code all the time. She'd roll her plaid burgundy uniform skirt up or wear bright purple canvas tennis shoes. Above the shoes, I noticed, pale ginger freckles dotted Samantha's shins, knees, and thighs.

Samantha was the girl who knew all the answers. I liked that. Every time Mr. O'Rane asked a question in orchestra class, Samantha was the first with her hand up. As she answered, I would look down and count the freckles on her calves.

This is like a crush, I thought, even though I'd really never had a crush before—on anyone. *This is weird. Really weird.*

I don't know why I decided to challenge Samantha for first chair, but I did, and so there we sat one day in front of the orchestra class. She played the Brandenburg Concerto No. 4, third movement. I watched her closely, watched the wrinkles of concentration form across the bridge of her freckled nose, watched her feet planted firmly on the floor in those purple canvas tennis shoes. No question, she was good, and hungry to keep her seat. I was super nervous, and my stomach ached as it always did when nerves got the best of me. But I knew I was really good too, and I made it through the piece without a single error.

A few days later, Mr. O'Rane held me after class. "Alex," he said, "you made first chair."

Not long after, Samantha and I started talking on the phone at night. Soon she was coming over to hang out. We would play scavenger hunt with all the kids in the neighborhood. Sometimes we would go for walks or just sit on the couch under the blue-and-white-fringed blanket and watch TV. I knew Samantha liked boys. We even talked about the boys she liked sometimes. There was this boy, Wesley, who was in the chamber orchestra with us after school. I sat next to him in Spanish class. She would always talk about Wesley.

I've never had a friend like this before, I thought, my toes curling under the blanket. *This is weird and not right.*

I didn't know what it was and why I felt this way.

And when she'd leave, I'd go to my room and write about Samantha in my journal. I'd write long paragraphs describing hanging out with her and what we did, what we watched on television, how much I liked her.

Weird, I kept thinking. *This is really weird.*

There was this one night, the summer after seventh grade. It was June, school had just ended, and the desert was getting really hot. Samantha had been over to hang out all afternoon, had stayed through dinner, and was planning to spend the night. We had been swimming in the pool and were lying poolside, warming ourselves on the concrete.

Samantha was wearing a pink-and-purple-striped two-piece. I was wearing a red one-piece with little anchors embroidered into the fabric. My mom only let me wear one-piece bathing suits because that was the rule at church—for modesty's sake.

I lay there on the pavement, the water from my bathing suit pooling on the concrete and then evaporating into the dry night air. I could feel Samantha lying just a few feet away. She was talking about something—I don't know what; I couldn't follow the words. I could just feel her a few feet away.

I wanted to hold her hand. I really wanted to hold her hand.

But I did not hold her hand. I just lay there and felt the dry, hot desert air press down on my back and a knot of nausea in my belly. That's how I felt whenever I was nervous.

THE SUMMER BEFORE NINTH grade, my parents moved me from University Prep to Encore, a private performing arts high school in the next town over. Encore was supposed to be a harder school, and I'm sure they thought I needed the discipline. The ambition and determination that got me to first chair in the school orchestra could make me pretty hardheaded and difficult at home. I would yell and slam doors. My dad once took the door off my bedroom for a month just to spare the house the noise.

But one of the good things about growing up in church was that it gave us this extended family, so when things were too difficult at home, my mom could just send me over to the Flores', where she felt I'd be safe. By high school, I was hanging out at the Flores' house all the time. Brianna, Pamela, and I, we'd lounge around on the big living room couches and watch television, or sit on the hammock in the backyard, picking roses from the Flores' rosebushes, or talk and goof off on the grass. Sister Flores made the best food in the world—Salvadoran food, *pupusas:* thick little tortilla-like corn cakes filled with cheese or beans or shrimp. She'd form a ball of *masa* in her hands, roll it out on the counter, sprinkle or spoon in the fillings, lay another *masa* circle across the top, crimp the edges, and brown the *pupusa* in a big skillet on the stove.

Not long before, Pamela had introduced me to smoking pot. She showed me how to rig cardboard paper towel tubes with perfumed dryer sheets so that after we took long pulls of smoke we could filter the smell through the tube, exhaling undetected. I didn't know how to explain it then, but I think what drew me to pot was that it calmed the anxiety I had about my future and how I would get out of Victorville. It also calmed the anxiety I had picked up from my parents. I knew how badly they wanted things to be okay for me. I felt the long, long hours my dad was gone. I would hear his car start in the early desert dark and pull out of our cul-de-sac, heading toward the highways that took him from the high desert to sell mortgages to clients in suburban Los Angeles—families just as anxious about making ends meet as he was. My parents were always stressed, and they hated where we lived, the rows of identical houses, day after day with identical worries, with the only break being church and its promises of safety and happiness forever. I could feel their anxieties mounting. Of course I didn't make it easier for them, but when I was high, I felt it all sort of blur out and the pressure ease. I could talk to them and feel that everything was really going to be okay. We all just wanted to feel okay, to feel safe.

Most of the time Pamela just hung around the house with her friend Jenny. Jenny was really, really tall and had long black hair; her last name was tattooed across her lower back in cursive writing, embellished by stars and butterflies. I was both fascinated and repelled by Pamela's relationship with Jenny. Jenny was from Los Angeles; she had met Pamela at a party in the desert. They were gay or at least experimenting with their sexuality, and they clearly loved each other, and this was something I'd never seen before: a gay couple. Not in Victorville. Especially not a Mormon girl. Jenny and Pamela always seemed to be in some sort of fight. It was clear that they were a couple, but everyone pretended not to notice. Until I asked directly.

"Yeah," Brianna told me one afternoon out on the hammock, "Jenny is Pamela's girlfriend."

Brianna was so abrupt about it, so blunt—trying to pretend that Pamela's having a girlfriend was totally obvious and she was okay with it. But I could sense that it made her uncomfortable. Her eyes did not leave the ground after she told me, and she started to swing the hammock underneath us a little bit faster. Having a gay sister was not in the standard Mormon family plan, and I don't think Brianna knew how to absorb the idea. As I watched her sit with her discomfort, I realized I wasn't uncomfortable at all—just curious.

A few days later, I found Pamela alone in the upstairs bedroom she shared with her sister Angela. Sister Flores had decorated the room in an Audrey Hepburn theme. The walls were painted purple. A chandelier hung from the ceiling, and photos of Audrey as Holly Golightly in *Breakfast at Tiffany's* adorned the walls.

"So." I pushed the words out, tentative but determined. "Are you gay?"

Pamela was sitting on her bed. She fixed me with a look. "No," she said. "It's just—it's just Jenny. Just this one."

She paused for a moment.

"Alex, I just know someday I'm going to marry a returned missionary and have kids." She put the words out there with a sense of conviction. She wanted me to believe her, and she wanted to believe it herself. I could feel that deep, familiar pull inside me, longing for everything to turn out okay for Pamela, and for me too.

I nodded. "Totally."

I felt how badly she wanted it to be true, the pressure of her hope, her expectation.

That's what Pamela always said after that. It was just this one girl. One girl and then she would straighten up and get married in the temple, just as we had all been taught. The way we knew, the right way. The way that would get us safely home, home to the houses with bedrooms we would decorate for our daughters and kitchens where we would stand over the stove and make them warm *pupusas* to eat.

DAD STARTED HEADING OUT Sunday evenings on the long drive to start his workweek. His business was slowing down, and I could tell it made him worried. He started putting in a few extra hours. When Dad was away, Mom started spending more and more time at the Flores' house, and Sister Flores started coming over to ours.

They would sit at the kitchen table, or one would sit while the other cooked dinner. Sometimes they talked about my mom going back to nursing and picking up shifts at the hospital, but my mom said she wasn't ready yet. They'd have the television on, dialed into a Lifetime movie or maybe the local news.

One afternoon over at the Flores' house, my mom and Sister Flores were sitting in the kitchen talking, with the television on, and pictures flashed across the screen of gay people getting married in Vermont. California had just come through a long fight over gay marriage, and the issue was a very big deal for Mormons. You have to be married in a Mormon temple in order to get into the highest levels of heaven. At church they told us that it was up to us to protect the family, that legalizing gay marriage would destroy the family and go against God's plan, that families—straight families—were meant to be forever, and that if gay people were allowed to get married, they could sue and shut down the Mormon temples where eternal marriages took place.

"It's just so wrong," my mom said to Sister Flores, almost offhandedly, as a gray-haired woman kissed another gray-haired woman on-screen. One woman wore a purple pantsuit. The other clutched daisies in her hands.

I had been passing by the kitchen but could see the images on the TV. I stopped just within earshot to hear what they'd say next. My parents didn't talk much about these things to me, but I was not surprised by how my mom felt.

"You know," Sister Flores said in a confiding tone, "Pamela was gay once. Or thought she was."

I froze in my tracks, waiting to hear what my mom would say next.

She must have just nodded or not known how to respond to Sister Flores's confession about Pamela. I didn't hear her say anything at all.

CHAPTER 4

Opening Up

I FIRST MET YVETTE IN April of my sophomore year. I was starting a recycling program at my school. I asked my mom to drive me to Home Depot, where I got giant plastic garbage bins, and I took them to the Flores'. Sister Flores had a ton of craft supplies, and I figured she would have spray paints so that I could stencil recycling signs on the sides of the cans. I was right, of course: she had paint in every color, and she was happy to let me use it.

Brianna and I dragged the garbage bins into the backyard and rolled them over onto their sides on the lawn between the hammock and the roses. We shook up the rattling spray-paint cans and aimed them at the stencils we'd taped to the sides of the bins. Pamela opened the sliding door from the house out to the yard.

"Honey, I'm home." This was her typical greeting. That and asking where the food was.

She stepped into the backyard, and right behind her came this pretty girl. She was petite—like five foot one—but wore giant wedge heels and short shorts that showed off the curves at the tops of her legs. Her long black hair fell to the lower part of her back.

"Brianna, Alex, meet my friend Yvette," Pamela said.

Yvette smiled but didn't say much. Pamela talked with Brianna for a few minutes, and I kept my eyes on my stencils and the spray paints, wondering who exactly Yvette was but not knowing quite how to ask. Later that night, after I had finished my trash cans and Yvette had left, I made Pamela fill me in. She had met Yvette at a rave near Los Angeles. She was eighteen years old, Pamela said, and gay.

A few days later, Brianna and I were sprawled out on the couch at the Flores' house, watching a Disney movie. Ashley bounced in with a brand-new kite.

"You guys!" she said in her comical, high-pitched voice. "Let's go to the park."

On our way out the front door, we met Pamela and Yvette, and they both turned around and walked with us to the neighborhood park.

We all started taking turns trying to launch the kite, running back and forth across the park lawns. After a few tries, Yvette and I peeled away to go sit on the swings.

"How do you know the Floreses?" she asked.

I told her about church, how my mom was friends with Sister Flores, and I told her about the first time the Flores girls burst into my house without permission.

Yvette had perched her small frame on the edge of the swing. Her dark hair grazed the small of her back, the top of her hips. She kept asking questions, about what I liked to do, about school, about my family. She seemed really interested in me, and I found myself opening up more and more to her as we sat side by side on the playground swings while Brianna, Pamela, and Ashley dissolved into laughter on the grass lawn behind us.

I barely knew her, but I realized I wanted to tell her everything. She had such a great way of making me feel comfortable and fully myself.

Over the next week at the Flores' house, while Brianna, Pamela, and Ashley crashed out on the couches in front of yet another Disney movie, Yvette and I would go upstairs and sit on the beds in Pamela's room. She would sit on Pamela's bed and I would sit on Angela's. We'd clear a couple of spaces amid the piles of clothes and books and dishes—the room was always a disaster—and sit cross-legged and talk under the chandelier and the watchful gaze of Audrey Hepburn.

I told Yvette about how rough things were at home sometimes, mostly on account of my own stubbornness. I told her about my dad's long hours and my mom's sensitivity, the way she had cried when my brother joined the military, the way she would spring me out of school for donuts and bad television sometimes, anxiously longing to keep her family together. I told her about playing the cello and how happy it made me. I told her about how badly I wanted to get out of Victorville, how bored I had felt for most of my life, how I was always making trouble, how much I wanted to be a lawyer and live in New York City someday.

Yvette told me that she'd never live in New York, that Los Angeles was the place for her—really, the best place of all, in her opinion. She told me that she'd lived there for a little while, in a brick-faced third-floor walk-up in a neighborhood near downtown full of real *pupuserias* and Korean liquor stores. She loved to drive the city at night, she said, the long boulevards from downtown to the Westside—Pico, Olympic, Wilshire—how the city changed as you headed west and toward the sunsets, which the smog made even more beautiful. But she had to leave LA to move back to Tucson, where she was from, to look after her grandparents. Her dad was dead, she said; her mom was not well. Yvette visited California as often as she could.

Yvette didn't have a job, this much I knew, but she did have a red Jeep and never seemed to be hurting for money. How that worked, exactly, I wasn't sure. But one day, in the upstairs bedroom,

I found out. Yvette told me that she made her living by growing and selling pot. I thought it was crazy, this petite, pretty, openly gay eighteen-year-old who made her own money like that and knew her way around the big city. I'd never met anyone quite like her.

The spring days at the Flores' stretched out, full of bad television reruns like *Boy Meets World,* smoking pot with the two older sisters when the parents weren't watching, and Salvadoran food, or tray after tray of cookies fresh from Sister Flores's oven. It was the spring when MGMT's "Electric Feel" video broke.

Oooh girl. Shock me like an electric eel. Baby girl. Turn me on with your electric feel.

The people in the video all seemed so happy and free to me, and the lush rivers and thick forests seemed just the opposite of Victorville.

Do what you feel now, electric feel now.

I could feel something building between me and Yvette, a friendship, maybe more, and tension building between me and Brianna too, because Brianna didn't like Yvette. She thought she was a bad influence on Pamela, who by then was getting closer and closer with her girlfriend Jenny, spending nights at Jenny's house, with the parents seemingly oblivious to what was going on. Maybe Brianna thought Yvette, who had never hid that part of herself, brought it out in Pamela. I wondered what it was like to be gay and not feel weird about it. But even this I did not really know how to ask.

One Saturday afternoon in May, when we were all sitting around at the Flores', Yvette decided she'd had enough of Disney movies and cookies. "Let's go to LA," she said.

"No thanks," Brianna said immediately.

"Alex?" Yvette looked at me and smiled, a question mark in her eyes. "I'll drive," she volunteered.

I wanted to go so badly. My mind immediately started devising ways to get out of town overnight without telling my parents. Of course they would never let me. I was only fifteen years old! But maybe if I told them I was spending the night with Jenny, Pamela's girlfriend, who they loved—and they seemingly had *no clue* that she was gay—it just might work.

"Give me an hour," I said and headed back to my house to leave a note and pack. Yvette came with me.

I knew it was wrong, of course I did. I even felt bad as I wrote my parents the note and left it on the kitchen table, telling them that I'd be at Jenny's for the night if they needed to find me. I changed into my cutest outfit: a red miniskirt, a white T-shirt, and flowered shoes. I threw shorts and a T-shirt into a duffel bag. I felt very nervous, and so, so excited.

I headed for the front door and pulled it shut behind me. I had asked Yvette to park and wait for me down the block, a safe distance from my house. There she was, in her red hardtop Jeep, smiling behind the wheel.

I climbed up into the front seat of the Jeep. My belly felt as tingly and nauseated as it did that night lying out by the pool with Samantha. I was so nervous I had absolutely no idea what to say.

It was about seventy miles to Los Angeles. We headed out from Victorville, past Apple Valley, past the stands of Joshua trees, into the foothills on the east side of the San Bernardino Mountains. Yvette loved reggae, and she played reggae as the Jeep rolled down I-15, over the rocky top of the Cajon Pass, down through a layer of smog into the eight-lane traffic of Los Angeles. Open spaces filled in with miles of strip malls, warehouses, auto dealerships, apartment complexes.

"Can I hold your hand?" Yvette asked.

I nodded.

I had held hands with a boy before—a dreadlocked twelfth-grader—and I'd even kissed him one afternoon, sitting in the cab of his truck in the school parking lot. At first, it had felt like nothing, kissing him, but then I'd felt kind of grossed out. I'd even felt my throat tighten a bit, as if I were going to gag, and not just on the smell of cigarettes in his car ashtray. This car ride with Yvette, holding hands—this felt so totally different, an enormous arc of intense emotions pressing from my heart against my ribcage. I didn't have words for any of it, the nervousness, the excitement, the anticipation, and, yes, some worry too. What would I tell my parents when I went back? Could I tell them anything? Surely they wouldn't approve. Was it better to just disappear in the city for a few hours, me and Yvette, anonymous, not to be found out?

We reached downtown as the sun was going down over the city, and it's true, the smog did make it more beautiful, a violently red and purple sky behind the skyscrapers. As we headed west, Yvette pointed out the neighborhoods where she had lived the last time she was here before she'd had to move back to Tucson. We soon reached the end of the freeway, and the ocean: Santa Monica.

Yvette parked the Jeep and checked us into a little hotel a few blocks off the Santa Monica Pier. Right away, we took blankets from the bed and closet and headed down the cliff to the beach. The air was getting cool and damp, and it carried the smell of night-blooming jasmine. To our left was the famous pier-top amusement park at Santa Monica, with yellow and green and purple neon, and the great Ferris wheel going around. Bright lights reflected on the soft black water below, the water moving through and around the pylons holding up the pier. I found it beautiful and thrilling, even more charged with electricity being here with Yvette. I could feel all the excitement, the miles of anticipation from our long drive into the city, build up in my body, building to this moment.

I knew she was going to kiss me, and I meant to let her. Even though I had kissed a boy before, I knew this was going to be different. I just tried to keep breathing. Sure enough, as soon as we set the blankets down and sat, she grabbed my hand and kissed me. Lots of kissing, all kissing. As the traffic wound on and the Ferris wheel turned and a stray person or two made their way down the wide, sandy beach, as the night got later and later. My phone batteries died, and it was like we were a million miles away from Victorville and no one could find us. Between kissing and the sounds of the ocean, I thought the night was just perfect.

I don't know why the cops didn't come to kick us off the beach, but they didn't. It must have been five in the morning when we finally made it back to the hotel room for just a few hours of sleep before I roused and remembered to plug in my phone.

Immediately, the screen filled with notifications of text messages, and I felt panic in my belly. I read the transcript of the night on the screen. Pamela had gotten super worried. My mom had been asking a lot of questions. The night had grown longer and Pamela hadn't heard from us. Finally, she had told my mom that I had snuck out of the house. I knew I was in big trouble.

It was time to go back to Victorville—this much there was no escaping. I woke Yvette and we started the drive away from the ocean, back through the congested miles of malls and auto dealerships, into the desert, over the mountains, and home. I was sick with nervousness, and Yvette was nervous too, which only made my panic worse, because I had come to think of her as the worldly one with all the answers.

"I promise," she kept saying, "I'll see you again soon."

When we pulled into my neighborhood, I could see a cop car parked in front of my house. I told Yvette to drive around the block and drop me off down the street.

I walked through the front door. Everyone was waiting at the kitchen table. My mom had been crying for hours; I hated seeing her that way. My dad was deadly still. Sitting with them at the table was a female cop, really short, really skinny, with her dark hair pulled back in a ponytail and no makeup. She was terrifying.

As soon as I walked in, the cop told my parents she wanted to speak with me alone first, and they nodded and let her, both of them still sitting at the kitchen table, my mom's sobs now tinged with a touch of relief.

The cop took me into the living room. We were both standing.

"I can't believe you did this to your mother," she said. "On Mother's Day of all days."

I had completely forgotten: Mother's Day. The pit in my belly got even deeper.

"You know they tried to file a missing person's report on you? Where were you?"

"I went to Redlands with some friends for the weekend, friends from school."

"Yeah? Redlands?" The cop was not buying it. "You keep this up," she continued, "and you'll end up dead or in jail."

Seeing my mom so upset sobered me. They grounded me for a couple of weeks. I knew I deserved it, but being grounded wasn't enough to kill my hunger to see Yvette again, to get out beyond the blocks of beige stucco houses in the desert, sit on the beach, see the lights of the city reflected on the ocean. Yvette had such independence, her own way of moving through the wider world. I wanted that, and I wanted to be with her. Would it really be so bad if I left again? I wondered. My parents would be upset, yes. I felt badly about that, but what could they do except let me back in the house? They were my parents. They had always loved and taken care of me, through the good times and the difficult. Surely that wouldn't change.

One day, when my mom was at work, I snuck out and went over to hang out at the Flores' house. Brianna, Ashley, Pamela, Jenny, Angela, and I sacked out on the couches, television on in the background. School was out by then; it was June. The desert was getting hot, and the beach beckoned.

"We should go to Venice," Pamela said.

Pamela, Jenny, and Yvette loved Venice Beach because it was quite the scene: a wide sandy beach backed by tall palm trees, a wide asphalt boardwalk, and what seemed like miles of funky beachfront shops. There were basketball courts and beachside gyms—world-famous Muscle Beach—as well as street artists and performers, old and new hippies, psychics reading tarot cards at little batik-draped card tables

along the boardwalk, and all kinds of unusual characters. The more
we talked about it, the more excited we got. Jenny got off the couch
and went to the computer. Within a few minutes, she had booked us
all a room at a funky boutique hotel right on the boardwalk.

Even though I was grounded, even though I knew it would
upset my parents, I also felt the pull to go, to get away from the
boredom and do something exciting. I asked Jenny to take me home
to pack while Pamela called Yvette to bring her into the plans. At
my house, I threw shorts and T-shirts into a beach bag. Then I
sat down at the dining room table to write my parents a note. My
stomach hurt. I really did not want them to worry. I did not want
them to be hurt or upset. But I had to go. All I wanted was to feel
the way I had felt being with Yvette a few weeks before. I couldn't
do that at home. There was no way I could sit on the couch at my
parents' house and hold her hand the way we had sitting on the
beach in Santa Monica.

"I'm sorry," I wrote. "I'll be back soon."

I left the note right there on the dining room table and hurried
out the front door and into Jenny's black Honda.

I'll just be gone a couple of days, I thought, trying to calm my guilt.
*I'll come home, chill out the rest of the summer, go back to school, and be a
really good kid.*

By the time we got to Pamela and Ashley's house again, Yvette
had arrived. Pamela and Angela got in with Jenny; I switched into
Yvette's car with Ashley. We started our caravan out of town. Down
through the mountains, over the Cajon Pass, into the outskirts of
Los Angeles, past the miles of auto malls and apartment buildings
and warehouses, into East Los Angeles, over the river, through
downtown. By the time we reached Venice on the far west side of
town, the long June day was ending. The sun was starting to set.
Dusk was settling in. We exited the freeway, drove down through
Santa Monica, and exited into the heart of Venice. Murals of Jim
Morrison loomed over us on the sides of old brick-faced hotels.

There were vintage shops with mannequins dressed in 1960s and 1970s gear in the windows, and coffeehouses and community grocers. The sidewalks were crowded with people.

We found our hotel, parked on the street, and spilled out of the cars, laughing and lugging our duffel bags and backpacks. Jenny went into the hotel first, to check in. The lobby was done up in bright graffiti murals, and everything about the place felt hip and modern. Yvette and I stood out front on the boardwalk, just breathing and taking in the scene. We saw this one guy wearing roller skates and a Speedo and Hula-Hooping. Another man in a silver turban zoomed along on Rollerblades carrying an electric guitar and mini amplifier, singing songs that sounded like they were written in another language.

Jenny came out to let us know we could go up to the room. After stashing our gear, we left the hotel to watch the sunset and catch the evening action at Venice. We stumbled past T-shirt shops, smoke shops, souvenir shops, again and again and again, rows upon rows of cheap plastic sunglasses for sale at one stand, fresh-made sandalwood and patchouli incense at the next. Yvette smiled at me and took my hand. I let her hold my hand in public, looking around to see if anyone was looking at us. There was no way I could hold hands with Yvette anywhere back in Victorville. At least I didn't think I could. I had never seen gay people around town before. I had never seen two girls holding hands in public. All I saw were people, like my parents, going about their lives, doing what they thought they had to, moving from their stucco houses to the freeway, to their jobs, to the big-box stores, and back to their houses. If there were gay people in love anywhere in that town, I never would have known it.

I loved the craziness of Venice—the randomness, the way the crowds of people swirled, the mix of cheap tourist traps and remnants of old-school hippie culture from the 1960s. I was so excited to be there, feeling free with my beautiful girlfriend, taking in the chaos with my friends. For the first time, I felt free, I felt fully myself and alive, and I knew I couldn't go back to hiding this piece of myself.

The next morning, I was roused from sleep by Yvette.

"Alex," she whispered.

Groggy, I opened my eyes.

"Alex," she whispered again, urgently.

I got up on one elbow. Pamela and Jenny were curled up in one bed, Ashley and Angela were crashed out on pillows and blankets piled on the floor.

"Alex, I gotta go home."

Yvette stroked my head and told me her grandma was getting really sick back in Arizona. She had to go be with her. She had to leave right away.

I didn't want to move from that spot. I wanted to keep going, with Yvette and my friends. I wanted to stay in Los Angeles and see the whole city, to stay in the beautiful chaos of it all.

When I had first realized that I liked girls, first thought about Samantha, the very idea of being with a girl scared me and I didn't want to be in that world at all. But now that I was in this world, with this beautiful girl who made me feel amazing, I realized how impossible it would ever be for me to fit back into the world of my religion and my family.

There was no place for girls who liked girls in Mormonism. They couldn't get married in the temple. I had told myself that my friends and I would have our wild days but we would go back someday and take our places in the community as we had been raised to do. We would end up following the plan as we were supposed to. Now I realized that was impossible. For a girl who liked girls, there was no place in the plan, and really no going back.

All of this I thought about as I sat there in the dark, my girlfriend stroking my head. Still, I didn't want to move from that spot. I didn't want to leave the dark hotel room on the boardwalk in

Venice, with my friends crashed out all around me. I knew that Yvette had to go home, and that meant I did too. But go home to what? After feeling this new sense of being alive, of being wanted and understood, it became harder to go back to my hometown in the desert. It became harder to live in a world fenced in by anxiety and boredom. I just couldn't.

CHAPTER 5

"Get Out. Just Go!"

Coming home from Los Angeles that second time, I did not find police cars parked in front of my house. There was no police officer waiting in the kitchen, and my mom wasn't crying at the kitchen table. My parents knew I'd come back and say I was sorry, which I did. I knew they would ask where I'd been, and they did. I told them. They grounded me, and that was pretty much that. We didn't talk more about it.

I spent the next month stuck in my bedroom reading and practicing my cello while the miserably hot and gray summer days ground on. I'd text back and forth with Brianna, Ashley, and Pamela. Pamela was especially persistent, asking if I was gay. I told her I wasn't; it was just Yvette, just this one girl—the same thing she'd told me months ago. It was hard to think of myself as gay. Pamela was the only gay person I knew, and she was so different from me. She was square shouldered, abrupt and direct in her manners. From what little I knew, she seemed to fit the stereotypes about lesbians. I did not.

Yvette went to Arizona to help her grandmother. But soon, she was back in Victorville. She must have loved those long drives across the desert alone in her Jeep. One Friday night, I asked my parents if I could go see Ashley. They weren't thrilled about it, but they relented.

Thirty minutes later, I was in the front seat of Yvette's Jeep, holding her hand.

"I missed you," she said.

"Thanks," I said. "I missed you too."

We headed for the outskirts of town, parked the car, and started kissing. The radio was on. Invisible radio waves from Los Angeles arced up and over the mountains and in through the speakers of the car.

The hours with Yvette just evaporated. Once in a while I'd squint at my phone to see what time it was. It was getting later. Texts from Ashley and Brianna were piling up on my screen. I knew I should probably go home. But it felt so amazing to be with Yvette.

We kissed and she told me about Arizona and the little house where her grandmother lived on the dusty south side of Tucson. We laughed about the way everyone had crashed out on the floor of the hotel room in heaps in Venice.

Then we were quiet and Yvette's long dark hair fell all around me.

In the quiet, as we were kissing, I started to wonder at the way I felt. I had never felt so electric. I had never felt so tender. I had never felt so *pretty*. That sounds funny now, I suppose, but that's how it felt. That's the best word I had for it. I really didn't know how to put what I was feeling into context. I thought back on Pamela's question: Was I *gay*? Was I *gay* like her? My mind really had to struggle to connect my feelings about Yvette to that word, to that idea. What exactly did it mean to be *gay*? I had no idea. It's not like they were showing a lot of gay kids falling in love on television or in the movies. All I had to go by was Pamela and her girlfriend, Jenny. Those were the only gay people I knew.

But as I felt Yvette's hands on my neck and my back, I remembered seventh grade and how I'd felt about Samantha. I remembered watching her in orchestra class, looking at her shoes and freckled legs while I listened to her play cello, then that night at my house, lying on the hot concrete next to the pool, wanting to hold her hand so badly. It wasn't just about holding hands or kissing; it was a bigger sort of wanting, and it came from a very basic place in me. I had been attracted to the best parts of Samantha: the way she'd been the first to raise her hand in class and know all the answers, the way she'd bent over her cello so intensely and gotten lost in the music, and the way she'd quietly stood up for herself even when other kids had whispered about her grandmother's trailer park. My attraction to Yvette was the same. I loved her long dark hair, yes. I loved her curvy legs and her platform heels. But I also loved her independence, her devotion to her grandmother, her fearless negotiation of Los Angeles, and the way she knew how to make anyone she talked to feel comfortable—especially me.

I knew what I was feeling was no accident. But was I *gay*? I still didn't know for sure.

When I stopped answering my texts that night, Ashley called my house, looking for me. She talked to my mom and blew my cover. As Yvette drove me back into town, I could definitely feel a new level of anxiety building in my belly. By the time Yvette dropped me off down the block from my parents' house, it was hard to push the feelings away and pretend like I wasn't nervous.

My legs tingled and my stomach hurt as I walked past the beige stucco houses to my cul-de-sac. I didn't know what would happen when I reached home, though I sensed that something was coming.

I didn't know that my whole world was about to change.

THE NEXT DAY STARTED out quietly enough. Maybe too quietly. I slept late. I heard my mom and dad leave the house early to run errands. By the time they came back, it was noon, and I was just getting dressed.

"Alex," my mom called from her bedroom.

I went down the hall. Mom met me at the doorway; Dad was sitting on the edge of their bed. I stepped into the space between them.

"Where were you last night?" Mom asked.

"At Ashley's."

"Ashley called looking for you."

I looked down at the floor. I thought about making up a story to cover my tracks. But this time felt different.

"Honey, what's that on your neck?"

"What's what?" I answered her, confused. I turned to face the mirror on the wall above the dresser and saw a purple hickey blooming on the left side of my neck.

"Alex, are you having sex?" my mom asked, the tone in her voice climbing higher.

"No, Mom," I said. I took a deep breath, then the words just tumbled out. "I like girls."

Silence. "What?"

"This hickey is from a girl. I like girls." I was surprised by how quiet and sure my own voice sounded.

Then my mom started screaming. "Oh, no!"

Dad said nothing. He just hung his head and studied the wood floor.

Mom kept screaming and started crying, and I pushed quietly past her to get back to my own room so I could figure out what to do next.

Within a few minutes, my phone started buzzing on the dresser.

It was my sister calling from Arizona. "What's going on?" she asked. "Mom just called me, and she's hysterical."

"I told her everything."

"What do you mean you told her *everything*?"

In the background at my sister's house, I could hear the baby crying. "I told Mom I like girls."

That was the first my sister knew as well. I could feel her blood pressure dropping. She became calm, very calm, even as the noise of her kids spiraled upward in the background.

"Okay," she said, then drew a long breath. "It's going to be okay."

Down the hall, I could hear my mom sobbing in her bedroom.

"We'll figure it out," my sister said. "You'll be fine."

I could tell my sister was struggling with the news, but she tried to stay calm and reassuring.

Mom appeared in my bedroom doorway. Dad had not moved. He was still sitting on the edge of the bed, not doing anything, not saying anything, just looking at the floor.

She took my cell phone from my hand and scrolled down through text messages and voicemails. "Who is this person?" she demanded through her tears. I had programmed Yvette's contact under a fake name.

When I saw how furious my mother was, it hit me that Yvette could be in real trouble—trouble with the police. She was, after all, eighteen and I was only fifteen. I said nothing. My mom continued to search my phone.

Then came the words that changed everything.

"Go." Her voice was hot and bitter. "Get out. Just go!"

Mom continued to look at the cell phone. She did not look at me.

Was she telling me to leave the house?

"Take what you need, Alex," she said. "Because the next time you come back everything will be in garbage bags in the front yard."

I went numb. I could not believe what I was hearing.

But I did what she said.

While Mom stood there, crying and angrily clutching the cell phone, I grabbed a black backpack embroidered with my initials. I pulled some shorts and T-shirts from my dresser drawers and got my toothbrush and makeup bag from the bathroom.

I headed down the stairs, leaving my parents behind me, my dad still frozen in his seat on the edge of the bed, my mom still sobbing in my bedroom. I felt like I was going to throw up, but my feet and legs kept moving.

I walked down the block to Ashley's house.

"What's wrong?" Ashley could see the distress in my face, even though I couldn't yet put many words together.

"I need to use your phone."

With Ashley standing at my side, I dialed Brianna. I heard myself tell her that I had been kicked out of my parents' house and needed her to come pick me up. Then I told Ashley I needed a moment alone. I stepped into the bathroom and shut the door.

Yvette was driving when she picked up the phone.

"I told my parents I like girls," I said.

"Oh shit. How'd they take it?"

I could hear the desert wind on Yvette's end.

"They kicked me out."

"Damn."

"And they're looking for you."

Yvette went quiet. I heard her pull to the side of the road. There was silence for a few moments.

"They could call the police," she finally said.

"I know. I think they want to."

Another long pause.

"Did you tell them my name?" she asked cautiously.

"No," I said, "and I won't."

Even in my situation, it felt good somehow to be able to protect Yvette.

Brianna and her mom came to pick me up. Not a word was said about anything that had happened back at my house. I'm not sure if Sister Flores knew that I'd be staying the night, or why. I'm not sure Ashley told her anything. When we got to the Flores' house, Brianna's mom disappeared into her room, and I took my bag upstairs to Brianna's room. Brianna was emerging from the garage with a Costco-size tub of cookie dough. She shot me a giant but sort of helpless grin. We stood at the island in the kitchen, placing precut hunks of chocolate chip cookie dough on baking sheet after baking sheet. Brianna always liked to eat in a crisis. So that's what we did. We sat at the island in the kitchen eating chocolate chip cookies as the afternoon turned into evening and night fell. Eventually, we crashed on the couches, soaking up the air-conditioner and the television.

Even after Brianna was asleep, I didn't cry. But my heart was racing and my head was panicked as I lay there in the dark thinking.

I told my parents I like girls, and they kicked me out of the house.

It wasn't like I hadn't told them hard things before. When I first started smoking pot and my grades dropped, I had told them about the drugs, and they had been calm and understanding. They had really held it together. Maybe because my older brothers once experimented a little with smoking pot, my parents had felt they knew what to do.

But having a daughter who liked girls—a gay daughter? This was totally different. They had no idea what to do with me.

I can see how terrifying it must have been, for my mom especially, because our religion told her there was no place for people like me, no place in the faith and the community that held her world together, and no place in God's plan. After everything that has happened, I can now see how scared my mom and dad must have been, and I feel bad for them. But in that very moment, when I was fifteen and lying on Brianna's couch in the dark, with no idea where I would go or what would happen to me, all I could feel was the crushing weight of my mother's shame and my father's silence.

ONE WEEK PASSED. I heard nothing from my parents. Not a word. Their silence was both painful and frightening. My worry started to take more practical shapes. School was starting soon. Would I even go? Would I have clothes or school supplies if I stayed at the Flores' house? Would my parents come for me before school started?

Brianna and I filled our days doing what we always did to break the boredom of late summer and numb the stress I was under. We hung out on the couches in the living room with Angela and Pamela. Nobody seemed to know what to say about the situation I was in, so we carried on as if nothing had happened. We ran the air-conditioner on high to fight back the desert heat. We watched movies and music videos. We smoked. We made tray after tray of cookies, lining up row after row of frozen hunks of Costco chocolate chip cookie dough. We sat at the island in the kitchen and ate them.

One night at dinner Sister Flores told me that my parents had called to check up on me but weren't ready to talk to me yet. Other than that, Brother and Sister Flores made no mention of my situation. We just didn't talk about it. Not about my getting kicked out of the house or being gay, or about what that would mean to my life and my family. It strikes me now that even as the bishop of our congregation, Brother Flores had nothing to say. Part of this is a good thing: nobody quoted scriptures from the Old Testament about gay people being an abomination; nobody told me God hated me.

But they also did not say anything reassuring, anything that would have made a huge difference to me or my parents, like "God loves everyone alike" or "This is nobody's fault" or "It's all going to be okay." Looking back, I'm sure that Brother and Sister Flores were as scared and overwhelmed by the idea of Pamela being gay as my parents were about me. They probably had no idea what to say, and our religion gives parents of gay children very little support.

A second week evaporated. Still no word from home. Finally, the Sunday night before Labor Day, Brianna's parents came into the living room together. Brother Flores broke the silence.

"Your parents asked us not to tell you, Alex, but we feel we should."

Tell me what?

I held my breath. I felt the anxiety wind up in my stomach once again.

"They are coming to pick you up and take you to Utah to stay with your grandparents," he explained.

I exhaled. That sounded like a good idea. I had always loved visiting my grandparents when they lived in Ojai, in a big old house surrounded by orange groves and vegetable gardens, with cats and bunnies roaming in the yard. A few years ago they had moved to southern Utah, but I always looked forward to visiting them and had found it calming to stay there. It would probably be good, I thought, for my parents to have a little space from me and for me to have a little space from them while we figured things out. As kind as the Floreses had been, I couldn't stay on their couch forever.

I went upstairs and started packing my bags, rehearsing in my head what my parents might say when the door opened, and what I could say to them.

I'm sorry? I was sorry for so many things, for leaving home and making them worry, for being a difficult kid. But I couldn't say I was sorry for kissing Yvette or telling them that I liked girls. I couldn't go back.

Within an hour, there was a knock on the front door. Brother and Sister Flores invited my parents in. Brianna stood just behind her parents. My mother stood in the entryway crying. My father thanked Brother and Sister Flores for keeping me, then put his arm around Brianna's shoulder and gave her a hug. I watched from the living room. No one spoke to me, until my dad looked up and waved me over.

"Alex, it's time to go."

I grabbed my backpack and headed for the front door. On my way out, I hugged Brianna and Brother and Sister Flores and thanked them. Then I followed my parents out into the hot desert night.

CHAPTER 6

Welcome to Utah

I LOOKED UP TO SEE my mom's white Pontiac Aztek packed with my belongings: clothes in suitcases, bags of my shampoo and shower gear, and my cello.

My eyes met my father's.

"You'll be staying with your grandparents for a couple of weeks," he explained, "so we can decide what to do."

I got into the backseat, my dad got behind the wheel, and my mom, still crying, sat up front.

No one said anything as my dad drove out of the neighborhood, down the long avenue, and onto I-15. NORTHBOUND: LAS VEGAS, read the green highway sign.

I waited for a while for someone to say something, studying the backs of my parents' heads as the weight of their silence settled on all of us. The stucco houses and strip malls of Victorville eventually ended, and then there was only the occasional gas station, and miles and miles of brushy foothills and desert, with peeling billboards for Las Vegas resorts, blown tires strung out along the sides of the highway, and giant power lines overhead. Still, neither of my parents said anything. Eventually, nearing the desert town of Baker, I got drowsy, grabbed my pillow from the back, curled up, and fell asleep.

I opened my eyes when we stopped for gas at the Nevada state line. We pulled off the highway, past a casino built to look like a castle. Another giant neon sign in the shape of an Indian headdress advertised a casino called Buffalo Bill's. Yellow roller coaster tracks wound between the neon signs and around the hotels.

The car came to a stop at a gas station, and my dad got out and started to fill the tank.

"Alex," my mom said, turning around in her seat, "do you want something to eat?"

I studied her face in the gas station light. She was not crying now, but her eyes were puffy and her face lined.

"No, I'm okay," I said in the darkness of the backseat.

In the days and months to come, my mind would go back to that moment many times. Maybe if I'd said yes we would have found an all-night casino restaurant where we could have sat down together and seen each other face-to-face. Maybe we would have ordered pancakes and eggs and started to talk over bottomless glasses of orange juice. Maybe she would have told me what she and my dad had planned for me, how they planned to make it all better, and I would have had the time to talk them out of it. Maybe I could have run, right then, right there.

But none of that happened. My dad finished filling the tank and got back in the car, not saying so much as a word. Then it was back to the highway, to the desert dark, and, for me, back to sleep.

IT WAS EARLY MORNING when I woke up next. Through the car windows, I could see the red-rock walls of the Virgin River Gorge, layer upon layer of sandstone hewn away by the river, like a smaller version of the Grand Canyon. We exited the gorge, and the desert leveled out again. WELCOME TO UTAH, read a giant sign at the edge of the highway, at the outskirts of St. George.

St. George was the first Utah town on I-15, the place where the rest of the world ended and the Mormon world began. It had been founded in the nineteenth century by Mormon pioneers, who had laid the whole town out on the same grid system Brigham Young and other leaders had used to organize every other Mormon town in Utah, Idaho, and Arizona, with the church tabernacle at dead center and all the streets—north and south, east and west—numbered outward from that point until they reached the red sandstone cliffs that marked the edges of town.

We pulled off the highway one last time and turned onto St. George Boulevard, passing outlet malls, then a string of gas stations, fast-food restaurants, and 1950s-era motels. St. George had grown a lot over the years, attracting many older Mormons like my grandparents, downsizing from their old rickety clapboard two-story house in Ojai with its porches, groves, and gardens to a compact one-story stucco house in a planned subdivision at the edge of the St. George grid. My grandparents must have felt more secure there, with all the neighbors being Mormon, everyone believing and feeling the same way, and everyone on the block attending the same congregation in the giant church building down the street. In some St. George neighborhoods there was a church building every few blocks, all of them designed alike.

My dad brought the car to a stop in my grandparents' driveway. It was Labor Day morning, and the streets were quiet and empty. I reached into the back of the Aztek, grabbed my purse and a pink-and-white-striped bag with some shampoo and a blow-dryer. After the long night in the car, I was ready for a shower.

My grandparents met us at the front door, and I followed my parents into the house. My grandma opened her arms, and I set down my bags and hugged her.

"Are you ready?" my father asked my grandparents.

Ready?

My mother saw my wondering look and paused. "We're going to meet a woman," she spoke haltingly, "who can help you with school while you're here."

My grandfather picked up the pink-and-white-striped bag I had just set on the tile entryway floor.

I searched my parents' faces, then my grandparents' faces. Except for my mom, who was crying again, everyone was so calm. Everything was so still. I felt in my gut that something was definitely not right. But no one said anything.

I followed my grandparents and parents back out to the driveway. We all got into the Aztek. My dad pulled out of the driveway. We drove for a few minutes more, then pulled up in front of another house—a house I'd never seen before.

It was a brown stucco house with a tile roof, just like my grandparents' and every other house on the block. In fact, it could have been on a block in Apple Valley or Victorville, or any of the desert towns along I-15, where identical stucco houses huddled up, one against another, and beyond the back fences desert stretched away, except here in southern Utah every subdivision had its own giant church building or two, and the desert sandstone was red.

In the front yard of the house, there was a tiny patch of dried grass and some oleander bushes cut short and browning at the leaves. I could see a faded red-and-yellow plastic playhouse on a bed of rocks in the backyard. In the distance was a tall ridge of mountains.

Wordlessly, my parents and grandparents got out of the car and started unloading my stuff from the trunk. I sat frozen in the backseat.

"What are you doing?" My voice started to shake. I screamed, "What is this place? Where am I?"

A woman came out the front door and greeted my parents on the driveway. She looked to be in her thirties. She had olive skin and long wet curly black hair, and she was wearing skinny jeans and a T-shirt with a South Pole logo in big cursive letters.

"Hi, Tiana," I heard my grandmother say, her voice low and still.

"Johnny is just waking up," I heard Tiana tell my parents. "He will be out here soon."

Selevia "Tiana" Siale gave my grandmother a big hug, then turned to shake hands with and hug my parents. It was the first time my parents had met Tiana in person, but everyone acted as if they'd known one another for years. They all exchanged these deep, familiar smiles tinged with grim resignation. Everyone seemed to know exactly what would happen next—except me.

Something was not right.

I reached for the car doors and locked them.

Wesley "Johnny" Siale—everyone called him "Johnny"—appeared on the driveway, olive-skinned like Tiana but heavyset. He wore a giant oversize white T-shirt, basketball shorts, and bright green Nike shoes.

Johnny greeted my parents with a big smile and a handshake.

My throat tightened, and panic uncoiled in my belly. Who were these people? Why were we here? I looked to the dashboard of the car and saw my father's phone resting there.

My parents, grandparents, Johnny, and Tiana all picked up my stuff—my suitcase, my purse, my pink-and-white-striped bag, and my cello case—and walked toward the house.

I grabbed my father's cell phone and looked down at it in my hands. Who could I call? Who could help me? Not Yvette. If I called her using my dad's phone, my parents would have her number. I tried Brianna first, and the phone rang four times before it went to voicemail.

I hung up and started to dial Ashley when I heard the locks unclick around me.

Johnny stood on the driveway, holding the car keys.

The car door opened and Johnny's huge hand reached in, grabbed my arm, and pulled me out of the car and onto my feet on the driveway.

Still gripping my arm, he looked me right in the face. "Don't make it hard" was all he said.

That's when the tears came to my eyes. I stopped feeling the ground under me. I was terrified.

Johnny led me to the house and through the front door, down a short hallway, and into the living room.

Mom and Dad were sitting on a big brown vinyl couch. My grandparents were standing next to them, with Tiana at their side.

"Mom? What is this place?" I asked through a hot haze of tears.

"Alex, you need to stay here with the Siale family for a little bit," she said, sounding resolute. "You need help. They're going to help you, and you shouldn't run away."

Run away? I took my eyes off my mother and scanned the house: a kitchen, a second-story loft, doors to bedrooms, a side door to the backyard. And no telephone in sight.

"Mom," I heard myself cry out, "*please.* No, please! *Please don't leave me here!*"

I looked to my dad. Silent, with his eyes on the ground.

Johnny's voice broke in. "You can be here three months," he said, "or you can be here three years. It's up to you."

That's when it all hit me: *My parents are sending me here because I am gay. There is no other reason.*

"Mom, please, don't leave me here!"

Yes, I had been acting up and making my parents worry, but it was clear to me that I was here because I had told them I was gay.

We were all crying: my mom, my dad, my grandparents, me.

Tiana gently interrupted, saying to my parents, "Do you have the papers I asked you to bring?"

My dad stood up and helped my mom up from the couch. She was crying hard, almost sobbing. I was sobbing too, and terrified.

"Mama, *please*."

These people, they were total strangers. I had never seen them before in my life. Why would my parents leave me with total strangers? They must have been really desperate.

My mom reached into her purse, pulled out some school and health insurance papers, and handed them over to Tiana.

That's when I got angry.

"I hate you!" I yelled. My mom, dad, and grandparents gave me that sad, knowing look, then turned their backs and left the living room. They didn't even say goodbye.

I heard the front door open and then click closed.

I tried to follow them down the front hallway, but Johnny stood between me and the door, crossing his arms.

Outside, the car engine started. My stomach sank as my parents drove away.

CHAPTER 7

I'm Going to Be Here a Long Time

As my parents drove away, I closed my eyes and my mind followed their car down the highway, out of Utah, through the Virgin River Gorge, past Las Vegas, through the desert, and back home to the people who knew me: to Ashley and Brianna and Yvette.

When I opened my eyes, I saw Johnny still standing between me and the front door, his large body solid and imposing.

A series of questions formed in my mind: *Who are these people? What is this place? How can I get out of here?*

I turned around to try to make sense of my surroundings. A short hallway led from the front door to the living room. I looked up to the high living room ceilings and saw an open second-story loft space that held a row of narrow beds. Another door from the living room led into the first-floor master bedroom. To my right, there was a counter separating the living room from the kitchen. In the kitchen, I noted, there was a sliding glass door that led to the backyard and a hallway that seemed to lead down to another bedroom.

The living room was dominated by the brown sectional couch, with the vinyl especially worn and faded in a spot near the center. The couch faced a large-screen television on a low table, with video-game boxes, cords, and controllers heaped in front of it on the floor. A bookshelf was pressed up against the wall near the master bedroom. The living room walls were white and bare, the carpet beige and dingy, and the doors made hollow sounds when they opened and closed. It was pretty much your average tract house.

My suitcase, purse, bag, and cello case stood in the living room. Tiana moved toward them.

"We're going to need to go through these with you," Tiana explained, opening the suitcase first. I wanted to protest, but I was too afraid. Not only was I totally stunned by being left with total strangers but Johnny and Tiana were physically much bigger than me. I was completely intimidated.

Tiana opened the suitcase on the floor and kneeled in front of it. Johnny stood by her shoulder to watch. I sat down on the living room floor.

First, she lifted out the scriptures my parents had packed for me—my combination Bible and Book of Mormon with my name embossed in gold on the front cover—and set them on the floor beside her. My parents had also packed a new journal for me. At church they had always encouraged us to keep a journal, as a way of reflecting on ourselves and how we could keep our lives as close to God's plan as possible. I had always used my journals as a safe place to sort through my feelings. When my parents kicked me out of the house, Pamela had gone back over to get my old journals with all the details about my relationship with Yvette and keep them safe. The new journal my parents had packed for me was big and sort of girly, with little brown birds nestled in leafy boughs printed on the cover. Tiana picked it up and set it on top of my scriptures in a pile. My makeup and blow-dryer went into another pile. I wouldn't be seeing them again any time soon.

Next, Tiana began to sort through layers of clothes my parents had packed: the clothes I regularly wore to school—shorts and T-shirts mostly but also a few tank tops.

"You know this is immodest," Tiana said, holding up a gray tank and looking accusingly in my eyes.

I nodded. Modesty was a big deal at church. We heard it all the time: no short shorts, skirts to the knees, no two-piece bathing suits, shoulders covered. My mom often fussed at me for wearing tank tops to school. Tiana sorted the gray tank into the pile with the makeup.

"Immodest," she said again, fixing me in her stare as she lifted a pink tank from the suitcase before setting it into the pile.

"Inappropriate." She held up a white miniskirt. "And you are too obsessed with name brands," she said as she disdainfully handled an Aéropostale sweatshirt and set it in the pile. I had never thought of myself as especially brand focused. I had, however, noticed that Tiana was wearing a South Pole–branded T-shirt.

Tiana continued her commentary as she worked down through the layers until the suitcase was entirely empty. Then she scooped up just about everything besides my scriptures and my new journal, dumped it back into the suitcase, and looked up at Johnny.

Johnny picked up the suitcase and my cello case and walked them out to the garage while Tiana disappeared for a moment into the master bedroom.

She returned clutching a black garbage bag, which she opened and dumped out in front of me. Long skirts and old oversize T-shirts emblazoned with the names of Utah vacation spots and church camps landed in a heap on the floor.

"These are the clothes you will wear while you stay with us," she said.

It looked to me like my new wardrobe came straight from Deseret Industries, a church-owned chain of thrift stores.

"Okay," I said as I slowly sorted through the pile, then put it all back into the garbage bag. The few things my parents had sent, they really didn't add up to much. But giving them up felt like another tie had been severed, another tie to my family, my home. All of it gone so fast—nothing to hold on to.

Tiana led me to the bedroom off the kitchen, and Johnny followed us down the hall. The bedroom door was open. There were little girls' beds on one side of the room and on the other side a pile of blankets on a thin pink mattress on the floor.

"This is where you will sleep," Tiana said.

I could hear the door from the garage open again and the sound of kids coming into the house. Tiana went out to meet them, and Johnny shut the door behind her.

"Change clothes," he said.

I stood with my scriptures, my new journal, and my garbage bag of thrift store castoffs in my hands. I waited a few moments, expecting him to leave the room so that I could change.

"Change clothes," he said again. "I'm not moving."

My stomach sank, the hairs on my neck bristled, and adrenaline rushed through my bloodstream. Left once again alone to face Johnny, I took in the size of his shoulders and his fighting stance, and I knew I had reason to be afraid.

I turned my back to him and set my scriptures and journal on the thin pink mattress, then pulled an oversize blue T-shirt and a long green-and-brown skirt from the garbage bag. My face burned with anger and shame as I lifted the gray polo I was wearing over my head, curling my shoulders inward to become as invisible as possible, then pulled the T-shirt over my head. I unbuttoned my shorts and stepped out of them, feeling his eyes on my back.

"Okay," I said, my back still turned to Johnny. "I'm finished."

I heard him open the door and head out to the kitchen, joining the rest of the Siale family for lunch.

I stood in the bedroom for a few minutes, trying to swallow my anger and collect my senses, before Tiana called me out to the kitchen.

"Everyone," Tiana said, "this is Alex."

I counted seven kids seated at the kitchen table, eating ramen from plastic bowls.

Sifa was tall, with dark hair, broad shoulders, and a quiet smile. I found out later that he was actually Tiana's nineteen-year-old nephew, sent by his parents to stay with Johnny and Tiana because of the trouble he'd been getting into at home. He'd been running with a rough crowd in Salt Lake City, drinking and hanging out with kids who were supposedly gang members. He could be loud and funny sometimes, but his goal was to keep the peace in the house.

Then came Calvin, who was eighteen and Tiana's brother. Calvin had moved in mostly just to get away from home, where he was being bullied by another member of Tiana's family. Calvin was shorter than Sifa and quiet—very quiet. He had been at the Siales' a long time, and I soon discovered that he would do anything to stay out of Johnny's way.

Next came Johnny and Tiana's boys: twelve-year-old Victor— Tiana and Johnny's first child, born when Tiana was nineteen and Johnny was sixteen—eleven-year-old Joseph, and nine-year-old Sione, all of them dark haired and heavyset like their mom and dad. Victor was the star of the family, the football player. Joseph was a bit slow, and Johnny would pick on him for it. Sione was short for his age but somehow managed to avoid Johnny's teasing. His parents even let him wear his hair in a ponytail.

Johnny and Tiana's two daughters were the youngest: Olivia was eight. In time, I would come to know her as the family tattletale— just her way of pushing back against the fact that Johnny picked on her for being "lazy." Four-year-old Grace sat on Tiana's lap, smiling brightly, the baby of the family. Olivia and Grace shared a bedroom, and soon I'd be sleeping on their floor. Sifa especially always looked out for Grace. He spent a lot of time with her.

"You hungry?" Tiana asked.

"No, thank you," I answered and left the kitchen, ignoring pangs of hunger. I hadn't eaten since we'd left California.

"You're not helping yourself," Johnny called after me.

I took a seat on the living room floor.

After lunch, Johnny sat down on the couch, and the boys sat down with him. Olivia and Grace went to their bedroom to play.

"Alex," Johnny said, squaring his shoulders and addressing me directly. "Here is what you need to know for today. Number one: don't talk to the kids."

The boys sat on the couch, looking up at their father.

"Number two: don't take anything that's not yours. Number three: do what we say and it will be fine." Again, he reiterated the haunting words he had said when my parents and grandparents were here: "You can be here three months or three years; it's up to you."

Three years?

I felt the adrenaline surge again and my heart rate quicken.

"Number four: remember that we know everyone in this town. Tiana and I, we've both worked in the juvenile system here in town. We know everybody. We know the police, the schools, the courts. They all know us and trust us. They know we take in troubled kids. It's your word against ours.

"Number five," he continued. "The more uncomfortable you are, the more you will grow. You remember that."

"When do I get to talk to my parents?" I asked.

"Once a week, if you act right."

"When do I get to see my grandparents?"

"That's not going to happen for a while. If you show that you are worthy of trust, we may take you to church with us, but even there we don't want you speaking to your grandparents."

My mind started to piece things together: I had no contact with my friends or family. Just about everything I owned had been taken from me and locked up in the garage. Two strangers were in charge of my day-to-day movements. And they could keep me here as long as three years—until I turned eighteen.

"You got it?" Johnny asked.

"Yes." I nodded. My nightmare was becoming all too clear.

"Okay." Johnny had ended his speech. "Sione, get me the controllers."

Sione got off the couch, turned on the television, and brought back the video-game controllers.

I sat on the floor, numb and apparently invisible, while Johnny, Sifa, Victor, Sione, and Joseph played Call of Duty, the sounds of gunshots and explosions ricocheting from the bare walls.

I let myself zone out and watched the screen for what must have been an hour, trying to come to grips with my circumstances. When I felt I could not bear another minute in the same room as Johnny, I opened my mouth. "Can I go to my room?" I asked. I was really not sure what I should do with myself.

"Go," Johnny said, not taking his eyes from the screen. I looked at Sifa, who let his eyes briefly meet mine.

I've got to find a way out of here, I thought as I returned to Olivia's room and sat down on the mattress. *I've got to find a way out.*

I had no phone, no car, no driver's license, no money, except for a couple of quarters floating at the bottom of my purse. I had no way to get in touch with friends and no idea how to tell them where to find me. I knew I was a few blocks from my grandparents', but I could not map out the neighborhood or even the way back to the interstate. Still, this did not discourage me.

A few days, I thought. *Just give me a few days. I'll figure out something. I always figure out something.*

I had always figured out something, getting into trouble and out of it, with Ashley and Brianna, and then with Yvette. I knew I was strong and had a stubborn streak a mile wide. I'd find a way.

A pang of hunger hit my stomach. An idea came to me.

I'll stop eating. I'll just stop eating, I thought. *Then they'll have to take me to the hospital. That's how I can get out of here.*

My mind worked out a plan as the afternoon stretched into evening, with the sounds of video games coming through the thin walls of the house. Nighttime fell, and I didn't leave the room for dinner, and to my relief no one came to get me. I stayed on my mattress, staring at the ceiling, feeling the stifling weight of the desert heat trapped in the house, unrelieved by air-conditioning.

Olivia came in bathed and ready for bedtime. Tiana tucked her in but did not say a word to me. I lay still, my fingers curled into fists, gripping the certainty that in just a few days I would find my way out of here.

That first night I was too angry and too afraid to cry.

I WOKE UP LATE the next morning, groggy and disoriented, trying to gather my senses before opening the bedroom door. The kids had left for school. The house was deadly quiet. I stepped into the bathroom, took a shower, and changed into fresh clothes, then walked toward the kitchen.

From the kitchen, I could see Johnny asleep on the living room couch. Tiana must have left for work, I gathered, though I had no idea where that was.

A phone. I've got to look for a phone.

I scanned the counters and then looked over toward a small built-in desk stacked with junk mail and school papers. School pictures of the children were thumbtacked to the wall over the desk. As quietly as I could, I moved my hands through the papers. My fingertips found a cordless phone.

My pulse quickened. I picked it up, pushed the button, put it to my ear: no dial tone. The phone was disconnected. I felt the breath go out of me.

It's okay. I'm going to get out of this. I've been in sticky situations before. I can find my way out.

The front door opened, and Johnny stirred from his sleep. Tiana had come home.

"It's time to get you enrolled in school, Alex," she told me.

School.

The idea that I might get to go to school while I was with Johnny and Tiana made me hopeful—hopeful for a chance to leave the house, any chance, and for contact with other people. But that wasn't the plan.

"We'll take you to register at the alternative high school today," Tiana explained, "but you'll be doing your lessons at home here with us."

Tiana took a folder of papers from the kitchen desk and put them in her purse, then I followed her through the front door to the driveway and into her blue TrailBlazer. As the car slowly drove down the block, I tried to read and memorize the house numbers and the street names, tried not to lose my sense of direction as we left the neighborhood and headed to town.

At the school office, Tiana walked in and handed the woman at the enrollment desk the folder of papers. "I'd like to enroll her," Tiana said, gesturing toward me with her hand.

The woman at the desk scanned the papers in the folder.

"You're from California?" she asked me.

I nodded.

This is my chance to ask for help. Maybe she can help me, I thought in a panic.

But I remembered what Johnny had told me: *We know the police, the schools, the courts. They all know us and trust us. They know we take in troubled kids. It's your word against ours.*

I said nothing. I watched as Tiana handed the woman papers my parents had signed giving Johnny and Tiana legal authority over me. My parents had signed me away to strangers. I could barely believe my eyes.

The woman scanned the papers silently. "Okay," she said without lifting her eyes from the papers, "these only apply if she stays in the state of California."

Tiana exhaled forcefully and shifted her weight.

"You're going to have to go to the district office and get Utah state guardianship for residency forms. You'll have to have them notarized and"—the woman raised her eyes to look at me—"are you over fourteen years old?"

I nodded.

"She will have to sign them as well."

As we walked back to the car, I felt like a tiny door had opened. What if I didn't sign? What if I dug in my heels and insisted on going back to my parents? Would they have to send me home?

That night, back at the Siale house, I took out the journal my parents had packed for me. I opened the cover and started my first journal entry.

Tuesday, September 7, 2010

Today the woman drove me to the school to enroll me. The school said they couldn't and that we had to go to the district office because the guardian papers my parents signed were only legitimate if I stayed in California. Thank God for that! The lady at the district office told us that if I'm over fourteen I have to sign a paper saying its okay, that I'm okay with it. I was so happy.

I brought quarters I found at the bottom of my bag if maybe I could find a pay phone. I didn't find one. I haven't eaten anything since Sunday. They will have to take me to the hospital soon.

I closed my journal, then closed my eyes. I kept thinking about my mother and the way she had sobbed when it was time to leave me behind. I could not believe that she wouldn't come to her senses. I could not believe that she and my dad wouldn't change their minds and want me back home soon. Then I thought of Yvette and her long dark hair and how badly I missed her, missed the feeling of being with her and talking to her. I was as in love as any fifteen-year-old had ever been. And it hurt. It all hurt. I felt the fighting instinct in me give way to pain, and the tears finally came to my eyes. I knew it was likely that no matter where I hid it the Siales would find my journal and read it. I knew that they wanted information on Yvette so that the police could locate her and press charges. I wanted to protect her from that, but I also needed a place to have my thoughts and feelings. Perhaps if I only wrote her first name, she would stay safe. I turned back to my journal.

> *I feel like dying. Yvette is the only reason I'm not. All I can do is cry. I feel so much hatred toward these people, my parents, grandparents, and Mormons in general. I feel so hopeless. My stomach hurts so bad. I need to eat, but I won't give in. I swear.*

THE NEXT DAY, I woke up, got dressed, and stayed in my room as long as possible, trying to avoid Johnny, trying to avoid breakfast and the kitchen so they could not force me to eat. I heard the sounds of the kids getting ready for school and then leaving. The front door closed. I heard Johnny move around the living room for a few minutes, then settle onto the couch. Once again the sounds of Call of Duty filled the house.

Around lunchtime, Tiana came into my room and announced that she was taking me, Grace, and Johnny to lunch. We loaded into the blue TrailBlazer and headed into town, to the McDonald's on St. George Boulevard near the highway.

Johnny, Grace, and Tiana stood in front of the cash registers, their faces turned up reading the menu board.

"What do you want?" Tiana asked me as she stepped forward to order.

"I'm not hungry," I said, ignoring the deep, hollow feeling in my stomach. "Can I use the bathroom?"

"Go ahead," Tiana said as she followed Grace out to the playground, trays of food in her hand.

My mind was racing. I opened the bathroom door. Inside, there was an older Hispanic woman wearing a burgundy McDonald's uniform top and a black visor and holding a plastic broom.

"I need help," I told her.

She shook her head. She didn't speak English, but her brown eyes were warm and kind and she seemed to sense my distress.

"Please," I said. "Do you have a cell phone?" I pantomimed raising a phone to my ear.

The woman nodded and drew a phone from the pocket of her black uniform pants.

I went into a stall and motioned nervously toward the door.

The woman nodded again and moved her body and her broom between me and the door, watching for it to open.

My hands were shaking as I held the phone; my pulse was racing. At first, I didn't know who to call. The Siales knew the police in town, they'd told me. The police probably wouldn't believe me or help me. I thought about my parents, but they had sent me here in the first place. I dialed Yvette.

"Hello?"

"Yvette?"

"Alex? Where are you?"

"My parents. They've sent me to this place. With these people I don't know." Just as the words started tumbling out, Tiana came through the door.

"Hand me the phone, Alex," she said.

A silent apology formed in the McDonald's worker's eyes.

Tiana handed the phone back to the worker and grabbed my arm. "Damn it, Alex," she cursed at me loudly. "I told you: no phones."

Her grip firm around the soft flesh of my bicep, Tiana pulled me to the play area.

"Pack up your lunch," she ordered Grace and Johnny. "Meet me at the car." Tiana turned toward the glass doors leading to the parking lot.

Panic leapt into my throat. I could not get into that car. I could not go back to that house.

"No! Help! Help me!" I cried out, loudly, to all the people in the McDonald's.

"Shut the hell up!" Tiana started dragging me toward the doors.

"Help!" I screamed, looking around at all the moms and their kids bustling to the play area and bending over their Happy Meals. "Help me! Don't let her take me! Please!"

No one even looked at me.

Tiana forced me out the doors and to the car, cursing under her breath. "Get in the car!"

I thought of breaking Tiana's grip and running. I looked out at St. George Boulevard, at the row of 1950s-era motels and fast-food restaurants, and at the row of red cliffs behind them, like a wall. Where would I go? My mind froze, and I felt Tiana push me into the backseat.

Johnny set Grace next to me and shut the door.

Tiana started the engine and steered the TrailBlazer down St. George Boulevard, toward the red-rock mountains at the edge of town, her neighborhood in their shadows.

"Never again," she said, "will you leave my sight without my permission. Not even to use the bathroom."

"You shouldn't have done that," Johnny said from the passenger seat, staring straight ahead, shaking his head, and laughing in low tones. "Yeah, you're going to get it now. You think you're smarter than us? You think you can get away?"

Johnny and Tiana both laughed then, and the hurt in my belly deepened.

When we got back to their house, I went to the room I shared with the girls and stared at the walls, hiding myself, blanking away the hours. I heard the family gather for dinner in the kitchen. But I did not join them. When the sun went down, I lay down on the mattress and opened my journal. On the next page, I wrote a letter to Yvette.

September 8, 2010

I spoke with you today on the phone, and hearing your voice for that second made me feel like everything was going to be okay. I can't explain to you how amazing it was to hear your voice.

The lady came in. She saw me using the phone. She grabbed the phone and yelled for the man. They dragged me to the car. They laughed at me and told me I was going to be here for the rest of my life. Writing these letters to you that you'll probably never see is the only thing that is keeping me from killing myself. I'm praying so hard. I never thought I would ever be in this situation. My parents don't want me. They are giving guardianship to these people. I know I only have three years until I'm an adult and can leave, Yvette. I don't think I can handle three years. Killing myself seems like my only escape. My body feels weak. I haven't eaten since the last time I ate with you. I'm trying to starve myself so they will have to take me to the hospital, but now . . . I don't think they will.

Today I stopped drinking. I'm trying to get to the hospital as quick as I can. Yvette, I really hope you get to see these letters, and I hope I get to be with you when you read them. I love you more than I thought I could ever love anyone. I pray I'll get out of here.

I was deep in my letter to Yvette when Johnny opened the bedroom door. There was no knock, no warning. Suddenly, he was standing over me, looking down at me. I lifted the pen from the paper and shoved the journal beneath the pillow.

"Stand up," Johnny said.

I came to my feet in front of him.

He made a fist and punched me in the gut, knocking the wind out of me. I doubled over and choked for breath.

"This is what happens when you try things like that. We warned you."

Satisfied, Johnny left me there doubled over and walked out of the room.

I crumpled onto my mattress on the floor, trying to find breath. A terrible thought formed in my mind: *I'm going to be here a long time.*

As I lay there in the dark, I had no idea that back in Victorville, at that very moment, Ashley was frantically searching for me. Her parents had told her I had been sent to one of the youth treatment centers in southern Utah, one of the reform schools where parents all over the country—some Mormon, some not—shipped their kids to get straightened out. These were places that offered a mix of dorms, uniforms, discipline, and group therapy that they promised would bring kids back into line. Lots of kids got sent there, for lots of reasons: acting up, hanging with the wrong crowd, failing in school, smoking pot.

Tiana and Johnny, I would eventually discover, had both worked at these youth treatment centers in St. George, and everyone in the neighborhood—including my grandparents and the local Mormon bishop—looked to them as authorities on dealing with troubled teens. They claimed to have been counselors or "youth mentors," but really their jobs had been more like security guards—breaking up the fights that erupted among residents or intervening in suicide attempts. They had no formal education, no training in counseling other than what they received on the job, but they promised they could fix just about anyone—including a gay teenager like me.

When my mom had called my grandparents to get their advice on how to deal with me, my grandparents had turned to Johnny and Tiana. They had promised my parents and grandparents that they could cure me by using the same tactics at home as they did with the kids at work, but their at-home treatment would cost my parents thousands of dollars less every month than the centers charged. Yet they had no license to run a treatment facility, no real background in counseling, and very little education. My parents must have been truly desperate to believe them.

It could have been worse—Johnny and Tiana could have worked for the wilderness programs that took kids out into the southern Utah desert on the theory that being out alone with a backpack in the desert would set them straight. Word had it that kids had died out there from exposure. How was that supposed to fix things? How was getting shipped off by your family and put into a dorm under the watch of people like Tiana and Johnny supposed to help? Maybe it was the idea of being out in the desert, the idea that the harshness and loneliness would scare anyone straight. For Mormon families like mine, I'm sure sending kids to Utah, to the heartland of our religion, where everyone seemed to believe and feel alike, could look like a kind of answer when they had lost control at home. Maybe my parents had hoped that sending me away to live with strangers would change me, and I would come home fixed and we could all pretend like none of it—my telling them I was gay, their sending me here—had ever happened.

Back at home, Ashley had gotten a list of all the southern Utah treatment centers and was calling each one, saying that she was my mom and she needed to speak with me right away. She had also used the church website to download membership lists of all the St. George Mormon congregations, to try to find the one my grandparents belonged to, and through them maybe to find me. But so far, she wasn't having any luck tracking me down.

As I lay on the mattress, I had no idea Ashley was searching for me, and I felt completely alone. I thought about the blocks and blocks of St. George neighborhoods we had passed on our way back from McDonald's, each full of Mormon families, each neighborhood with its own big church building, everyone believing and feeling the same way, sure that it would all work out if we just stuck to the plan of salvation they taught us at church. I thought about the sad, knowing smiles my parents, grandparents, and the Siales had exchanged; they were sure what they were doing was the right thing for me, to try to fix me and make me fit into the plan—the plan that, as far as I could tell, had no place for gay people.

Then I thought about all the people in the McDonald's, the St. George families—the dads on lunch break wearing the pressed white shirts Mormon men wore to church on Sundays and work the rest of the week, the moms with their minivans in the lot and matching bobbed haircuts, the little blond kids eating Happy Meals—all the Mormon people who had sat there as Tiana dragged me out to the car, who had done nothing as I screamed and begged for help, not looking up from their lunches or daring to act. Everyone in silent agreement, believing it would all be okay if no one disagreed or stepped out of line.

California Mormons used to trade inside jokes about Utah Mormons. Because we California Mormons lived in a place where Mormons were a small minority, we had to stand up for ourselves and stand out, be different, and take the flak for it. But because Utah Mormons lived in a place where they made up the majority, they seemed so conservative, so rule-bound, like such comfortable *followers*.

In that moment, I held on to my faith, but I blamed Utah Mormon culture for the fact that no one had stood up or spoken out when I had so badly needed them.

I'm going to be here a long time. And no one in this town is going to help me.

CHAPTER 8

"You Think You're Gay, but That Is Not How God Made You"

THE DAY AFTER MY first escape attempt, I kept a very low profile around the house. Since my guardianship paperwork hadn't been straightened out yet, I wasn't enrolled in school, and no one told me what I should be doing with myself while the Siale kids were away during the day.

I discovered that Tiana worked the night shift at a local residential treatment center for teenagers sent there by parents—like mine, I guess—who felt they had no other options. All night long Tiana would sit in the dorms, watching girls sleep or stepping in to defuse fights and stop suicide attempts. She would always come home from work exhausted and angry, go straight to her bedroom, shut the door, turn on the television, and go to sleep.

Johnny did not have a regular job, for reasons I soon pieced together. He'd never managed to get an education, and he had an arrest record. He said he had worked, like Tiana, at a residential treatment center, but he'd had to quit because he had gout and his feet hurt too badly.

While Tiana slept off her night shift, Johnny sat on the couch playing video games. I stayed in my room, watched the clock, rode waves of hunger and dizziness, and nursed the tender spots on my arm and stomach where Tiana had gripped me and Johnny had landed his blow. The hours passed so slowly, and the house was deadly quiet except for bursts of video-game gunfire.

The afternoon stretched on and the September desert heat filtered in. From my mattress on the floor, I could hear the younger kids arrive home from school first and then, later, the older ones. I heard them come in through the front door, throw down their backpacks, and open the refrigerator. I thought about my school back in California and counted the school days that had passed. Three so far. I wondered what classes Brianna and Ashley were taking. I imagined coming home from school and practicing my cello, which was hidden away in the Siales' garage. I missed my friends, and I missed playing the cello, but most of all, I missed my parents. As angry as I had been at being left in this place, I missed them terribly, with an ache much greater than the hunger in my belly.

At dinnertime, Olivia came to get me from my room. Tiana had woken up and was pulling a tray of chicken out of the oven. Johnny was sitting at the kitchen table with the kids. I counted how many days it had been since I'd eaten. Four so far.

After the plates were cleared, Johnny asked the family to join him in the living room.

All the older kids—Sifa, Calvin, Victor, Joseph, Sione, and Olivia—sat down on the floor. I sat down with them. Johnny and Tiana took their seats on the couch, and four-year-old Grace curled up in her mother's lap.

Johnny straightened himself up, leaned forward, and put his hands on his knees. "Do you know why Alex is here?" he asked the kids.

Joseph, Victor, Sione, and Olivia raised their hands.

"Olivia?"

"Because she has a bad life."

"Yeah, but why?"

Joseph shot his hand in the air. "Because she likes girls when she is supposed to like guys."

My heartbeat quickened and my face flushed. I felt like I couldn't move. It was the first time it had been stated so boldly.

"Yeah." Johnny nodded. "That's right, and that's why we're going to help her."

The tone in his voice reminded me of the worst Sunday school teachers I had ever had: sweetness on top, but underneath it was grim, almost punishing certainty.

"She can stay here for as long as she needs," he continued, smiling. "It could be three months. It could be three years."

There it was again. *Three years.* Could they really keep me that long? Would my parents really let them?

Johnny fixed his eyes on me. "Alex," he asked, "do you understand the plan of salvation?"

Yes, I did. After all, I had grown up in church, and I had paid attention. The plan of salvation meant that we had all lived with God in heaven before this life, that this life was supposed to be a place where we learned by experience, making our choices and experiencing their consequences. That idea—that we learned by experience—had always meant something to me, strong willed as I was. In church, they also taught that Jesus had died to make a way for us to repent of our mistakes, and that if we lived righteously enough we could be together with our families in the celestial kingdom— the highest levels of heaven, where God lived—if our parents had been married in the temple. And families being together forever in the celestial kingdom was supposed to be the whole point. Temple marriages kept our families safe and connected into the eternities. Except when it didn't, as I had discovered when I realized that technically, due to my mom's first marriage, I was sealed to no one, and no one could tell me who I would belong to in heaven.

I understand the plan of salvation, I thought. *I don't need to hear it from you.*

But I didn't talk back. "Yes," I said.

Johnny smiled. "You know it doesn't apply to gay people."

My face flushed hot again.

"You can't get married in the temple, and you can't have kids," he continued. "In God's plan you're sinning if you don't get married, or have kids."

It was no accident that Mormonism made a big deal about marriage and families. For Mormons, heaven was all about families. I remembered the painted wooden tree that had been on the entryway table at my house back in Apple Valley, with all the names of my brothers and sisters on the branches and my parents at the root. I had never really thought about where gay people fit in all of this. Homosexuality was considered a serious sin, and the church was totally opposed to gay marriage—anywhere, by anyone, but most especially in the Mormon temple.

"How you gonna be with your family in the celestial kingdom if you're not married in the temple?" Johnny asked. "You'll be in the telestial kingdom." The telestial kingdom is the Mormon version of hell.

I could feel Joseph, Victor, Sione, and Olivia staring at me. I was tempted to look up at Sifa, to see if he was willing to offer some support, but I kept my eyes down.

"You've made some bad choices, and you think you're gay," Johnny pressed ahead, "but that is not how God made you. You are confused. We are going to help you change. That's why your parents sent you here."

I said nothing.

"Now, your parents are good people," he continued. "They'll make it to the celestial kingdom. You won't be there unless you change. But even if you are gay and you don't get into the celestial kingdom, God won't want to deprive them, so there will be a copy of you with them, but it won't really be you."

What? I knew what Johnny was saying about gay people lined up with what I had been taught at church. But never in my whole life had I heard his crazy version of God making copies of rebellious children so the parents wouldn't miss them too badly in the celestial kingdom. That was just plain wrong, and I knew it.

I began to sense that Johnny had a pretty twisted view of God.

"Is that what you want to happen, Alex?" he asked. "Do you want your family to be in the celestial kingdom without you?"

I kept my eyes on the floor, waiting for the lecture to end. Anger burned inside me.

"We're going to help you want to live by the rules and get ready to have your own family. Here's how it's going to work. Every day you're going to get up, help the kids get ready for school, do the chores, and cook the meals," he explained. "In the mornings, we will do group meetings with Sifa and Calvin. Us four, we will study the scriptures together and talk about making good choices. At night, there will be family prayer. You'll do personal prayer and scripture study too. And church on Sunday."

Sitting there on the living room floor, I tried to wrap my mind around what Johnny and Tiana wanted from me: to do chores around the house, to attend their group scripture study sessions, to be more religious. And this was supposed to change me? This was supposed to "cure" me from being gay? How? By being stuck in a house in Utah far away from Yvette and my friends? Cut off from my family? Not allowed to attend school? Not allowed to have my own clothes? My cello? Humiliated? Beaten? It didn't make sense. My parents could not have signed on to this. None of it made sense to me.

Another wave of hunger-driven dizziness came, cresting as hot anger. Again, I felt the strength rise in me.

I've got to find a way out of here. I've got to find a way out. I'll figure out something. I always figure out something. I am smarter than these people. I will find a way.

I SPENT FRIDAY SEARCHING in my mind for ways to travel the hundreds of miles back home. In my mind's eye, I could see the Siale house out on the edge of town with desert and red-rock canyons stretching out behind it, but I had no map and only the dimmest sense of how far it was to get into town. Between the house and town stood blocks and blocks of regular neighborhoods, full of Mormon people who knew Johnny and Tiana because they went to church with them. I remembered Johnny's speech the first day:

We know everyone in this town. Tiana and I, we've both worked in the juvenile system here in town. We know everybody. We know the police, the schools, the courts. They all know us and trust us. They know we take in troubled kids. It's your word against ours.

My word against theirs. As I had learned when I was screaming for help at McDonald's, this was not the kind of town where people would step into a difficult situation and come to someone's rescue. It was a mind-your-own-business kind of town. Don't ask questions. Stick to the plan. It was a place where people like me were supposed to be invisible. I thought about all the Mormons I'd grown up with, how we tended to stick together, how we wanted to believe we had all the answers, and how we turned our heads when we didn't. If I wanted help maybe I would have to find non-Mormon people in this Mormon town.

Late in the day, Tiana got home from work, went to the fridge, and realized the family needed some groceries for dinner. From my room, I heard her and Johnny arguing about who would go to the store.

Maybe this was my chance. I had to take any chance to get out of the house. I ripped out a page from my journal, wrote a note asking for help, added my name and my parents' phone number, and stuffed it into my pocket. I opened the bedroom door and stepped into the kitchen.

"I can help get the groceries for dinner," I volunteered. Since part of my job while there was to help with the household chores, I felt like they would be happy I was doing what they asked.

"I'll go," Johnny said, grabbing the keys from the kitchen counter. "You come with me. But you will do what I say."

When we got to the Albertsons, Johnny ordered me to keep one hand on the cart at all times. We moved up and down the aisles, adding ramen noodles, gallons of milk, and big bags of shredded cheese and store-brand cereal to the cart. I kept my fingers curled around the edge of the basket, but my eyes roved the store for someone who did not look Mormon, someone who might be more likely to help me.

At the checkout, I saw a woman in the line next to us. Her hair was cropped short and colored bright red. Her face was deeply tanned and wrinkled from the sun. Funky shell earrings hung from her ears. And she was wearing a tank top. A Mormon couldn't wear a tank top and wear garments—sacred Mormon undergarments, which all adult Mormons wear after they've gone through the temple and committed to the faith—at the same time. I checked her basket for another sign, maybe a beer, that she was not Mormon. But really the tank top was enough.

Keeping one hand on the basket, while Johnny turned his back, I slipped the note from my pocket and handed it to the woman. She seemed a little startled by it. Questions formed on her face.

Please. Please. Please, I silently begged.

Her eyes focused on mine, and she started to open the note.

Hurry. Help me. Please.

Johnny turned around, saw the note, stepped between her and me, and simply took the note from her hand.

And she let him.

Please. Please. Please. No.

Johnny read the note to himself and laughed out loud. "What a joke," he said, to no one in particular. Then he turned to the woman in line. "This is all a joke," he said.

She did not question him. Maybe she was intimidated by his laughter, or his size. Her turn came to check out, and she unloaded her basket onto the conveyor belt without saying a word to me. My heart fell.

After we checked out, Johnny wheeled the cart to the parking lot. I was still holding on to the edge, bracing for what came next. He opened the car door and ordered me to get into the backseat. There was nothing I could do. He straightened up and pulled his belt from his loops. Cars came and went. Families got in and got out. Kids scrambled and darted through the parking lot with their parents. I could see them at the edges of my vision as the blows fell, but it was like they could not see me. Not one of them said a word. Neither did Johnny. Neither did I. Maybe it was the hunger. Maybe it was getting so close to a chance at escape and failing. Maybe it was realizing that even non-Mormon people probably would not help me. I don't know. But in that moment, I could not find it in me to fight.

Johnny finished the beating and I curled up in the backseat. He put the rest of the groceries in at my feet, shut the door, and climbed into the driver's seat. Neither of us said anything the whole way home. The car pulled into the driveway. I helped carry the bags inside.

"Help me make dinner," Tiana said.

She boiled a big pot of water and put the ramen noodles in it. I stood over the stove, feeling the steam on my face, staring into the boiling water. When the noodles were soft, Tiana drained them and then showed me how to fry them, melting a big hunk of butter in a pan on the stove.

The kids sat down at the table. I sat with them. Without a word, Tiana put fried noodles on my plate.

Three months or three years—it's up to you. We know everyone in this town. It's your word against ours.

Johnny's words played back in my head. My body hurt from his blows. I hated him. I hated him so much. But it was going to take a long time to get out of here. If I could get out at all.

I lifted my fork and brought the buttery noodles to my lips. I could feel my body craving the savory, salty taste at the same time as I felt waves of anger and sadness flooding through me. By eating, I had lost again. None of my plans had worked. I hated feeling defeated, and I knew I needed a new plan.

"That's right, Alexie," Tiana said, giving me a nickname she and Johnny would use whenever they wanted to show tenderness. It was strange to me how she would sometimes treat me warmly, like a daughter, and other times so cruelly.

She put her hand on my shoulder. My first instinct was to pull violently away, but I forced myself to sit still and keep chewing. Johnny, I had already learned, seemed to be able to anticipate my every move. If I was planning an escape, he knew it before I did. But maybe I could find a way into Tiana's conflicted emotions and win her trust. Maybe in the complicated spaces between her anger and her exhaustion, between the hardness she had to wear on the outside and the loneliness she felt inside, I could find a way out of this house.

Late that night, back in my room, lying on the pink mattress, my thoughts turned for comfort to Yvette. I tried to imagine her face, her long dark hair, the way it whipped in the wind as she drove her red Jeep with the windows down. I wondered if she was still looking after her grandparents in Tucson or if she was back in Victorville. Did she miss me? Was she worried about me? I wanted so badly to have her arms around me. I thought of the afternoons Ashley and Brianna and I used to spend lazing across the couches and laughing. My mind went back to my parents. How long had it been since I'd had a hug from my mom? Five days since she and my dad had left me here. Almost eighteen days since they had kicked me out of the house.

I thought of Tiana's hand on my shoulder. Loneliness welled up inside me as I fell asleep.

Saturday, September 11, 2010
   Dear Yvette:
   I had a dream about you last night. You took me away from this place. I know I'm going to be here for a long time and I know that there is always a chance you could find someone else. You mean the world to me, Yvette, and I want you to be happy.
   Last night they took me to a grocery store and I had a note in my pocket saying that these people were bad and to please call my parents. It had their number and my name. I tried to pass it to a woman who looked like she wasn't Mormon. The man saw it. He laughed and said it was a joke. He took the note and took me outside. He took me to the car and locked the doors. I was praying so hard that nothing would happen. He took his belt off and beat me with it.

Sunday, September 12, 2010
   Yvette:
   Today is Sunday. I was woken up by the man. He told me to get up and get dressed. I got up and collected my clothes. The man was still standing there. I tried to walk past him to the restroom, but he wouldn't let me by. He said to get dressed right now. I asked him to please leave and shut the door. He just laughed at me. I got dressed as quickly as I could, and when I was done, he left. I cried and cried, but crying doesn't help. Baby, I'm afraid of what's going to happen next. My grandparents will be at church, but I'm not allowed to speak to them. I'm praying every chance I get for us. I'm praying for your grandparents. I hope they are doing well. I'm praying for you,

that you're okay and that you're safe, that you're staying strong. I
love you, Yvette.

ALL DAY AND ALL night my mind kept fighting, throwing itself
against the walls of the house, trying to imagine the world beyond,
the faces and the voices of the people I loved, the feel of my bedspread at home. I reached for God—not in the way the Siales wanted
me to but in my own way, drawing from a very personal, private
kind of faith my religion had planted in me when I was a little
girl. I had always been taught that if I prayed, God would answer.
Was that promise conditional on whether I turned out to be gay or
straight? Did God really care if I liked girls? Would God still hear
my prayers? The stubborn part of me wanted to believe in a God
bigger than all that, and I just kept praying in the hard hours. I held
on to everything the Siales had not taken and could not take away,
everything inside my mind and spirit.

But my body knew that I wouldn't survive unless I adjusted to
the everyday routines and played along until I could find a way out.
And I had to survive. That much I knew for sure.

CHAPTER 9

Free to Choose

A TYPICAL DAY IN THE Siale house started with Victor pushing me on the shoulder to wake me up. If I tried to look into his eyes, he'd turn away with a blank expression. Whether it was sadness or fear or guilt or indifference, I could not tell.

I would get up, shower, dress in the long skirts and oversize cast-off T-shirts that were my uniform, then go into the kitchen to make breakfast and pack lunches for the younger Siale kids. Breakfast was usually cereal that came in big bags from the grocery store or from the church food pantry, the bishop's storehouse.

After the Siale kids left for school, it was just me, Johnny, Sifa, and Calvin.

At ten A.M. every day, Johnny called us into a meeting he called "group." He would sit on the couch, rubbing his pained feet, while Calvin, Sifa, and I sat on the floor. He'd open group with prayer, then take out the scriptures. In his Book of Mormon, he usually turned to the early chapters in 1 Nephi or 2 Nephi. He'd pick a verse to read out loud, then explain what it meant and ask questions to make sure we understood it.

"Men are free to choose liberty and eternal life," Johnny read one day, "through the great Mediator of all men, or to choose captivity and death, according to the captivity and power of the devil; for he seeketh that all men might be miserable like unto himself."

He paused, then repeated the words for emphasis. "*Free to choose. Life, or captivity and death. Because Satan wants you to be miserable.*" He put down the scriptures and shifted his weight on the sofa. "Heavenly Father has given us all the power to choose. It's in the plan of salvation. You can choose to stay with the plan, or you can choose death and captivity. It's that simple." He fixed his eyes on each of us in turn. "It's your choice to be here. It's your choice to continue with the problems that got you here. Or you can choose obedience and happiness."

Then he'd address each of us with questions, going around the circle and putting us on the spot about our issues.

Calvin had been caught trying to buy a bus ticket out of St. George and go back to his family in California. Johnny would repeatedly lecture Calvin about taking responsibility for his situation and not running away from his problems, even though from what I could gather Calvin's problems stemmed from the fact that he had been bullied back in California. All the time, Johnny would ask Calvin, "Are you gay?" Calvin would simply say, "No." Johnny did it just to dominate Calvin, just to humiliate him. He had been totally broken in. Or just broken.

When it came time to talk about me, Johnny would launch into a familiar dialogue.

"Why do you think you're here, Alex?"

"Because I'm gay."

"Do you know why being gay is wrong?"

"Because it's not included in the plan of salvation."

"We are going to help you, Alex, help you find your place in the plan. You're going to pray and read your scriptures. You're going to learn to clean and cook for all of us so you can get married to a returned missionary and have a family of your own."

After group, I spent the afternoon doing homework packets we picked up from the alternative school each week. Nighttimes, I'd cook and clean for the family.

As far as I could tell, that was the extent of the Siales' strategy for changing me from gay to straight: prayer, scripture study, home-schooling, group meetings, and chores. And being cut off from all the people I loved.

Sometimes Johnny would press me for information about Yvette—where she lived, how old she was, her phone number—but I refused to give up any information.

Sifa was the example of how we could turn out if we did what Johnny said.

"Sifa used to be a really bad kid," Johnny would say, "and now he's not."

"Thanks to you guys," Sifa would say, in a tone that made it hard to tell whether he was thankful for what he had experienced at the Siales' or he was just thankful now to be left alone. "Thank you so much."

Group would close with prayer. Johnny would tell us to bow our heads, then do the same. "Dear Heavenly Father, please help these kids. Thank you for bringing them into our house."

After he finished praying, Johnny would set up the video games and get back to Call of Duty. Or, sometimes, Madden NFL.

During the afternoons, Calvin, Sifa, and I would drift uneas-ily around the house. I would clean the kitchen or the bathrooms. When my chores were done, Calvin, Sifa, and I would play cards at the kitchen table. Sifa was more talkative than Calvin. Calvin seemed to pull deep inside himself to avoid being noticed by Johnny, while Sifa tried to maintain the peace by keeping everyone happy, by playing with Grace when she was there or singing around the house in a sweet tenor voice—usually hymns from the Mormon hymnbook.

Sometimes I would write in my journal, or read. There was one bookshelf with rows of encyclopedias, a bunch of thick paperback crime novels that belonged to Johnny and some books published by the church. I picked out a biography of Joseph Smith and started to make my way through the pages during the long afternoons.

When the kids got home from school, Olivia and Grace would play outside in the backyard or in Olivia's room while the boys would join Johnny in the living room on the video games. Johnny's feet really hurt all the time from his gout. He'd manage the pain with pills or ask the boys to rub his feet for what seemed like hours at a time. He'd also drink something called kava, a traditional drink made from powdered roots. He taught me how to make the kava for him. I'd go into the pantry, and steep and squeeze a nylon stocking filled with the root powder in a big plastic bucket of water that stood on the pantry floor. Sifa and Calvin told me that you could get buzzed off kava, that the way Johnny drank it—every day, all afternoon—he must get pretty high.

Tiana would usually wake up around dinnertime, but making dinner was my job. I'd do as Tiana taught me, spilling value-size bags of chicken pieces across baking pans and placing them in the oven. I learned to cook ramen so many different ways: fried, boiled, mixed with SPAM and mayonnaise. The house would go through a giant mayonnaise container about twice a month. Sometimes there were fruits and vegetables in the fridge—apples, oranges, and carrots—but Tiana always said that they were expensive and told me not to let the kids have them.

Monday nights everyone would gather in the kitchen for Family Home Evening, just as we had in my own house growing up. There would be a lesson from the church lesson manual—about honesty or baptism or the importance of keeping the Sabbath day holy—and a game or dessert to follow.

Some nights Johnny just watched television—the St. Louis Rams or the Los Angeles Lakers—and ignored Tiana. Sometimes he yelled and screamed at her. Or threw things across the room. Usually, he would lash out if something made him feel stupid. Johnny hated feeling stupid. But Tiana knew how to calm him down. They'd go into the bedroom, a mix of affection and weariness on her face, and the house would settle into an uneasy quiet.

Some nights, when Johnny was bored or if there was an argument or disagreement between the boys, Johnny would make Calvin, Sifa, and Victor go out into the garage and fight. He would pass out boxing gloves, then push back the giant Rubbermaid tubs of football and other athletic gear to clear a space.

"Go," he'd say. "Go harder, or I'll take somebody's place."

They'd be out there for what seemed like forever. Then they'd come in, Johnny full of edgy energy, his voice still loud, the three boys looking tired and humiliated. Sifa and Calvin would say nothing and head straight for their room.

Having felt the force of Johnny's fists, I was both incredibly sorry for the boys and incredibly relieved that it was not me being forced to fight.

Sundays, of course, we would walk down the block to the big LDS chapel and spend three hours at our church meetings. My grandparents were in the same congregation as the Siales, and at first I was so eager to see them. But when they came and took their place two rows behind us in the chapel, they would not even look at me. If I looked back, they pretended not to notice. After sacrament meeting, they would disappear into their Sunday school classes without trying to find me and hug me. It was like they had a silent agreement with the Siales that any contact with me would ruin my treatment.

Everyone agreed I should be invisible. But being invisible hurt. How was it possible, I wondered, for my grandparents to pretend I wasn't there? How was it possible to refuse to see your own grandchild? I also wondered how they too could believe that leaving me with strangers and refusing to see me would help me or even cure me of my homosexuality. Most of all, I just hurt. I didn't have the words for it then, but now I realize how much I was aching for something familiar, some kind of reassurance, someone to say my name and give me a hug—the kind of connection everyone needs to hold their lives together.

The one Sunday we didn't go to church was during General Conference, when Mormons all over the world tuned in to watch addresses from our leaders in Salt Lake City. Back in California, we got it on cable. In Utah, it was on regular television channels. It felt like the world stopped when Conference came on TV.

Johnny and Tiana made the kids sit on the couch to watch the Sunday morning session. Calvin, Sifa, and I sat on the floor, looking up at the faces of our church leaders—men in dark suits and ties, all of them in their seventies and eighties—on the flat-screen.

I had spent enough time listening to Conference talks in my life to know that they were usually pretty basic. Pray. Keep the commandments. Pay your tithing. Serve the church. That sort of thing. I sat there, tuned half in, half out—just enough to know what was going on in case Johnny or Tiana asked me.

But I found my attention focusing in as a church leader named Boyd K. Packer came to the pulpit. "There is such confusion and such danger that our young people hardly know which way they can walk," he said, then he started to discuss two dangers: pornography and homosexuality.

People at church usually talked about homosexuality in one of two ways. Sometimes it was compared to a disability or a disease, like alcoholism, that some people had been burdened with for this lifetime, as a spiritual test of their strength and obedience. Other times the emphasis was that it was always a choice, something that could be changed with enough effort, cured, or just ignored altogether. Elder Packer, it sounded like, was in this camp.

"Some suppose that they were preset and cannot overcome what they feel are inborn tendencies toward the impure and unnatural," he said. "*Not so!* Why would our Heavenly Father do that to anyone? Remember, he is our Father."

God would never make someone gay, was what Elder Packer was basically saying. That's what the Siales seemed to believe too, that liking girls was not who I really was but some kind of trick my mind was playing on me, something I did just to be rebellious, and it could be drilled out. That just didn't feel true to me.

"Every soul confined in a prison of sin, guilt, or perversion has a key to the gate. The key is labeled 'repentance.' If you are bound by a habit or an addiction that is unworthy, you must stop conduct that is harmful. Angels will coach you, and priesthood leaders will guide you through those difficult times."

I felt a knot of anxiety form in my stomach. I knew that my parents and grandparents were listening, that the Siales were listening, that everyone around me, all the houses on the block, were listening to Elder Packer on television. Everyone believed that liking girls was something that could be fixed, something that *should* be fixed, and that people like the Siales knew how to do it.

I again remembered what Johnny had told me my first day in the house: *It's your word against ours. You can be here three months or three years.*

The panic had returned to my stomach.

CHAPTER 10

The Burden of Homosexuality

Friday, October 15, 2010

My anger is gone. I feel emptiness, like I can't be happy and I can't be sad. I can just be. Like I got rid of all my emotions and now I'm empty. I think I've been expecting to just go back to my normal self, to be how I was before I met Yvette, but I've realized I'll never be the same. Before Yvette, I couldn't love anyone but myself, I couldn't trust anyone but myself. And she changed everything. I cried over her, felt pain that I never thought I could. I felt happiness that I thought I could never feel before. Now I know I can feel that pain and that happiness and that love and trust. My whole perspective on everything has changed.

Maybe this is just a chapter in my life that I have to complete. A good chapter, finishing high school. Maybe to finish high school I have to be here. I don't know what to think. I don't know what to feel. Not anymore.

I think I get a phone call with my parents on Sunday, but
I'm not sure. If I do, I'm going to tell them I love them. Maybe
saying it will make this better.

At the bottom of the journal page, I drew a girl with sloped
shoulders, her face hidden by a frizzy mat of hair. I drew spirals,
a cluster of jewels, and a huge circle with a word written in the
middle: "begin." I etched in a bass clef symbol and some lines for
musical notation, my fingers remembering and hungry for my cello.
Vines grew from my pen up the side of the page, and amid the
vines, I wrote these words: "I'll never be the same."

I could feel the way that time at the Siales was changing me. But
their program of group meetings, housework, homeschooling, and
religious discussions seemed not to be getting the effects the Siales
promised.

In November, Tiana came home from work tired as usual but
seeming like she had a solution to a problem that had been weigh-
ing on her.

"Okay," she said to no one in particular as she crossed the living
room where Johnny, Sifa, Calvin, and I were sitting for group. "I
know what we're going to do."

She went into her bedroom, got a black nylon backpack out of
the closet, and set it on the kitchen counter. Then she left the house
through the kitchen door and stepped into the backyard.

She came back with gray rocks. They were round and smooth,
the kind you buy at the home and garden center to use as deco-
ration in the yard. I think Tiana had pulled them up from their
places at the edges of the lawn. She must have had five or six of
them.

One by one, she put the rocks into the backpack while we all
watched, then she zipped up the backpack and called me over.

"Alex." She straightened her shoulders and puffed out a heavy
breath. "You're going to wear this all the time now." She placed her

hand on the backpack. "This represents the physical burden of being gay. This is what your mind and emotions are putting you through because of the choices you have made. You are going to wear this every day so you can feel the burden. You ignore your emotions. This will help you feel them."

She handed me the backpack. I slipped it on and felt the weight of the rocks settle onto my shoulders.

"You will wear this from the time you wake up until you go to bed. It will help you feel what a burden you are carrying in choosing to be gay. You can choose to be gay, but you know it's not in the plan of salvation. That's a heavy burden, Alex. You need to feel it to help you make the right choices."

I looked at the backpack, studied the straps and the shapes of the rocks through the fabric, but I could scarcely take in the reality of what she was telling me. I would be wearing this backpack every day? To represent the "burden" of being gay? It was like she was speaking a foreign language.

That first day, I moved through the hours with the backpack resting on my shoulders, making dinner for the kids, cleaning the kitchen, then heading to the bathroom for my shower. I closed the door, set the backpack on the linoleum floor, and exhaled. I took off my T-shirt and looked in the mirror. The straps had left pink marks on my shoulders.

It's not so bad, I told myself as I stepped under the running water. *I can handle this.*

I went to sleep that night with the backpack next to my bed.

The next day, I tried to get used to the feeling of the straps on my shoulders and the load of rocks pressing into my lower back as I got the kids ready for school and out the door. But by midmorning, after group, I felt a tightness in the muscles around my shoulder blades.

At first, the tightness went away as soon as I took the backpack off at night, as soon as I made it to the privacy of the bathroom, where I could set down the backpack full of rocks, pull off my oversize T-shirt, and exhale. I would press my fingers into the pink marks on my skin and try to straighten my shoulders, to undo the cramping. It worked at first.

But after a few days, the pink marks grew red, and the tightness deepened into a persistent cramping that never went away, even after I set my backpack at the side of my bed and lay down for the night. Lying there on my mattress, I could feel one shoulder blade creeping higher than the other, trying to accommodate the weight of the backpack.

Johnny kept pressing me to give him information about Yvette. When I refused, he ordered Calvin or Sifa to get another rock. "Make sure it's a good-size rock," he said, "or you'll wear a backpack too."

They silently went along with it, just to stay out of Johnny's way. I couldn't blame them.

One night after dinner, Tiana asked me if I was hurting. I told her I was, even though I hated letting her know how I was really feeling.

"Sit down," she said, gesturing toward the kitchen table. "We're going to write a letter to your parents."

She rummaged in the kitchen desk drawer for a pen and a blank sheet of paper, set them down on the table, and sat down beside me.

"Here's what you need to say: Dear Mom and Dad. Thank you for sending me here. Now I know that I'm not really gay. I was just on all these drugs."

I stopped writing and stared down at the table.

"You finish the letter," Tiana said, "and we take a rock out of that backpack."

Anger rose from my belly to my throat.

Trapped. With rocks on my back. In a stranger's house far from home. Nowhere to run.

Tiana started in again, dictating the letter. "I'm getting clean now and I really needed it. Getting clean is really hard, but I'm doing it and they're helping me."

I let my hand follow the words.

It was a bitter feeling, giving in to Johnny and Tiana, to their game of rocks given and rocks taken away. But really I had nowhere else to go.

A WEEK AFTER I got the backpack, one night Tiana took me to work with her at the treatment center. Wearing my backpack, I got into the blue TrailBlazer, and we drove these long roads at the base of the red-rock mountains until we got to the facility—a set of stucco and cinder-block buildings clustered around a green lawn and hemmed in by chain-link fences, in a neighborhood of warehouses and office buildings just a block off I-15.

We arrived just in time for the nighttime group meeting, the last event of the day before the girls went to their beds in the dorms. It was Tiana's job to monitor group, then sit in a chair in the dorms all night.

When we walked into the facility, I felt a dull sense of fear settle into my stomach. I almost could not believe my eyes. There were other girls wearing backpacks, moving heavily through the halls, gathering for group meeting. Their backpacks were weighted like mine. But they curved around their backs and didn't make the heavy clunking sound mine did as the rocks fell into one another when I walked. *Backpacks full of sand,* I realized. *They're wearing backpacks full of sand. To feel the burden of . . . what? What are they here for? Are they gay like me?*

Another girl walked past me into the group meeting. She was wearing what looked like a bike helmet, with a mirror hanging from a wire in front of her eyes so she would have to look in her own eyes all day long. I could imagine what they had told her, whoever had come up with this kind of "treatment"—something about looking yourself in the face so you could see your reflection and the unhappiness your choices produced.

I felt dizzy.

This cannot be right. I wonder if their parents know about this.

Sitting at the edge of the group meeting with Tiana, I started putting more of the story together. I believed Tiana was trying to do to me at home what she observed someone do at the residential treatment centers: isolate me from my family, take away all my stuff, make me attend group, wear the backpack. They could put a Mormon spin on it because they were in their own home and because my parents and grandparents were Mormon too. And they felt like they were right, all of them—that I had to be broken, that I could be cured, that it would happen in time—because that's what they had heard from the leaders of our church. I knew they were wrong, but it didn't change the fact that I was trapped, a prisoner in their home.

There is no way out of this, I thought. *I used to get away with a lot, messing around with Brianna and Ashley, taking off for LA. But this is karma. This is payback. I am never getting out.*

EVEN NOW IT IS hard to explain everything I was feeling. The physical pain of the backpack dominated my reality from the time I woke up until I went to bed. According to Johnny and Tiana's rules, I could go to bed as soon as the chores were done—as early as eight P.M. I couldn't wait for eight to come so I could disappear into the bathroom, take off the backpack, let the warm water run across my cramping shoulder muscles, and head for my mattress, where I would pretend to be asleep until real sleep finally came.

But the physical feelings were just a tiny part of it. At first, after my parents had left me, I felt angry, indignant, determined to find a way out. Then the loneliness settled in. I missed Yvette, and my parents, and Ashley and Brianna. I wanted someone who'd known me forever to laugh with me and say my name. I wanted to know where I was on the map—in my own house, in my own town. I missed the routine of going to school every day and I missed eating cookies and hot *pupusas* at my friends' house. I felt so lost, so alone.

But as the weeks wore on, the loneliness started to change shape. I came to terms with the idea that there was nothing I could do to escape my situation. I started to feel like a stranger in my own life. Sometimes I felt like part of me was pulling away deep down inside, away from the surface, away from where anyone could see me or touch me.

But at other times I felt like part of me was trying to swim to the surface, trying to come up for air, starving for a feeling of normal, or for normal human contact: a hug, a touch on the shoulder.

Most days I just went through the routine, numbed out by sadness.

All I could do, I figured, was to play along with the Siales' rules, as best as I could figure them, and survive.

CHAPTER 11

Invisible

IN LATE NOVEMBER, THE days got colder and shorter. I had been there almost three months. When I arrived, the late summer desert heat had kept temperatures in the 80s and 90s. But now I found myself awakened in the middle of the night by the chill. The Siales did not turn on the heater in the house, and I had one thin blanket to use on my mattress on the floor. As I lay there, the cold would creep into the cramped muscles in my neck and shoulders and around my shoulder blades.

I started wearing extra layers of clothes, both to ward off the cold and to deal with the deepening pain of the backpack of rocks I wore. Every morning after my shower, I'd slip on several oversize T-shirts and a sweatshirt before putting on the backpack to go make breakfast and lunches for the kids. On colder days when I thought I could get away with it, I'd wear a coat too. Having that extra layer helped blunt the bite of the backpack on my skin, but it did not dull the pain in my muscles.

Fall also meant football season, which was a big deal in the Siale household. Johnny had worked as a football coach's assistant, and all the Siale boys had played in tackle football junior leagues from the time they were small. Every week, Johnny and the boys went to see the football games played at the local high school. One Friday night I got to come too.

After finishing the dinner dishes, I headed to my room to change my clothes and get ready. But first, I sat down on my mattress and took out my journal. Balancing the book on my knees, I wondered if I should try it just one more time. Should I write a note and try to find someone to help me? Johnny knew all the coaches and many of the people in the stands; he watched football with them week after week. They all knew him, and he knew all of them. Chances that anyone there would be willing to help me, to believe me, were incredibly small, and just thinking about the risks (another beating? more rocks in the backpack?) made me wince.

But I had to try. I felt my pulse quicken as I heard Johnny walk down the hallway, gathering the kids into the car. I quickly scribbled a note in the journal:

> *Help. These people are crazy. My parents don't know what's going on. Please call the police for me.*

I tore the sheet from my journal and shoved it into my pocket.

I got into the car with the Siale kids. It was the first time I had been to the high school, and I watched carefully out the windows as we drove, trying to put together a map in my head of how I could get there on my own someday. It was only a nine- or ten-minute car ride along the road at the edge of the neighborhood, with red sandstone foothills on one side and tracts of family homes and church buildings on the other. The stretches of sagebrush and rabbitbrush were broken up by a field of black lava rocks. Right after we crossed the lava rocks, the road turned right and headed to Snow Canyon High School.

It was a big school, a set of square, modern-looking buildings with panels of glass and panels of stucco that matched the red sandstone in the canyons all around. We drove past the Future Farmers of America building at the north end of campus, and the LDS Seminary building, where most of Snow Canyon's students attended church meetings one period of the school day. Both Snow Canyon High School and Snow Canyon itself were named after Lorenzo Snow, one of the early prophets of the Mormon Church. In my mind, I could see the pictures of him from my Sunday school classes, with his long white beard.

The football stadium was built into a canyon behind the school, with bleachers on one side of the field and concrete stands on the other. Johnny parked the car in the lot behind the stands and looked at me in the rearview mirror.

"You can leave your backpack in the car, but stay close to me."

The kids piled out and I did as I was told, slipping off my backpack and leaving it on the backseat floor, then sticking with the family through the parking lot to take our place in the stands. Lots of people greeted Tiana and Johnny on the way. We were surrounded by Siale family friends and neighbors. If I was going to find help at the game, I knew it would take some careful thinking.

The game started. Johnny and Tiana watched it closely, standing and cheering with every rise in the action. The boys did too, following their father. Olivia and Grace played on the steps of the stadium, too young to care about football. I spent my time scanning the crowds. Who here would help me? I looked up and down the rows of Snow Canyon families from the neighborhood, dressed in their green and gold Snow Canyon Warriors gear. They looked like the people I had seen in the parking lot at Albertsons the last time I had tried to escape, or the people in the McDonald's: regular St. George people, who would probably believe whatever Johnny and Tiana told them, and who probably believed I deserved to be where I was.

A family sitting close by caught my attention. They were being really loud and funny, and something about the way the dad laughed made me feel safe. He was tall and bald, and he was wearing a Snow Canyon Warriors T-shirt. His wife was blond and had pretty, soft features. She laughed with her husband. Her elementary-school-aged daughter sat next to her.

Throughout the first and second quarters, I tried to tune in through the noise of the game and the crowd to bits of their conversation. They were visiting town. They had come to see their nephew play for Snow Canyon. They didn't live in St. George. This fact, with the warmth of the father's laugh, gave me a spark of hope. If they weren't from the neighborhood, maybe they didn't know the Siales. Maybe they would believe that I needed help. Maybe they could help get me out. I looked around me at the crowd in the stands, following every play in the game with rapt attention. Johnny was too, but I knew that he also had one eye closely on me. I figured that at the end of the second quarter—when the team came off the field and the crowd started moving for the refreshment stands and the restrooms—that moment of confusion would be my chance to reach out and pass the note.

The tension in my belly started spiraling upward. I put my hand in my coat pocket and held the note between my fingers. I kept my eyes on the field, listened to the crowd cheer every new first down, but out of the corner of my eye I focused on the minutes and seconds ticking down on the scoreboard.

The mom, I thought. *Get it to the mom.*

She was sitting about ten feet away from me. Between us sat another man. I would have to rely on him to get the note to the blond mom in the laughing family.

The clock ticked down to 0:00. People all around us stood up. I took a deep breath, shoved my hand into my pocket, and grasped the note.

I turned to face the man next to me. "Can you give this to the blond woman?" I asked.

He looked at me quizzically but with just a hint of warmth, an openness.

Wordlessly, he turned and tapped the blond mom on the shoulder. Her eyes turned and met mine.

I formed words with my mouth: *Help me.*

She paused. As the crowd started moving around us, her eyes stayed with mine. She nodded, as if she were taking the words in, and put the note in her pocket.

Next thing I knew, Johnny was at my shoulder. "Did she just pass you something?" he demanded of the man sitting next to me.

The man paused.

Please. Please. Please. Please. I prayed, silently.

The man looked at Johnny, then saw the pleading look in my eyes. "No," the man said.

I did not turn to face Johnny. I could scarcely breathe until he turned back to the boys and stepped away. In fact, I pretty much held my breath the rest of the game. I kept looking over at the blond mom. She kept looking back, meeting my eyes with what seemed like understanding. I silently begged her to do something, to come sit by me, ask my name, who I was, and how I'd gotten there.

I needed someone to see me.

Please. Please. Please. Please, I begged throughout the third and fourth quarters, as the navy, green, and gold Snow Canyon Warriors scrambled on the fields and the noise of the crowd rose and fell. Still, nothing happened. If the woman had read the note, she wasn't doing anything.

The clock ran down to zero again, and when I turned one last time to lock eyes with the blond mom next to us, she and the rest of her family had already left the stands.

Later that night, back at home, Tiana and Johnny came into my room before I fell asleep.

"You know those people you passed the note to?" Johnny said.

My stomach fell. I braced myself.

"That was Brother Taylor's brother and sister-in-law."

The Taylors were a Mormon family who lived in the neighborhood.

"They told us everything," Tiana said. "And we told them who you were and why you were here."

This time Johnny and Tiana did not need to yell at me or drag me by the arm and force me into the car and beat me.

It was their word against mine. I was surrounded by people who would never believe me. It was like no one could hear me or see me.

I already felt defeated.

AS FOR CONTACT WITH my parents, all I had was one phone call on Sunday afternoons—supervised, always supervised. I would sit at the kitchen counter and use Tiana's cell phone while she stood over me.

Thanksgiving, I told myself, would be different. My parents were scheduled to come for my first unsupervised visit. I counted down every day, imagining how it would sound for my mom to say my name, take me in her arms, or stroke my hair. That's what got me through the cold nights and the mornings making breakfast, through the group meetings, when Johnny told me that being gay had no place in God's plan, and through the weight of the rocks in the backpack.

For Thanksgiving itself, we went to visit Johnny's relatives in Las Vegas. My parents arrived in St. George the day after Thanksgiving. The plan was that they would stay at my grandparents' house. I would get to spend a little time with them, and I wouldn't have to wear the backpack.

It was about nine P.M. on Friday night when Johnny and Tiana dropped me off at my grandparents' house. "Don't be stupid," Johnny said to me as I stepped out of the car.

Tiana walked me to the door. When it opened, I could not wait to get into my parents' arms. I needed them to see me. I needed them to hug me. Most of all, I needed them to hear what I had to say.

We left Tiana on the doorstep and went into the kitchen to sit down at the table.

My mom smiled and wrapped her manicured hands around a glass of diet cola. My dad sat silently beside her.

"I have good news, honey," she said, smiling. "Your father and I are working on moving to Utah, so we can be closer to you."

I felt like the ground fell away under me. "No, Mom! Please! I can't stay here."

I could feel my mom pull back and stiffen a bit, the air between us change, a quiet settle in.

"I will not take you back to California, Alex."

"Why, Mom? Please."

"You can't go back. You need to stay here. The Siales are helping you."

"Johnny says I will be here until I am eighteen!"

"If you try, Alex, just try," my mother smiled, "that will never happen."

I paused. I needed to tell them. They needed to understand. "Mom, they hit me. They make me wear a backpack full of rocks."

I waited for the impact of the words to sink in. I looked to my mother, my father, sitting there with me at my grandparents' dining room table.

I said it again. "All day long. They make me wear a backpack full of rocks. It hurts." My words were calm and measured.

There was a pause. My mom did not look away, or look down. Her face did not change. "Honey, was it a bad idea to have an unsupervised visit with you?"

"You have to believe me. You have to believe what I'm saying."

"Alex, we have wanted to believe you. But you've lied to us before."

"Johnny says I will be here until I'm eighteen years old. I can't, Mom!" Tears began to roll down my face.

I thought about pulling down the shoulder of my shirt, showing them the outlines the straps had left in my shoulders, or taking their hands and guiding them to the knots in my back. But a wave of hopelessness washed through me, paralyzing me. I had hoped they would see me and hear me. But it was not to be.

My father stood up, turned without a word, and stepped into the kitchen. The conversation was over. I could feel my parents pull back from me into a defensive silence. And I pulled back from them, into sadness, anger, and pain. I could see that they didn't trust me. To them, I was the rebellious kid who had run away one too many times to be trusted.

We didn't say much to one another over the next hour. I tried to absorb whatever affection I could from my mother. Then we got into their car and headed back to the Siales'.

Sitting in the driveway with the engine off, I pleaded with my parents. "Please don't tell the Siales anything I told you."

My mom turned around and searched my face; my father looked straight ahead, at the garage door.

"We love you honey," she said.

It sounded like an apology.

THE WAY MY PARENTS and the Siales saw it, saying that I was gay, that I liked girls, was just an act—the act of a teenager out of control. They held Yvette responsible for my trouble and confusion. As I sat on the floor in group, day after day, Johnny explained it to me again and again: Yvette had "groomed" me, picked me out, confused me, made me use drugs, forced me into making out with her. In the Siales' view, I had to get away from Yvette and tell them all the details about her: first and last names, where she lived, her actual age. If they'd known she was eighteen when we dated and nineteen now, they would've reported her to the police. As they saw it, getting away from Yvette and getting in touch with my real feelings by confronting the pain of the backpack would snap me back into reality, back into my place in the plan.

One thing they had right was that every day, as I wore the backpack and went through the motions, I *was* getting in touch with my real feelings. The weight of the rocks, the bite of the straps into my shoulders, pressed me down into myself, down through the layers of boredom and shallow distraction that had defined my former life with my friends in Victorville. The weight of the backpack also pressed me down through the layers of what I had been taught at church, through the holes and gaps in the plan of salvation as it had been taught to me. It forced me to look more closely at all the ways I had acted out and tested my parents. I thought about the times I had caused them to worry, by driving to Los Angeles with my friends or smoking weed. I thought about all the arguments I had caused in the house. No question, I had been a difficult kid. But I had always told them the truth and taken the punishment.

The weight of the backpack forced me to look as well at my feelings for Yvette. Yes, I missed her. I missed her badly. I thought about her every day, wondering where she was, imagining how good it would feel to be with her again. But this was not about Yvette. This was about me, about the fact that I had told my parents I liked girls, and it had frightened them so badly they had pushed me out of the house and put me in a place where I couldn't be found, where no one would believe me, where I was invisible—and I would stay here until I broke. As much as they might tell themselves this was about Yvette, I knew this was about something deep inside me, an inseparable dimension of who I was. I had always been the girl who didn't fit into other people's expectations, the curious one, the hardheaded one, the one who stood on the edge of the crowd, who didn't believe everything they taught me, who dreamed of running away to the city.

I had always been different.

That difference could make me strong.

And I would need that strength in the weeks and months ahead.

Friday, December 3, 2010

    Last night we had group. Tiana and Johnny told me that next time my parents come it will be monitored. They're afraid I'm telling my parents bad things about them. I miss my parents so much. In thirteen days I will be able to see them. Although it will be monitored, I'll still be happy. Even though Thanksgiving was hard, I have to believe my parents. I do believe in my parents. I have to believe they will do the right thing, because they know the right thing. Yesterday Tiana said she had to make me feel small. But she didn't. I felt 5'6". I'm not going to let anyone make me feel small. I'm going to make myself happy. I'm not going to be sad for the rest of my life.

    Tiana and Johnny slept until about two this afternoon, and when they came out the sink was full of dishes. I was in the living room reading a book and she started yelling at me. She said she just might cancel my visit with my parents. But I know my parents won't let that happen. I told my mom that Johnny always threatens that I'll be here until I'm eighteen. At Thanksgiving she promised me that would never happen.

    I believe her.

    My back hurts so badly.

    Daisies are beautiful but flimsy against what nature throws at them. But a tree is strong and won't be broken against any kind of weather.

    I am a tree.

Sunday, December 5, 2010

    I had to wear this backpack to church today! They added rocks back. It is so heavy and it hurts so badly. I want to speak to my parents. It's 8:00 P.M. and I still haven't gotten to do that. I can't believe how fucked up my brain is. A couple of weeks ago I was writing about children and life, and now all I can think about is ending it. Ending it all. "To die will be an awfully big adventure." I wonder what happens after you die. I wonder if heaven exists. I hope it does, I really, really hope it does. Today Tiana and Johnny said that if I want this backpack off, then I have to tell them Yvette's real, full name, where she lives, her birthdate, and I have to tell my parents. I don't want her to go to jail. I think I'm quite content with this backpack. It's nine o'clock and I don't think I'll be getting my phone call. I am beyond tired.

At the bottom of the page I drew a house. It was burning.

FINDING OUT THAT YVETTE was nineteen only agitated Johnny and Tiana. To me, it was no big deal. Lots of high school kids in my town dated people who had just graduated. Yvette was just one of the girls in the group we ran with, just another one of Angela's friends. But to Johnny and Tiana, the fact that Yvette was nineteen confirmed their idea that she had groomed me, made a victim of me, taken advantage of me, changed me into someone I was not. There was no other option now: they told me I had to make a report to the police.

I had always wanted to protect Yvette, even when I couldn't keep her name safe in my journal. Was it really such a bad thing that we fell in love? It seemed too easy to pin it all on her when I knew very well what had landed me at the Siales' was something essential to *me*. I had always been different. I liked girls. Time at the Siales' only confirmed for me the reality of my feelings. Reporting Yvette to the police would change nothing.

Tiana must have sensed my hardening resolve. I could feel her anger and resentment toward me grow. She managed moments of tenderness toward me. Sometimes she would put an arm around me or offer an encouraging hug. I let her too, though it seems strange to admit it now. There were times when I needed those hugs, even when they came from her. I was so lonely, so hungry to be seen and loved. Still, I know she didn't like having me in the house. Who wants to take in troubled teenagers for money? But with Johnny out of work, I don't think she had many other options. The weight of the house rested on her, and in turn, sometimes she took it out on me.

A few days after she and Johnny confronted me about Yvette's age, Tiana came home from work one morning with another plan.

It was a Wednesday morning. Usually when she got off the night shift at the treatment center she would walk straight to her bedroom, close the door, turn on the television, and go to sleep. Today, though, she stopped in the kitchen, where I was sitting at the table, playing cards with Sifa, passing the time between our group meeting and lunch.

"Alex," she said, standing at the head of the table. Her eyes looked so tired. "You've tried to run away from us before, and now you're trying to run away from telling us the truth about Yvette. So here's how it is going to be. Until you tell us Yvette's last name and where she lives, not only will you wear that backpack of rocks all day . . ."

She paused, crossed the kitchen to the hallway, and put her hand on the wall.

"You will wear that backpack of rocks and face the wall, from breakfast through bedtime."

She explained, "You can have three bathroom breaks. You can sit down for lunch and for dinner. The rest of the time"—she placed her finger on a spot in the middle of the hallway wall—"I want you right here." She tapped the spot twice, forcefully.

It took a minute to absorb this new reality. When I did, knots formed in my stomach and I felt like I wanted to cry, but I held back the tears.

Johnny got up from the couch and joined Tiana in the kitchen. "You can start now," he said.

I slowly stood up from the table and walked across the kitchen into the hallway.

"Here," Tiana said, pointing to the spot where she wanted me. "No more running."

I stepped into place. My toes were about five inches from the wall. My eyes went blurry for a moment, then focused on the wall in front of me. It was totally bare, except for a triangle of pushpin marks at the upper right edge of my field of vision.

Johnny stepped in behind me and spoke into my ear. "Breakfast to bedtime. Until you tell us her last name and where she lives."

Tiana went to her bedroom and shut the door. Johnny went back to the couch.

And I stayed.

I stayed there at the wall.

Sifa did not say a word. Like me, he was terrified of Johnny. What could he say, anyway? What could he do for me? Nothing. In a few minutes, I heard him put away the cards, go into the living room, and sit down on the floor.

I am a tree. A tree is strong and won't be broken against any kind of weather.

During those first few minutes at the wall, I tried to mentally prepare myself for what was ahead of me. I reassured myself that I was strong, determined, and different. I would figure something out! I promised myself, urgently, that I would.

I thought next of Yvette, Brianna, Ashley, Pamela, and Angela, then of my parents, my grandparents just down the block, my brothers and sisters. I pictured their houses. I revisited the last time I had seen each of them. I tried to lose my mind in happy memories. I stayed there as long as I could, as if I were holding my breath underwater.

When I couldn't stand it anymore, I turned my head back to glance at the clock on the microwave oven in the kitchen.

Forty-five minutes had passed. Forty-five minutes.

I tried a new strategy.

One, two, three, four, five, six, seven . . .

I started counting.

Eight, nine, ten, eleven, twelve, thirteen, fourteen, fifteen . . .

An hour or two later the Siale kids came home from school and the noise of the house spiraled upward. Still, my mind pressed on with its chain of numbers.

Eight hundred eighty-four, eight hundred eighty-five, eight hundred eighty-six, eight hundred eighty-seven . . .

I breathed and counted, breathed and counted. Though my mind bolted wildly about, I found that first afternoon I could still bring it back.

Standing in one place, I had no way to shift or discharge the weight of the backpack, as I could when I was moving about the house. The tightness across my shoulders ratcheted up, and the arc of pain from the base of my skull to the base of my spine flared.

Two thousand fifty-three, two thousand fifty-four, two thousand fifty-five, two thousand fifty-six . . .

I held to the numbers until dinner was over and kids were in their beds.

That's when Johnny put his hand on my shoulder.

"Alexie," he said. "It's time to go to bed."

THE NEXT DAY AND the next day, there was more counting.

Ten thousand three hundred ninety-four, ten thousand three hundred ninety-five . . .

But then again sometimes my mind left the numbers and went other places. I would space out, letting my eyes blur and disconnect from the world around me. Or I would focus on the edges of the pain and try to figure out how pain worked, where it came from, and where it stopped. I tried to feel where my ribs anchored into my spinal column and where the base of the column stopped. I tried to dial my attention in through the fog of pain.

Hours passed with me replaying scenes in my head of things I should have done differently. I shouldn't, for example, have told my mom that I liked girls. In my mind, I saw her in her bedroom and my dad sitting on the edge of the bed, looking down at the floor. I relived the walk from her bedroom to mine. The phone call to my sister. My mom appearing at the bedroom door and telling me to pack and leave the house. I should not have told her that I liked girls. I should have told her that I was having sex with a boyfriend— something that would've still been unacceptable but not cause for sending me away.

Or, in another version of the story, as I rewrote it in my head, when my mom asked me if I was having sex, I said no. I just shook my head and walked out the door.

Or when my parents came to the Flores' to get me, I ran. I left my bags and ran.

Or I ran from the gas station at the Nevada state line. I just ran from the parking lot, crossed under the interstate, and hid behind one of the state-line casinos until Yvette could come get me in her Jeep.

I could run right now, from this house, down the block. Except for the fact that everyone in this town seemed to know Johnny and Tiana. No one knew me or believed me, and no one would come to my aid—that much my months in St. George had made clear.

Seventeen, eighteen, nineteen, twenty, twenty-one . . .

And when I had replayed all the missed chances of escape, my mind went running to God. Because there was no one else to help me and nowhere else to go. I had not wanted to face God for a long time. I wanted God to leave me alone. I wanted to run and hide myself, get lost in this crazy, beautiful world with my girlfriend, feel her lips on mine. I did not want anything to do with a God who did not want me.

That's how I felt until I was at the wall, hour after hour, day after day, the backpack biting into my shoulders.

Four hundred thirty-eight, four hundred thirty-nine, four hundred forty . . .

But pressed down inside by the weight of the backpack, I re-played in my head the stories I had heard at church from the time I was a little girl. I remembered all the Sunday school lessons about kids in terrible circumstances—lost in snowstorms, separated from their families, alone and afraid. I remembered a story from the Book of Mormon about a prophet named Enos who went into the forest and stayed there and prayed and prayed until he had his answer.

I am a tree.

Seven thousand four hundred thirty-five, seven thousand four hundred thirty-six, seven thousand four hundred thirty-seven . . .

And so I prayed. I prayed like a Mormon girl. I prayed like the girl I still was, gay or not, and had always been.

Dear Heavenly Father. Please help me. Please, please get me out of here.

The noises of the household swirled around me as I stood at the wall.

Sometimes Johnny would call out, "Look at that dyke."

I would shift my feet to try to shift the weight and to lessen some of the pain.

"You can't march away from this, you dyke. You are at a dead end," Johnny would say.

HERE IS THE PART that chilled me the most, the part that chills me still: people saw me standing at the wall, and no one said a word. There I was, in the front hallway of the house, positioned between the entryway, the living room, and the kitchen. Throughout the day, whoever came and went from the Siale house walked right by me. Already I knew from my escape attempts that I was invisible, that everyone trusted the Siales, and that I was just another problem kid who deserved whatever she was getting, a girl so broken and confused that she even thought she was gay. That's how they must have seen me, the visitors from church and the neighborhood who occasionally came and went from the house, not one even acknowl-edging me or asking the question about what was going on.

The across-the-street neighbors came and went. One of Victor's friends and his parents came and went. People the Siales knew from church came and went. Facing the wall, I could hear it all, the knock at the door, the hellos and how are yous. Not a break in the regular flow of conversation, even as they passed within inches of me to go to the living room or the kitchen. They all trusted the Siales, that the Siales were doing what was best for me. I knew I couldn't say anything to these people, because they'd never believe me.

The local Mormon missionaries came over for dinner about once a week. It is a Mormon tradition to feed the missionaries, the pairs of short-haired, name-tagged, white-shirt-and-tie-wearing nineteen-year-olds from Utah, Arizona, and Idaho who knock on doors and try to find people to teach and convert, even in places like St. George. On the nights the missionaries came for dinner, I would make chicken and potatoes, set the table, and take my plate to the wall. They'd knock on the door, and Johnny would greet them with a huge hello and shake their hands. The whole family would sit at the table with the missionaries while I stood at the wall about twenty feet away. After dinner the missionaries would take out their scriptures and read to the family or show a church video on a portable DVD player.

Facing the wall, I could hear it all. I knew they could see me. But they never said anything to the Siales, to anyone else in the ward, or to anyone in the outside world. Day after day at the wall, I thought about it. How it was that the missionaries couldn't see me, ask my name, question what was going on. They were not so different from me, those nineteen-year-olds in their name tags and ties. They were regular Mormon kids, just boys like the boys I had grown up with in my ward in Victorville. They were far from home. They couldn't see their families or friends or talk to them on the phone. Day after day they moved through a set schedule of praying, studying scripture, knocking on doors, visiting church members, attending meetings, following the incredibly strict rules that govern how Mormon missionaries eat, sleep, and live. In many ways, they were as locked into their missionary lives as I was locked into my backpack full of rocks. Locked into a set of rules that made it impossible for them to see me the way one human being sees another.

Was it fear, I wondered, their silence, their refusal to see me or talk to me? Was it fear that animated the conversations they would have at the dinner table with Tiana and Johnny and the kids? Or was this their own desperate hunger to fit into the plan, the plan that was supposed to order their whole lives? If they raised their voices, stepped out of line, broke the rules—both the written rules of missionary life and the unwritten rules of a community in which people like me are not seen—would they lose their place in the plan and all the guarantees that came with it?

Someday, somehow, I would get out of this house, out of this backpack. Even if it meant lasting a couple more years until I turned eighteen. I would get out. I would not stay invisible. I would have my voice back.

Would they ever get back their ability to see things they weren't supposed to see, to ask questions they weren't supposed to ask? Or would they be locked in for life?

What makes me different makes me strong. I will have my voice back. A tree is strong and won't be broken against any kind of weather. I am a tree. These are the things I told myself every day at the wall, the words that I tried to hold in the front of my mind. But as the weeks passed, I could feel my mind shifting, no matter how hard I tried to hold on. I could feel something deeper inside me, something that ran from the base of my skull through the arc of pain across my shoulders to the root of my spine, pulling me down and away from the surface, away from other people.

This was the part of me that made me strong. This was the part of me determined to find a way out. This was also the part of me that wanted to die.

The idea presented itself quietly at first. I don't know when. At about the same time I realized that no one could see me and no one would help me, I started to really feel the pull to kill myself. By December, I had started putting it into words in my journal. Seeing the words on the page, the idea of killing myself frightened me. But beneath the words and the idea, the pull itself had a reassuring kind of power.

I will get out of this one way or another.

I could feel that strong, stubborn force pulling me down into myself, away from the mind-bending boredom of the white wall I faced every day, away from the sequence of numbers that cycled through my head as I counted down minutes and hours, the word "dyke" hovering angrily in the air around me with the sound of gunfire from Johnny's video games, and the locked-in silence of all the people who came and went and kept me invisible. The pull was the place I went to be away from this situation I had no way out of. It was dark and warm and familiar, and it belonged to me alone. When I was in my thoughts of how to end my life, no one could touch me there.

I will get out of this one way or another.

Sometime in December—I don't know which day; it was hard then and it is harder now to distinguish one day at the wall from another—I decided that I would do it. I would give myself a way out, as a present to myself, on my sixteenth birthday: December 16th.

I had been looking forward to turning sixteen for as long as I could remember. I wanted my driver's license, and I wanted to celebrate with Ashley and Brianna, just driving around Victorville, being silly, maybe having a big birthday cake with lots of candles. But that life seemed so far away now. Like I was seeing it from the bottom of the ocean.

I woke up on December 16th and spent the first part of the day turning over my options in my head. Very quickly a plan came together: I knew where there was medicine in the house, and taking a bunch of pills would bring either death or a trip to the hospital.

I will get out of this one way or another.

When I came off the wall to make dinner, taking ramen noodles, soy sauce, pots, and pans from the pantry and cupboards, I quietly inventoried the collection of pain medications Johnny used along with his kava to deal with his bad joints and feet. He kept them in the kitchen cupboard, next to bottles of naproxen. As I boiled and fried the noodles, the Siale kids moving through the kitchen, I calculated in my head how much I weighed, how much Johnny weighed, how much he took, and how much I thought I would need to take to kill myself. I filled plates and set them on the table, then went back to the wall. I would not eat dinner that night, I resolved, so the medication would move through me more quickly.

After dinner, I scraped the leftover ramen from the plates, rinsed and stacked the plates in the dishwasher, then returned to the wall once again. I felt the minutes move past me as darkness fell across the house. I could hear Johnny shuffle from the couch to the kitchen and back, refilling his cup of kava. One by one, the Siale kids left the living room and went to their bedrooms to sleep, and Johnny went quiet. All I could hear were voices from ESPN narrating football highlights in the dark.

"Alexie." Johnny's voice rose sleepily from the living room. "Take your shower and go to bed."

He left the couch and shut the bedroom door behind him.

I stepped away from the wall and into the bathroom. I set my backpack down on the floor, then took off the sweatshirt and T-shirts I had layered on to dull the backpack's bite into my shoulders. As I did every night, I pressed my fingers into the red marks in my skin. I paused, I looked in the mirror, and I pulled my shoulders back and straight. The pain arced across my shoulder blades like wings, and I felt that deep, dark pull from the base of my skull to the bottom of my aching spinal column. My eyes met my eyes in the mirror.

I am so out of here.

I had always been stubborn. I could feel my stubbornness rise inside me again, now, as I deliberately took steps toward my own death. After showering, I dressed in my pajamas and robe and sat on my mattress to write a goodbye letter to my parents. I could hear the deep breath of sleep from Olivia's bed. I don't have the letter now, and I don't know what happened to it, but I remember telling them that I loved them and that I was sorry—very sorry—for the trouble I had been to them. I tore the page from my journal, folded it in half, and tucked it under the corner of my mattress on the floor.

I was so careful not to make a noise as I left the bedroom for the kitchen. I took the naproxen and prescription pain relievers from the cabinet. Standing at the kitchen sink, I filled a giant plastic tumbler of water, then swallowed every pill in the bottle and a third of the naproxen. As I swallowed, I found my eyes focusing on a fluorescent lightbulb above the neighbor's patio. I urged myself to work as quickly and quietly as possible.

I went back to my mattress and closed my eyes. Hours later, my eyes opened. It was still completely dark and very early in the morning. I felt an overpowering dizziness. My hands and feet were tingly and numb. I smiled as I felt that deep, dark, warm pull take me under. I was so happy it wasn't going to be painful. I was so happy to finally be getting out.

The next thing I remember was the feeling of a metal spoon being forced down my throat. My head pulled back by my hair. Hands prying my mouth open. Yelling. Tiana yelling so loud. Water pouring into my mouth. The smell of the bathroom floor. The taste of bile in my mouth. Fluorescent lights overhead.

"Stupid! What were you thinking, you stupid dyke?"

The metal spoon scraped the back of my throat. I could hear the shower turn on and feel icy cold water soak through my pajamas.

"Wake up, Alexie! Wake up!"

There really is no escape at all, I realized as the drugs left my body and I came grudgingly back to consciousness.

There is nothing.

THE SIALES WERE FURIOUS with me for my suicide attempt. Tiana pulled back the bits of affection she had been showing me and doubled down on my chores, and Johnny told me I was stupid for even thinking to try. They also seemed to believe that somehow my suicide attempt wasn't quite real.

"There is no way you took all those pills," Johnny yelled at me. "You would have died. You would have been dead by now."

Still, the Siales told my parents. We spoke a few days later, during our regular Sunday phone call. Mostly, my mom just cried. I hated hearing the pain in her voice. But it was also strange to me that neither they nor the Siales did anything. Hadn't I tried to hurt myself? Wasn't there some point at which I should be sent to a therapist, a counselor, anyone who could help me?

I would later learn that many kids who are sent to residential treatment centers feel the same way, that being cut off from your home and family can trigger suicidal thoughts. But kids in residential treatment centers who contemplate or attempt suicide, as I had, are put under the supervision of a doctor or a licensed therapist. At the Siales', I had no one except myself. Even after my attempted suicide, no one was brought in to help. If I was going to survive, I would have to make it on my own.

That same Sunday, Tiana took me to church for my annual interview with the bishop of our local congregation, the church I attended every week with the Siales and the same one my grandparents attended, even though they did not acknowledge me because that was against the rules of the Siales' program. It was customary for teenagers to have an interview with the bishop on their birthdays. It was all part of the plan. Strange how much of my life had changed since the previous year, yet this part had stayed the same.

Tiana drove me down the block to the church. We walked into the church building, straight to the bishop's office, and knocked on the door.

The bishop opened the door. He looked like a typical Mormon dad: white shirt, tie, graying brown hair, gentle expression.

"Hello, Sister Siale." He reached out and shook Tiana's hand. "Give us a few minutes?"

"Of course," Tiana said, then smiled and took a seat in the foyer outside the bishop's office.

I took a seat in front of the bishop's desk. My head was still foggy from my suicide attempt and I made no efforts to hide my desperation.

"Alex, how are you?" he asked.

Tears started to come down my face. I started to tell him everything: about the trip from home, the way the Siales treated me, the backpack, the wall, my overdose.

I reached for the box of Kleenex on his desk and paused.

The bishop began to speak.

"Well, your parents, I know, love you very much, and they are good people," he said when I finished speaking. "The Siales are really good people too." I knew he saw them the way the whole ward saw them. They were following the plan, going to church, raising their kids, teaching the five- and six-year-olds in Sunday school. They belonged in a way I could not. "They're just doing what they can to help. You used to do drugs, right?"

"Yeah, but I haven't in a long time."

"I think this is their way of helping you."

"Please don't make me go back. Please, Bishop."

I could feel my voice quavering in my throat.

"I understand the Siales' way of doing things is a little harsh, but it has helped a lot of people."

I guess I had hoped—really hoped—that the bishop would be able to see me, that the trust I had been taught to place in my church leaders from the time I was a little girl would not fail. I had hoped that he could come through for me, that all the stories I had heard about leaders in the church being inspired to help, would prove true in my case as well. But that didn't happen. He did not see me, did not hear me, even when I pleaded for help. I felt myself pull further away, down within myself, away from the sound of his voice. I went numb—this time mentally.

When the interview was over, the bishop walked me out into the foyer and shook hands with Tiana.

Within minutes of returning home, I was standing back at the wall.

FOR CHRISTMAS, MY PARENTS made plans to come visit me, and they asked the Siales if I could stay at my grandparents' so we could be together as a family. But the Siales told my parents that they didn't think I was ready yet. I would have to stay the whole Christmas with them, although my parents and I could have a supervised visit. Besides my parents, there would be about twenty people from Johnny's and Tiana's families in town for Christmas too. There was so much to do to get ready for everyone that I didn't have to spend December 24th at the wall. I spent it in the kitchen with Tiana.

"Hey, Alexie. Go make the kava."

Standing over the sink, shredding cabbage for egg rolls, I heard Johnny's voice from the living room. I set down my knife and the cabbage wedge. In the corner of the kitchen, on the floor, stood the big white plastic bucket. Balancing the weighted backpack, I squatted in front of the bucket. Using a big plastic soda cup from the local convenience store, I measured powdered kava root into a nylon, knotted the nylon at the top, and kneaded the powder through the nylon in the water. In a few minutes, Johnny would come to fill his mug and return to the couch. With family coming to visit, I knew the next days would bring a lot of kava making.

We stayed up late that night, Tiana and I, marinating chicken, rolling what seemed like hundreds of egg rolls, and frying them in the deep fryer. My job was to keep the oil clean and to help her set the tables for Christmas dinner. As we worked, Tiana seemed to unwind and relax a little. These were good moments, when Tiana would confide in me, tenderly tuck a strand of my hair behind my ear, even hug me. I was so hungry for any kind of tenderness that even when it came from Tiana I drank it in.

Her life was hard. I knew that. A great deal of weight rested on her shoulders, because Johnny had such a hard time finding and keeping work. It was all up to her, bringing income into the house, keeping the kids fed and cared for. The fact that Johnny yelled at her and was mean to her only made matters worse. Sometimes, when it was just us and she was feeling relaxed, she would talk to me. Tonight was one of those times.

"His temper, it scares me."

"You mean Johnny?" I asked her.

She nodded, using tongs to place another couple of egg rolls into the fryer basket. "Yes."

Something about her authority started to melt away as I stood by her side, listening to her talk about how Johnny treated her. It felt like Tiana was my same age, like we were both just teenagers trying to sort out our place in the world. Her face softened as she looked into the oil. I could see a sadness about her eyes, in the curve of her mouth.

"He calls me fat, you know," she offered with a chuckle.

"I know," I said. I had overheard their fights many times. "Doesn't it make you mad?"

"It just makes me want to eat more." She laughed, a short, self-deprecating giggle.

It must have been four A.M. by the time Tiana and I had everything ready and finally went to bed. By eight A.M. the next morning, I was awake again, wearing the backpack and facing the wall while the Siale kids opened their presents in the living room. My parents would arrive at noon. I could take the backpack off then.

Relatives of Johnny and Tiana arrived all morning—her parents lived there in St. George; his sister and brother had driven in from Nevada. I stayed at the wall as they all arrived, taking breaks only when Johnny asked me to refresh the kava in the bucket. Every time I kneeled in front of the bucket and kneaded the powdered kava in the nylon, I stared at the kitchen wall clock, counting down the minutes until my parents would arrive.

Just before noon, Tiana told me I could stand away from the wall and take off my backpack. I was putting it in the closet in Olivia's room when I heard my parents arrive.

Johnny greeted them at the front door. I rounded the corner from the hallway just in time to see him exchange hugs with my parents. "Merry Christmas," Johnny said.

My mom looked up and saw me watching her from down the hall. She walked toward me and hugged me. "Merry Christmas, Alex," she said. I had missed the feeling of being near her. I had missed it terribly.

My dad stood nearby, watching us. His eyes met mine, but we did not hug.

"Come in." Johnny waved both of them into the living room and started introducing them to his relatives.

After the round of introductions, my dad took a seat next to Johnny on the couch. "What is that you're drinking?" my father asked, referring to the mugs of kava several of Tiana's and Johnny's male relatives held in their hands.

"It's a tradition," Johnny said. "This is a root that takes away your body aches. Will you have some?"

My dad smiled, said okay, and followed Johnny into the kitchen.

I could see my dad relaxing as he drank the kava with Johnny and his relatives, settling into the couch, smiling, and starting to talk.

"What's this root called again?" he asked Johnny, then he asked my mom to write down the word "kava." "Maybe this would be good for my arthritis," he wondered aloud.

At about four P.M., everyone sat down to Christmas dinner of chicken, rice, and egg rolls. I sat next to my mother and leaned into her as she ate. I didn't feel like I could eat that day. My stomach hurt and I felt nauseated. She let me lean into her, into her familiar warmth.

When dinner was over, I helped clear and wash the dishes while the men went back to the couch for more kava and Tiana and my mom talked in the kitchen. I could hear my mom pleading with Tiana gently to let me come back to my grandparents' and spend the night. Just one night.

"I just don't think she's ready for an unsupervised visit," Tiana told her.

My mother paused. "Then can I stay here with her?"

Tiana hesitated but agreed. "You can stay in the upstairs room," she said.

As night fell, the Siale family relatives started to leave, one by one. My father stayed downstairs, drinking kava and laughing with Johnny.

Tiana showed my mom and me to our beds in the loft. I had hoped we would be alone so I could talk to my mom privately, tell her that I had tried to kill myself. I needed her to know as badly as I needed to feel her familiar warmth. But the next thing I knew Olivia and Grace came upstairs with their blankets and pillows and took their place on another set of beds in the loft. To say anything in front of them was to risk more days at the wall or worse punishments from Johnny and Tiana.

My mother and I changed into our pajamas and settled into bed. I hoped she could see the red marks on my shoulders, so that I wouldn't have to say anything. But her back was turned and she did not notice.

"Come here, honey." She gestured to me, inviting me to lie next to her.

As I lay down, I remembered the way we used to snuggle together under the blue-and-white fringed blanket on the couch back in Apple Valley. I started to cry. I curled up and pulled into her.

"They make me wear a backpack of rocks. They make me face the wall all day. It hurts, Mom," I whispered to her. "Please don't make me stay here. I want to die, Mom," I sobbed into her chest. "I want to die."

She stroked my hair. "We're trying to help you, Alex. And I'm trying to move here as soon as I can."

Downstairs I could hear my father talking with Johnny about football. My dad, who had never watched football, had never liked football, talking football and drinking kava with the man who called me a dyke and beat me.

I cried and held on to my mother, who was still my mother despite the fact that she had sent me here, despite the fact that she did not know how to be okay with me being different, with me liking girls, who was so hungry for the comfort of the plan of salvation her religion taught her that she was willing to send me away to live with strangers in the hope that it would save me too—if I was willing to change.

But toward my dad I could feel a sense of disappointment forming. He hadn't been born into this religion. He'd chosen it. He'd converted to be with my mother. I knew he didn't agree with all of it. There had been times when our eyes had met because we both disagreed when our more conservative Mormon friends and relatives started talking politics and religion. I knew he hadn't agreed with sending me here in the first place. But he never said a word. It was like he was so overwhelmed by his own worries about making ends meet, making enough money to take care of me and my mom, and fitting in, that he couldn't muster the energy to disagree.

I think deep inside me I hoped that he would be the one to

believe me, to hear me, to see me. He would finally come around.

But hearing him talking football and bonding over kava with Johnny, I felt my hope darken into resentment.

My parents both needed to believe that there was a plan that would make everything okay and keep them safe. They both needed that assurance to deal with everything life handed them—all the day-to-day struggles and challenges. They both needed to belong to a community that told them they were okay, even if it had no place for people like me, even if the demands it placed on me—to change who I loved, to change who I was at a basic level—hurt me.

Just like the people in St. George who saw Johnny and Tiana beat me in the grocery store parking lot but could not find a voice to intervene, just like the missionaries who saw me at the wall but could not say anything, to anyone, to question who I was or why I was here, my parents were locked in by their need to believe and belong, so locked into their hunger for answers that they could not be with me in my questions and struggles as a gay girl in a religion that was so impossible for people like me. I did not blame them then, and I do not blame them now. Still, the realization hurt. It hurt me deeply.

It was dark the next morning when my parents woke early to make the return trip to Victorville. It was still dark outside when they left. My mother hugged me and told me she loved me. I avoided my dad altogether. But I cried as I watched them drive down the block. I cried as I said goodbye to the hope that they would help me.

CHAPTER 12

Giving In

I'T'S HARD TO DESCRIBE the days at the wall, mostly because I don't remember them so well myself. I also didn't write much about them in my journal. Johnny had found my journal and was reading it regularly, I knew, so I had stopped writing in it as frequently. It was not a safe space for me anymore. I don't think I had a safe space, a space of my own, left to claim. Everything in my world, my survival—or so it felt—was dependent on my ability to get along with Johnny and Tiana.

I do remember the outlines of a few cold winter days in late December and early January when I dressed in the dark, layering on the extra T-shirts and my coat, put on the backpack, handled the morning chores, and reported to the wall. I remember placing my toes five inches from the wall and letting my eyes adjust to it for the first time each day. I started counting, or I tried to entertain myself by replaying some memory from my old life, like eating warm *pupusas* in the Flores' kitchen back in Victorville or taking my cello from its case in orchestra class.

Sometimes I conjured up a picture of my old bedroom, piecing it together detail by detail, as if holding on to the purple-and-green print of my bedspread or the shape of the handle on my nightstand drawer would help me keep my grip on reality. Even as I tried to reminisce, the familiar pain arced across my shoulder blades and from the base of my skull to the base of my spine. Sometimes I started my routine of shifting my weight around on my feet. I could hear myself breathing more and more heavily, and then it went dark. When I came back to my senses and turned my head from the wall to look at the blue numbers on the microwave oven clock in the kitchen, hours had passed. I had no idea where the time went. It was freaky. But as I discovered, these are things the mind does to protect itself. When there is nowhere to go, it creates new places of its own where it can hide.

Some days I had what you would call panic attacks while standing at the wall. I felt my stomach get nervous—as it often did—but then, all of a sudden, my pulse shot up and my heart started racing. It felt like I was going to die. I don't know how I stayed on my feet.

I remember one gray January morning feeling so heavy and hopeless. I moved through my routine of morning chores. When the kids left, as I was cleaning up the breakfast dishes, I took a knife from a drawer and slipped it into the waistband of my pants. Just a regular-size kitchen knife. The blade felt cold against my skin. As soon as my chores were over, I went to the room where I slept and slipped it under my mattress. For a couple of nights that followed, I reached my hand under the mattress, brought out the knife, and held it close to my belly. I tried to work up the courage—is *courage* the right word?—to end my own life. But I couldn't. I knew I couldn't.

I couldn't.

I just could not do it anymore. I had always had a fighting spirit. Even my suicide attempt was in its own way part of my fight to control who I was and where my life would take me. My fighting spirit had gotten me into trouble at times, to be sure. But now I could feel something in me surrendering and lying down. I felt cold inside and started to analyze my best chances of survival. The only thing keeping me on that wall was my stubbornness and my determination to protect Yvette. I wanted to protect her, I reasoned with myself, because I loved her. But I could not take another day. Down to my bones, I could not take it. As much as I wanted to keep Yvette safe, I had to focus on my own survival. No one else was on my side.

I figured that if I confessed, I would get out faster, and if they did press charges against Yvette, the legal process would take a long time. They would have to interview me in person as well, really get my testimony, and if I was free, I could tell them the truth—I was no victim, at least not to Yvette. So I came off the wall, finally, one late morning in mid-January. Tiana had just gotten home from work and was in the kitchen fixing herself something to eat.

"Tiana," I raised my voice. "I'm ready to quit."

Johnny got up from the couch and came into the kitchen; Tiana crossed from the kitchen sink to the hallway.

"Okay, honey," Tiana said in a soothing tone, putting her hand on my shoulder. "Why don't you put that backpack down for a moment and sit with us?"

I stepped away from the wall. My eyes refocused. I took the black backpack off and set it on the ground. My shoulders stayed cramped, and my feet still ached. I still felt numb and hopeless. But I was finally off the wall.

"You understand that we just want you to be honest, to face the consequences of being dishonest," Tiana said. "We just want you to focus on getting better and living the values we teach in our household and your parents teach in theirs."

The truth is, I couldn't give them that much more detail about Yvette. I knew her last name. I knew the name of the town where her grandparents lived, the town she'd grown up in and went home to when she hadn't been hanging out with us in Victorville or visiting Los Angeles. I knew that she drove a red Jeep. I did not know the license plate number. I knew her cell phone number and her birthday. I did not know her home address. I really did not.

I took a deep breath. "I understand. I'm ready to be honest and tell you everything. I'm ready to focus on what I need to do to be better."

A last name. A birthdate. A phone number. That's all I had. And I gave them everything. Tiana wrote the details on a pad of paper, and Johnny stood over us, resting his weight against the kitchen counter, his arms crossed over his chest, his knuckles curled into his biceps.

ALL I CARED ABOUT was that I did not have to stand with my toes five inches from the wall. All I cared about was that I no longer had to count numbers higher and higher, or watch my own mind struggle to maintain a grip on reality, or feel my pulse spike without reason.

It did not matter to me that I still had to wear the backpack and do my daily chores around the house. At least I could move, giving some relief to the muscles around my spine.

As soon as I had given Tiana and Johnny Yvette's last name and confirmed that she was over eighteen, they called my parents, and my parents filed a complaint against Yvette with the Victorville police. My parents, the Siales, everyone kept telling me that it was Yvette who had picked me out, "groomed" me, given me drugs, and forced me to be with her. No one seemed to be able to understand that I had wanted to be with her. I had fallen in love for the first time. With a girl. In their eyes, reporting her to the police was the right next step.

"There is a detective in California who wants to speak to you," Tiana said. "This is a very dangerous situation for you, Alexie. You don't have experience dealing with law enforcement like I do. You need to be fully truthful with them or else you might get in trouble yourself. Do you understand?" She looked at me, intently. "You need to tell them what I tell you," she insisted.

"Okay," I said. If it meant staying off the wall, that was enough for me.

We both sat down on her bed. She placed herself right beside me, and she took out her cell phone, dialed a long-distance number, pressed the speakerphone button, and laid the phone on the bedspread.

A man's voice came from the other end of the line. "Victorville police."

"Detective, this is Tiana Siale," she said.

The detective had been expecting her call.

"I have Alex here with me, and she is ready to share with you details about the case we've been discussing."

"Alex," he said, "I need you to tell me about Yvette Espinosa. I need you to tell me what happened."

Tiana leaned over and started to whisper in my ear. She told me to say that Yvette had pressured me into smoking weed. She told me to say that the weed had clouded my thinking, that Yvette had forced me to have sex with her for drugs. I said everything she told me to, even though it wasn't true.

"Did you go out of state?" the detective asked.

"No."

The interview continued, getting even more graphic and detailed. Tiana whispered specific details about sexual acts, details I was embarrassed to say out loud. I had never talked about my relationship with Yvette to Tiana or Johnny, or written any of this down in my journal, which I knew they had been reading. I had no idea where Tiana had come up with all the specific sexual details she insisted I tell the detective. But as soon as she whispered them into my ear, I spoke them into the telephone. It was like I was a pawn in a conversation between two adults about sex, a conversation I barely had a role in.

At one point in the conversation, Tiana's voice rose as she whispered me instructions. I faltered and stopped speaking, frozen, terrified of what would happen next.

"Is someone telling you what to say?" the detective asked.

Tiana spoke over me. "No, detective, she's just a little confused."

"Stop doing that," the officer told Tiana.

But she did not. We finished the interview, with Tiana still whispering instructions in my ear, and then we hung up the phone.

Tiana took the black backpack from the floor and put it into her closet.

"You did well, Alexie," she said. "It's the only way—being fully honest and facing the consequences of your actions. Now that you are honest about things, see how the burden lifts?"

Now that I was free from the wall and from the pressure of keeping Yvette safe, I started to focus more on getting along with Johnny and Tiana. It seemed the surest way to gain the small moments of freedom that made it possible to survive.

I had always followed the rules of the house and done all the chores that Johnny and Tiana had assigned to me. If I didn't, I understood quite well it would have been worse for me. I had felt the pain of Tiana's grip and the force of Johnny's blows. I had seen the role physical force played in their punishment of their own children, especially the boys. I would far rather cook breakfast, lunch, and dinner for a family of seven than be taken into the garage and disciplined. No question there.

There were other parts of the household routine that I quietly resisted, especially the group talk therapy and scripture reading sessions Johnny convened every morning. From the very first day, I had found them ridiculous.

I had always been a bit of a rebel when it came to my Mormon faith. But the way my parents had raised me and the years I had spent going to church three hours every Sunday had made an impact on me. I knew how to pray. I knew my scriptures. I knew what it felt like to want there to be a God, to want safety and protection, to want to have all the answers. I had absolutely felt that hunger. I knew the basic teachings of my faith. I knew them well enough to understand the places where the plan of salvation could not offer security to people like me.

When I had started at the Siales' five months earlier, I sat through the morning group sessions, cross-legged on the floor, and privately rolled my eyes while Johnny read out of the Book of Mormon or lectured me on the plan of salvation. Who was he to be lecturing me about my own religion? Especially when he started elaborating on Mormon doctrines in a way that made no sense—telling me, for example, that God would not let me as a lesbian into heaven but he would provide a perfect copy of a non-lesbian me so my parents, who would get into heaven, wouldn't miss me in the eternities. I knew that was not Mormon doctrine, but Johnny had treated it as if it were.

So much had happened over the months that had worn me down. By January, I just wanted to survive. I needed the Siales to approve of me. What's more, I wanted them to love me. I had been cut off from my family and friends and anyone who would say my name or touch me or laugh with me. The Siales were now all I had.

A good way to make Johnny and Tiana happy, I decided, was to participate more intently in group. I started to bring my own copy of the scriptures and follow along with whatever passage Johnny was reading. If he asked a question, I would try to answer it.

One day during group, sitting on the worn beige carpet, scriptures open in my lap, looking up at Johnny seated on the couch, I decided to go one step further. I raised my hand.

"Here, in the Book of Alma, it says that God sent his son to take away the sins of the world," I said.

Johnny seemed a bit startled.

"How exactly does it work that Jesus's death pays for everyone's sins?"

It was a serious question.

Johnny looked at me and paused. "Alexie, I don't know what you're doing, but you got to do it for the right reasons," he finally said. "I think you just opened your book to whatever page and asked just to be asking."

Clearly I needed to work harder to convince Johnny that my newfound interest in the scriptures was real. So starting the next day, every morning, after chores were done, I got my scriptures and took a seat at the kitchen table, and I returned to the table with my scriptures every night, after the dishes were cleared and the kids were ready for bed. Sifa and I used to pass these long stretches of downtime playing cards or reading the household collection of crime novels with gory black-and-red covers. But no more. I started participating more in group, and not just because I was trying to beat the system. I really did feel that my survival depended on it, and I was determined to survive.

It started working. The more I talked in group, the more I let Johnny tell me that God had no place for gays in the plan of salvation, the more I expressed a willingness to change my heart to be as God wanted, the easier my day-to-day life became. Coming off the wall, of course, was a huge first step. Getting rid of the backpack was an amazing second. The relief of not having the cut of the straps against my shoulders and that arc of pain across my shoulder blades is almost indescribable. I still had to follow the routine and all the rules. I still was cut off from my family, my friends, and just about everything a sixteen-year-old girl considers normal life. But I could once again feel a bit of space between my vertebrae. That felt like an enormous victory to me. Even if I was a prisoner in the world the Siales defined for me.

LUCKILY FOR ME, THAT world was not limited to the four walls of the Siale household. On Sundays, I got to walk the three blocks to the big LDS Church just down the road. For the first few months at the Siales', my heart was so angry at the people at church. Many of them had seen me wearing the backpack or even facing the wall, and no one—*no one*—seemed to think anything about it.

But as I resolved to do whatever I could to get out of the Siales' house, I knew that acting the right way at church would go a long way toward gaining their trust. I started to speak during testimony meetings, standing at the microphone in front of the whole congregation and praising the Siales for helping me. They even arranged for me to play the cello one Sunday in church during a special musical number, even though I had not been allowed to practice for months and the cello went back into the garage right afterward.

Right about at the time the backpack came off, Johnny and Tiana told me I would be allowed to go to some of the activities they held at church every week for the Young Women's program. The best news of all was that neither Johnny nor Tiana nor anyone in the Siale family would be attending with me. I would have one hour a week to myself. One hour without supervision. The news felt almost as good as getting the backpack off.

The Young Women's leader for my age group of girls was named Sister Jeppsen. Sister Jeppsen had four grown kids of her own. She drove a big green passenger van, and she wore her auburn hair in this awful permanent wave with short curly bangs. But she always brought us something sweet to snack on, and she had a wonderfully warm laugh. Even when my heart was angry at the rest of the ward, Sister Jeppsen seemed like someone I might be able to talk to. Maybe even someone I could ask for help.

"Don't you dare," Sifa warned me one Sunday night after church when I confided in him at the kitchen table. "You know her husband is really good friends with Johnny. You'll ruin this for me and for you if you cause any trouble."

He paused. "I can't take it, Alex," he said, pleading. "You know Johnny will punish me if he thinks I help you or keep any secrets from him. I just can't take it anymore."

Even knowing that, there was something in Sister Jeppsen's voice that felt like a warm hand on my shoulder.

One Sunday in church Sister Jeppsen announced that the following Saturday the Young Women would get to go on a special outing to see the waterfalls outside a little town called Gunlock about twenty miles away.

"The rains have been pretty good this month," she told us with a huge smile and excitement in her voice. "The waterfalls will really be running. It should be beautiful."

Even though I was not close to the girls in my class—I did not go to school with them, and their parents had probably told them to keep their distance from me—it sounded wonderful.

That night, as I was clearing the plates from Sunday dinner, I took a deep breath and asked Tiana. "Sister Jeppsen is taking our class to see the waterfalls at Gunlock on Saturday." I let the words hang in the air and kept on clearing dishes, trying not to betray how badly I wanted to go.

"Olivia, Grace, go get ready for bedtime." Tiana seemed not to have heard me at first, being preoccupied with the household evening routine.

"Can I go?"

There was a pause. "Yes," Tiana said.

I held my breath and smiled inside. This new plan was working. Slowly I was gaining some of my freedom back.

When Saturday morning came, I got up extra early and held my breath all through breakfast and morning chores. I was so nervous that something—*anything*—might set off Johnny or Tiana and ruin my hopes. But my fears were unfounded. About ten minutes before we were supposed to meet for the outing, Tiana told Johnny to drive me to church. It was close enough to walk, but in their eyes I was not ready for that kind of unsupervised time.

Twenty minutes later, I was riding in the front passenger seat of Sister Jeppsen's van while the rest of the girls chatted and joked in the back. We headed out of our subdivision, down the long rural route that led toward Gunlock. On the east side of the road, red-rock hills stood a thousand feet high. On the west side, a vast red desert plain dotted with tamarisk trees stretched away. I watched the scenery go by outside the window, taking in the view.

Gunlock was a tiny town, with one small post office and a big LDS Church. Just five minutes beyond it, a reservoir came into view. Sister Jeppsen parked the van in a gravel lot, and all the girls piled out. Several of the girls were wearing navy, green, and gold sweatshirts from Snow Canyon High. Everyone seemed to have a daypack or a water bottle, except me.

"Here, Alex." Sister Jeppsen pressed a cold water bottle into my hand with a smile. Without my saying a word, she had noticed.

It was just a fifteen-minute hike to the falls, down from the parking lot into a dry slot canyon. The other girls were caught up in chatting about school, so I stayed in my own thoughts. After so many months stuck in the Siale house, the freedom of moving on a trail felt amazing. The air was cool, but I could feel a bit of sun on my face. I took in the feel of the rocks under my feet and the smell of the water from the reservoir.

"How you doing there, Alex?" Sister Jeppsen asked, suddenly hiking next to me.

"Doing great," I said, and I meant it. I stopped there, though I wanted so badly to tell her everything that had happened in the last five months, from the time my mom had told me to leave the house to my escape attempts and the beatings that had followed, the backpack, the wall, the suicide attempt. I wanted not to be alone with it all. I wanted someone to know. But I remembered Sifa's warning and I said nothing.

They weren't the biggest waterfalls you could imagine, just twenty feet of falls pouring from the top of a red-rock cliff into a green pool below. But I was so grateful to see them.

As I felt the spray from the falls on my face, I felt more committed than ever to doing whatever it would take to convince the Siales to let me have more moments of freedom. It was, I realized, my only way out.

IT WAS AROUND THIS time that I began to get closer to Sifa and Calvin. We all attended group together, but Sifa and Calvin didn't have to do any chores or cook for the family. As Johnny often reminded me, one of the goals of my treatment was to help me get ready to meet a nice Mormon man, preferably someone who had served a mission for the church, and to marry him and raise a family, all according to the plan of salvation. The boys had to work and help pay the household bills. Calvin I had never trusted because I could see how dependent on Johnny and Tiana he had grown, how desperate he was to make his situation better. Still, I came to understand and pity him. Sifa too had been pretty broken in, but he still had a spark of playfulness about him, and somehow it raised my spirits a bit to hear him sing around the house.

In late January, our group grew by one when a kid named Dante arrived from San Francisco. I was with Tiana on her night shift at the residential treatment center when he arrived. I went with her at night because I didn't want to stay in the house alone with Johnny. After her shift ended, we drove to the Greyhound station. Dante stood on the curb, tall, light skinned and light eyed, with golden hair that he wore close to his head. The waistband of his pants sat just below his skinny hips, held up by a belt cinched tight. He moved back and forth from foot to foot, blowing into his hands to keep them warm. A backpack was all he'd brought with him.

A few years back, he had been a resident at one of the local treatment centers, sent by his family and paid for by state funds as an alternative form of punishment for getting caught with pot. Now he was eighteen years old, and he had nowhere to live. Dante had contacted Tiana and asked her if he could stay with Johnny and her for a while.

Tiana got out of the car and greeted Dante with a big hug. He climbed into the backseat of the car, stuck his hand out, and introduced himself with a broad smile. I saw a glint in his light-colored eyes that made the nerves in my stomach jump a little.

At group the next morning, Dante joined Calvin, Sifa, and me in our session. Johnny welcomed Dante and ran down the list of house rules: don't talk to the Siale kids, don't talk to the other kids in treatment, don't steal, follow directions. Dante was also reminded that everyone in town knew and trusted Johnny and Tiana, so if he tried anything, he wouldn't get any help. Johnny did not make him give away his own clothes, though.

"You are welcome to stay here as long as you are working to become honest and accept the consequences of your choices. While you are here, you have to live by the values we teach in our home," Johnny explained. "We do group with prayer and scripture study. You will be a part of that."

Dante interrupted. "But what if I don't believe in your religion? What if I don't believe in it at all?"

Johnny repeated himself. "While you are here, you have to live by the values we teach in our home. You will also attend church with our family."

We went around the circle, introducing ourselves and explaining, with help from Johnny, why we were there with the Siales.

When it came to me, I told Dante, "I'm here because I like girls."

I hated confessing to the group, but I knew I had to do what Johnny and Tiana expected me to.

"I'm here because Tiana helped me a lot in treatment," Dante said. "And because I have nowhere else to go."

"You need to take responsibility," Johnny stopped him. "You are here because you're into drugs. Until you can learn to be honest about your choices and take responsibility for the consequences, you have to stay under my supervision."

A few hours later, Dante and I were sitting at the kitchen table. School had just let out, and Olivia was sitting with us, eating an after-school snack.

"I don't think it's right that you're here because you're gay," Dante said.

I swallowed hard and looked at Olivia. "I don't want to talk about it," I said right away.

Dante looked at me for a few seconds, then drew a cell phone from his pocket and put it on the kitchen table and silently offered to push it across the table to me.

"No," I said. "I don't want it. We're not allowed to have cell phones here."

I kept my eyes on Olivia, silently hoping she would not say anything.

He had just arrived. I had no reason to trust him. I was terrified, in fact, that Dante was going to get us all in trouble.

OVER THE NEXT FEW weeks, I learned more and more of Dante's story. Calvin would head out in the morning to attend Snow Canyon High School. That left me and Dante in the house together. We weren't supposed to talk to each other, but every other day we grabbed a few minutes of conversation, whispering at the kitchen table, while Johnny dozed on the couch or passed time drinking kava and playing video games.

Dante had grown up in Northern California. He had a family back at home but had always been a bit restless, always getting into some kind of trouble, smoking a lot of pot, doing poorly in school, and fighting at home. His parents had sent him to treatment in St. George, hoping it would straighten him out. He'd worn the uniform, gone to group, slept in the bunks, the whole routine. That's where he'd met Tiana.

When he turned eighteen, back in California, his parents told him it was time to leave the house, and he moved to San Francisco.

He found a place to crash in the city with a bunch of guys. Dante liked both girls and guys, and he started a relationship with one of the guys in the house. When they had a fight and broke up, the ex-boyfriend kicked Dante out. He had nowhere else to go, so he'd looked up Tiana and asked if he could crash with her and Johnny for a while.

Over the weeks, I told him about my own struggles with my parents, about meeting Yvette, running off to Los Angeles with her, falling in love, and getting kicked out when I confessed it to my parents. Dante told me that his last girlfriend had been fifteen. It did not escape my notice that Dante was an eighteen-year-old who had dated a fifteen-year-old, and no one had made a big deal about it. Apparently in this household, being straight and dating underage didn't mean getting reported to the police.

"We need to get you out of here," Dante said one day. "I'll run with you. We gotta get Calvin out too."

I thought of Calvin and his sweet, sad face, the way he cowered a bit whenever Johnny walked into the room. Calvin had it worse than any of us with Johnny. Johnny could sense the hurt in him, the fear in him, and he zeroed in on it, taunting Calvin and asking him if he were gay. I wondered if Calvin would ever have the guts to run. And where exactly would we go? I had just been making progress getting Johnny and Tiana to trust me. The idea of running terrified me. But something about having Dante there sparked a boldness inside me I thought the days at the wall had killed.

One day, when Johnny got up to refill his kava, he walked in on us whispering at the kitchen table. Dante and I had to devise a new form of communication.

Silently, over the next few days, we worked out a system using a book in the bookshelf on the living room wall. At night, Dante would write a note in the dark up in the loft when he was supposed to be sleeping, and in the morning, when the house was quiet, he would slip it into the book. I'd retrieve the note later in the day and write my own note back to him after my bedtime. Back and forth we went, trying to devise a plan to get out of there together, speculating on who, if anyone, in the ward we could ask for help in getting home.

Our system of communication lasted for just a few days.

"ALEXIE," TIANA DEMANDED LATE one afternoon. "I need to see your journal. Bring it to me."

I was starting preparations for dinner. Calvin was doing his homework. Dante and Sifa were reading on the living room floor. We exchanged glances.

"I don't have it," I replied.

That much was true. During one of our furtive talks at the kitchen table, I had asked Dante to keep my journal for me. I was afraid that Tiana and Johnny would take it. I wanted to keep it safe, and he had promised that he and Calvin would hide it for me and make sure my parents got it if anything happened.

"What do you mean you don't have it?" Tiana's voice started to rise.

I looked at Calvin. A panicked look crossed his face. He was silently begging me not to tell.

"I threw it away," I told her.

"When?" She was now yelling.

"When?"

Tiana came into the kitchen and got right in my face. "All of you! Outside! Outside!"

Tiana took me by the arm out through the kitchen door, around the back, to the side yard, where the trash cans were lined up against the side of the house. Dante, Sifa, and Calvin followed, with Johnny close behind them.

The afternoon was gray. I could feel the cold concrete under my bare feet, and Sifa, Calvin, and Dante shoved their hands deep into their pockets.

Tiana pulled a lid from one of the trash cans. "You!" she screamed at me. "Find it. Now!"

I slowly started to sort through the trash, lifting away layer after layer of junk mail and empty food containers.

"You threw it away, huh?" she yelled. "If you threw it away, you're going to find it."

I kept my head down and did as I was told, but I could feel the humiliation rising in me. Just when I was beginning to gain ground, to get some glimpse of freedom, I had ruined it by trusting Dante. I had ruined everything.

Just as I reached the bottom of the first trash can, Dante spoke up.

"Okay, okay," he said. "She didn't throw it away. I have it. I'm keeping it for her."

"You *what*?" Tiana's voice was furious.

"I have it," Dante said again. "I'm keeping it safe for her."

"You three! You've been talking! I knew it."

Calvin's eyes dropped, and he looked like he was about to cry. Dante's face only hardened.

"Inside," Johnny ordered, his voice low. "All of you."

Ten minutes later my backpack was back on my shoulders, and all four of us—Dante, Sifa, Calvin, and I—were lined up, facing the wall. I wore my backpack. The boys, they held stacks of encyclopedias, ferried by Johnny from the living room shelves and loaded into their arms.

THE NEXT MORNING AFTER breakfast, Johnny made Calvin stay home from school. He made Dante, Calvin, Sifa, and me sit at the kitchen table, and he put a blank piece of paper and a pen in front of each of us. We were all angry, each blaming the others for the trouble we found ourselves in. "Write it all down," Johnny ordered. "Tell us everything. The more honest you are, the better it will be for you."

Johnny knew how to play us one against the other, to use our fear and desperation to humiliate us, making us give away the small hoard of secrets we had accumulated together, the small bit of shelter we were able to offer one another.

"You know," Johnny taunted us as he circled the kitchen, "I already know at least some of what you're up to. You think everyone in this room is keeping secrets? You think you can trust each other?"

I shot Dante a sidelong glance. I had always known he would be trouble. Why did he have to tell them he'd hid the journal? I could have just gone through the rest of the trash cans. Given the situation, I coldly calculated my best strategy. I knew I had more on him and Calvin than they did on me.

I started to write.

We talk to each other whenever we get a chance. We hide notes in the bookshelf on the wall. Dante has been trying to get us to run away.

I paused.

Johnny's voice broke in. "The more you tell me, the better it will be for you."

My grip tightened on my pencil.

Calvin and Dante drink Johnny's kava. They sneak cups of it when no one is looking. They get high on kava.

They had drunk kava. At least once. That much was true.

Sifa has a girlfriend. He sneaks out at night to see her after hours. She goes to Dixie High School. They stay out late making out.

Sifa was supposed to be getting ready to go on a volunteer mission for the church. He was not supposed to be dating. That would really get him in trouble.

But I knew that the worst thing I could tell Johnny and Tiana was how we all felt about Grace, their youngest daughter. She could misbehave terribly and be rude to the three of us, but Grace was her daddy's favorite. Johnny absolutely adored her.

Calvin and Dante talk about how much they hate Grace. They laugh at her and fantasize about cruel things that could happen to her.

I put my pencil down and pushed the paper away from me. A combination of relief and cold apathy flooded me. I had given away our secrets. I had sold Dante and Calvin out. I tried to care, but I couldn't. I just couldn't. I would do what I had to do to survive.

Johnny picked up each of our papers and read them silently. Dante, Calvin, and I all watched him as he read the papers through, his face betraying no expression.

"You two," he pointed at Dante and Calvin and set the papers down on the counter. "Let's go."

Johnny walked the boys into the garage. The door closed. From the living room, I could hear Johnny yelling, then Calvin crying and begging. Dante did not utter a sound. Once in a while I could hear a blow land or a body knock into a bin of sports gear. Calvin started whimpering. It went on for what seemed like forever. And I felt cold inside.

The next day, the boys had to stand against the wall, holding a stack of encyclopedias.

I had always been a person who let her feelings guide her. Letting my feelings guide me had even gotten me in trouble from time to time. But what was really troubling to me was the fact that my feelings seemed to be disappearing as I gave in to Johnny and Tiana. I had confessed. I had heard the sound of blows landing in the garage. The next morning, I saw them take their places at the wall, holding encyclopedias. It had been a relief to tell on Dante and Calvin, just as it had been a relief to give up Yvette and have the pain of the backpack taken from me. Had I become like all the people who had passed through the house, seen me wearing my backpack, and said nothing? Had I become like the people who had seen Johnny beating me outside the grocery store or Tiana dragging me through the parking lot and said nothing? Dante and Calvin were suffering as I had, and I did nothing. I said nothing.

I know I was doing what I thought I had to do to survive, but now I feel incredibly guilty about it. I feel guilty about the way Johnny and Tiana rewarded me for confessing. While Calvin and Dante stood and shifted their weight from foot to foot, I got to sit on the living room floor and watch television with the family. Sometimes in the evening Tiana asked me to rub her feet. I was happy to do it. I wanted them to love me. I wanted everything to be okay. It was, most of the time, as long as I did what they said. If I said my prayers and read my scriptures and cooked and cleaned and got the kids out the door on time, it would be okay. I could go to church and cook dinner for ten. It would be okay, in the long run, wouldn't it? That's what Johnny and Tiana kept trying to tell me. Stick with the plan and it will be all right.

But once in a while there were days when the old cruelty glimmered through even when I stuck with the plan. Johnny would put me on the wall just because I didn't mop the floor right—just because he wanted to, really. Or Tiana would have a hard day at work and she'd snap at me. Then she'd catch herself, pull me close, and hug me. I would let her.

"I love you, Alexie. I love you like I love my own children."

Her words were chilling, but true.

WHY DIDN'T WE JUST walk out the door, the three of us? I ask myself that question all the time. Strong as they were, Johnny and Tiana could not have stopped three of us. At least one of us could have gotten out and found help. Or so it seems to me now. But back then, after five months away from my family and friends, I had become convinced that no one on the outside would help me. They had all moved on with their lives, Johnny and Tiana had told me, and they were doing just fine without me. I thought I would have to steal a car, find directions out of St. George, and even then, where would I have run to? Where would we have run to, Dante, Calvin, and I?

Sifa tried to run away once, before I had arrived at the Siales'. Every day he reported for work at a chocolate factory in St. George some people from church owned. He stood there all day making chocolates, earning paychecks he split between Johnny and Tiana and his savings for his mission. One day, he left work on his lunch break and walked away. I guess he wandered around St. George for a few hours, on foot, no money, nowhere really to go. Late that night, the bishop brought him back to the house, and he stayed. He stayed until he left on his mission to Mexico.

Calvin also tried to run away, in February, just a couple of weeks after Johnny and Tiana put him on the wall. He didn't come home after school one day. I think he started walking from Snow Canyon toward town. How far could he make it in an afternoon? Not far enough—not far enough to get out of range of being found. All Johnny and Tiana had to do was call the police, and one of the police officers we knew from church, one of their friends, set out in his squad car looking. After Calvin was brought back, Johnny and Tiana restricted his activities even more. Running did not make things better. In fact, I don't think Calvin ever left St. George. Years later, I would see him in the grocery store, a gallon of milk in each hand, to feed the Siale family. Or so I imagined.

Dante was eighteen, so Johnny and Tiana really couldn't keep him here against his will. He was bolder too, more daring than either Calvin or Sifa. He'd seen a bit more of the world than they had, and at least he knew where the Greyhound station was in town. He spent a few days at the wall, silently figuring his next move. It was probably better to be homeless than it was to be subjected to this form of "treatment." He was just gone one day when we all woke up, and Johnny and Tiana never said a word about it. Months later, I tried to find him on the Internet. "Teen Crashes Stolen Vehicle into Local Store," read the headline, and there was Dante, in a mug shot, light eyed, handsome, and defiant as ever.

One of the things I've learned since this all happened is that LGBT kids like Dante and me end up in state custody more frequently than straight kids. Thirteen to fifteen percent of the kids in the juvenile justice system identify as LGBT—that's almost twice the rate of LGBT people in the U.S. population at large.[1] Why do so many of us end up in foster care or so-called treatment centers or state-run shelters or group homes or jail? Why are so many homeless kids LGBT? Twenty to forty percent of all homeless youth are gay. Thirty-nine percent of gay homeless youth say they were kicked out of their homes; forty-five percent have had a run-in with law enforcement or the juvenile justice system. Of the thousands of teenagers who will sleep on the streets or under bridges in Utah tonight, fully half of them are LGBT kids, the majority from Mormon families.

Most experts surveyed about LGBT youth in the juvenile justice system say that families hold the key. When gay teenagers experience conflict or rejection over their sexuality at home, they are at greater risk for physical and mental health problems, including depression, drug use, and alcohol abuse. Those who are kicked out of their homes and have no stable place to live are much more likely to commit survival crimes like theft and prostitution. LGBT kids who are bullied at school are more likely to skip school and get charged with truancy, or fight back and get charged with assault or disorderly conduct. Research even shows LGBT kids are more likely to be profiled by police as delinquents, and a gay teenager who has a run-in with the law is more likely to be detained—held in jail—

---

1. Katayoon Majd, Jody Marksamer, and Carolyn Reyes, *Hidden Injustice: Lesbian, Gay, Bisexual, and Transgender Youth in Juvenile Courts* (San Francisco and Washington, DC: Legal Services for Children, National Juvenile Defender Center, and National Center for Lesbian Rights, 2009), http://www.equityproject.org/wp-content/uploads/2014/08/hidden_injustice.pdf.

than a straight teenager. Those who are detained face a higher risk of physical and sexual assault while in custody, plus they are less likely to complete school or move on to a healthy life when they get out.

I can't speak for every gay teenager, but I know that all I wanted was to go home. Even after my parents sent me away to the Siales and didn't hear me or help me when I told them how bad it was, I wanted to go home and be with them again. No matter how hard or wild a kid acts, that hunger for home is basic—as basic a need as eating or sleeping, as basic as breath itself. It's the best thing any of us has, really, the promises we make to one another, to look out for one another and give one another shelter, even if we make mistakes or things turn out differently than we'd hoped. The idea of home is the best thing we have, and sometimes it's the only thing. Once that bond is broken, we may go from place to place to place, looking for somewhere to be, and we may even find a place that works well enough. For a while. But that brokenness stays inside us, changing the way we love, making us restless, making it hard to stay anywhere at all.

CHAPTER 13

Going Back to School

W HAT I WANTED MOST of all was to go home. But I was also hungry to go back to school. The Siales had enrolled me in an alternative school, which meant I did homework packets at home, because Tiana thought I wasn't ready for regular school; I couldn't be trusted. It was better for me to take care of the kids, do the laundry, cook and clean. Day after day, my mind ached with boredom.

But the more I tried to get along with the Siales and go along with their system, the more Tiana seemed to soften on the school idea. By the time March arrived, she agreed to let me enroll at Snow Canyon High School.

"Tell them you moved here to help your grandparents," Tiana instructed me as we crossed the lawn from the parking lot to the glass-paneled administration building. Snow Canyon had a big campus, with the football stadium and baseball and athletic fields out back and Future Farmers of America and LDS Seminary buildings on the north end of campus. Taking it all in, I felt excited but also nervous.

"Remember we know all the teachers here and everyone who works in the office," she told me. I felt the familiar pang of dread.

She opened the door and we walked into the office. Sure enough, the staff and the counselors greeted her by name. The principal was a neighbor and went to church in the same congregation as the Siales and my grandparents.

"This is Alex," she said. "I'm here to get her started in school."

A woman working in the front office set a stack of papers on the counter. When they'd brought me to Utah, my parents had sent along a form authorizing Johnny and Tiana as my caregivers to enroll me in school. The State of Utah required different forms, though, authorizing Johnny and Tiana as my legal guardians. Because I was over fourteen, I had to sign the forms as well, and I tried to push back, tried to resist by withholding my signature. But after a long tearful conversation on the phone with my mom, I had given in. Still, even with the proper forms on file with the district, Johnny and Tiana had kept me out of school for months, providing only minimal homeschooling.

I couldn't help but look around the office to see if someone looked friendly enough to help me. But my various failed escape attempts had taught me that pretty much everyone would be on the Siales' side. I resolved to keep my head down and not say anything. The last thing I wanted was to go back on the wall, especially when I had just earned the right to attend school.

It took about forty-five minutes to fill out the paperwork, and then Tiana took me to the store to buy me a few new things for school because the long skirts and oversize thrift-store T-shirts I had been wearing since I had arrived at the Siales' would not do. She picked out a pair of jeans and a couple of T-shirts and a backpack. A new backpack. Not the black nylon backpack she filled with rocks for my punishment. *A different backpack.*

For the first time since I had arrived at the Siales', I felt a bit of hopefulness flutter in my stomach. I let the feeling dance a bit, as nervous as it made me. Because I did feel nervous. Nervous about doing something that might upset the Siales and being taken out of school again. Everything depended on my not screwing up this new chance at a bit of freedom.

I CLUTCHED MY PRINTED schedule in one hand—geology, English, animal science, math, cooking class—swung my backpack over my shoulder, felt the familiar weight of it, and with it a surge of panic. I took a deep breath, reminded myself that this backpack was really different, and walked into my first period geology class. I'm sure I mustered a brave smile, but all I remember is how terrified I felt.

I found a desk in the last row.

This boy in the seat in front of me turned around. He looked like the classic Mormon kid: blond, blue eyed, and totally clean-cut. He wore a striped polo shirt tucked into his Levis, with a leather belt. "Hi," he said, offering his hand to shake mine. "I'm Spencer. What's your name?"

"I'm Alex."

"Are you LDS?" he asked, smiling warmly.

"Yes," I told him. Of course he was too. He went to church every Sunday.

"Are you new here?" he asked.

"Yes."

"Well, you should come over to my house for Family Home Evening next Monday."

The Siales were super strict about holding their own Monday-night Family Home Evening, as church leaders encouraged all Mormon families to do. Without fail, every Monday night there would be some kind of religious lesson at the kitchen table and dessert to follow. Even when I was standing at the wall.

The suddenness of his invitation startled me. Was Spencer just being sweet, or was he actually flirting with me?

I knew my chances of getting permission to leave the Siales' and visit Spencer were very slim. But maybe if I brought Spencer—a *boy*—to Family Home Evening at the Siales', I could show them that I was taking it all to heart and changing a bit.

I returned Spencer's warm, friendly gaze and tilted my head a little bit. "Would you like to come to Family Home Evening at my house instead?"

I WASN'T TRYING TO meet anyone, really. Moving through the halls at Snow Canyon those first few days felt overwhelming, even a bit dangerous in the way freedom can feel dangerous to someone who has been living without it. I just wanted to keep my head down, blend in, and not attract attention.

It worked in most of my classes, except for foods.

Nothing and no one escaped the attention of Jason Osmanski, and he wasn't the kind of kid who believed in blending in either. A lanky redhead, Jason had a giant rainbow patch on his backpack. Some days he carried a purse or wore lip gloss. He was gay and very out.

I was desperately trying to avoid him. But just a few days in, my foods teacher assigned us to the same table and the same group.

"You're new."

"Yes."

"What's your name?"

"Alex."

"Alex, I'm Jason. Where are you from?"

"California."

He paused and gave me a careful once-over. His eyes were full of mischief. "We should totally talk more. What's your cell phone number?"

"I don't believe in cell phones."

"You don't have a cell phone?"

"No."

"Alex, are you on Facebook?" he asked one day as we were

standing over the stove, melting chocolate for brownies. I held the wooden spoon and stirred the pot.

"I am not on Facebook."

Every day in class, Jason would ask me a few more questions. The more I held back, the more intrigued he became.

"We should totally hang out. Okay, so can I come to your house?"

"No, I have too much family."

"So," he smiled, taking on a motherly tone, "you're going to come to *my house.*"

"No."

Jason seemed to sense both how badly I wanted to talk to him and how terrified I was to do so. And it made him press further.

"Alex, do you have a boyfriend?"

"No."

"Do you have a *girlfriend?*"

I drew in a quick breath. "No."

"Do you have anyone to sit with at lunch?"

"No."

"Okay." Jason smiled. "You're sitting with me at lunch."

It seemed impossible to resist him.

"And after class, you're coming with me. There is someone you need to meet. She is the most amazing teacher at Snow Canyon. She's the advisor of the Gay–Straight Alliance," he said. "And I am the president."

THE FIRST THING I saw when Jason opened the door to Delsy Nielson's classroom was a quote from the rock band the Killers spelled out on the wall: "Are we human, or are we dancer?"

Jason pulled me through the door.

There stood Delsy Nielson in a sundress and sandals, her shoulder-length brown hair perfectly straightened and her nails painted pink. She had warm brown eyes and an open, generous way about her.

"Delsy," Jason said, "I'd like you to meet my friend Alex. She's new to Snow Canyon."

"Alex," Delsy said, reaching forward to take my hand, "what a pleasure to meet you."

"Now, Jason," she continued, "I have to tell you something. The fairies in my garden are out again."

I looked up at the other quotes lettered across the classroom walls: "I sound my barbaric yawp over the roofs of the world." "In the end only kindness matters." It was the place—and it really felt like the only place at Snow Canyon High—where the kids who were different, the artists and the outcasts, could find a bit of refuge. Delsy stayed in her classroom every lunch period just so those kids would have a place to go.

Jason went there frequently, and he belonged as well to the debate team, which Delsy coached. She was also an advisor to the school's environmental club, the PEACE club: Protecting Every Aspect Concerning Earth. She led school cleanups and took her kids on field trips to Zion National Park, where Gordon, her husband, drove a shuttle bus. I walked slowly around Delsy's room while she and Jason caught up, talking in tones that were playful but also serious. I looked at the Led Zeppelin and Beatles lyrics on the walls, and at a big bulletin board papered with pictures of trees her students had drawn. The trees came in all imaginable colors and designs, each one different and a reflection of the student who drew it.

I looked at all the books on her shelves. There were about a dozen copies of *Night* by Elie Wiesel and *To Kill a Mockingbird*. A square blue bumper sticker with a yellow equals sign was on a file cabinet that stood front and center in the room, where all the kids could see it.

When the bell rang to signal the end of lunch, Delsy called out to me across the room. "Alex, please come back anytime," she said. "And why not join the debate team?"

And after Spencer showed up on the Siales' doorstep for Family

Home Evening the next Monday night, there was only one favor I wanted to trade for my good behavior. I asked Johnny and Tiana if I could attend the debate club meetings after school.

They said yes. What it was that won them over, I'm not exactly sure. Maybe it was Spencer. Maybe it was my new effort to comply with the rules of the house and my "treatment." Maybe it was my attempts to bond with Tiana. Maybe they were just getting tired of me and wanted me out of the house. Whatever it was, I did not stop to ask. I saw the opening, and I took it.

JASON AND I BECAME fast friends, and over the next few weeks, during foods class, lunchtime in Delsy's room, and debate club, he told me his story. It had not been easy growing up gay in St. George, Utah.

"I was about seven years old," Jason told me one day when we were melting gummy bears over the stove in foods class. "My family was going to this Southern Baptist church and the pastor gave a sermon about homosexuality and how evil it was."

Jason's parents were not LDS. They had been living in Las Vegas, had fallen on some hard times, and had moved to St. George to make a fresh start.

"His sermon made me reflect on how I felt about my best friend Justin. I didn't know what to call it. I had been calling it 'admiration.' But that pastor, really." Jason smiled and stirred the pot. "He was the one that gave me the word."

For years, Jason struggled silently with the idea that he might be gay. "I prayed every single day, asking God to take it away from me, and when God didn't, I got very depressed."

I reflected on my seventh-grade crush on Samantha in orchestra. I remembered lying by the pool, wanting to hold her hand but feeling so *weird,* and so *not right.*

"Sure, I thought about committing suicide," Jason told me in Delsy's room at lunchtime. "It got so bad that one day after eighth-grade summer vacation, I lay down on my bed. I lit some candles and wrote a note to my mom, apologizing."

He spoke so steadily, like he'd told the story a million times, like it was a story that deserved—even needed—to be told. Somehow, Jason's willingness to tell his story made me feel very safe.

"When I held the knife to my wrist, I thought of my mama and what it would do to her to find me like this."

My mind raced back to all the times I had gotten stoned or wanted to escape or to run away. How many of my ups and downs were linked to my sense of shame or my confusion about liking girls?

"So I called my cousin's girlfriend, Ashley," Jason said, shifting his weight in the desk as we sat in Delsy's room, then pausing to take a sip of his chocolate milk. "I told her, 'I don't know what to do anymore. I'm depressed. I'm sad all the time. I think I'm gay.' And you know what she said?" He paused. "'That's nothing to be sad about, Jason.'"

Jason gave me a kind, deep smile. I felt the warmth of these words, and the way they had liberated Jason, wash over me.

It had been hard for Jason to keep his sexuality a secret from his parents. He wanted them to know, needed them to know, and needed to know how they would deal with it. When he was fourteen, he located an online support group populated by older gay men. The advice they gave him was to definitely tell his parents, but do it in a public place.

"So we went to Walmart one day." Jason laughed as we waited for debate club to begin. "I was shaking the entire time—I was that scared. I went to the pharmacy and got a piece of paper and wrote, 'Will you love me no matter what?' I handed the note to my mom. 'Of course,' she said. 'What's going on, honey?' I wrote down the words 'I'm gay,' handed the paper back to her, walked into the next aisle, and sat down in front of the mascara. There I was, crying and shaking."

I thought of how I had blurted out the words "I like girls" up-stairs in my parents' bedroom. I had been in fighting mode. Was fighting my way of crying? I remembered the disappointment on my mother's face, the sound of her pain in my ears, the way my father had looked at the ground and had not known what to say.

"My mom walked down the aisle toward me, pulled me up, and hugged me, and we both started crying, together," Jason said.

At Snow Canyon Middle School, as the only out fourteen-year-old gay kid on campus that he knew of, Jason had faced some pretty harsh treatment. He lost friends. He was bullied. He was called a "faggot." Kids spread rumors that a person could catch being gay just by touching Jason. He was shoved into lockers, sometimes while teachers just watched. Some teachers didn't believe him or accused him of making it all up just to get attention. His locker and backpack were searched for porn by school officials. The principal even considered having him change his clothes for gym class in a separate room.

But there had been one teacher—a U.S. history teacher—who'd stood up for Jason.

"These kids were joking around, saying the word 'faggot'—not directly to me, but loud enough for me to overhear," Jason remembered. "And the teacher said, 'This is a safe room. I will not accept any sort of discrimination in this classroom, joking or serious. If I catch any of you engaging in that type of behavior, you will automatically fail the semester.' And that put a stop to it. It was the first time I experienced teachers standing up for gay kids. Delsy is the second."[2]

All his experiences had made Jason think about how many other kids at school needed safe spaces. Jason was definitely out and visible as a gay teen. "I flew out of the closet," he explained one day, waving his hand across his tight shirt and purse. Because he had come out, other kids had started entrusting him with their secrets.

2. Erik Eckholm, "Gay Utah Teenager Takes Another Step in 10-Year Journey," *New York Times,* January 1, 2011, http://www.nytimes.com/2011/01/02/us/02utahside.html?_r=0.

Most had said they were bisexual. Jason had thought the same of himself at first.

How many of those kids, he then wondered, felt as he had—alone, ashamed, possibly suicidal? They needed not to be alone anymore. They needed allies. They needed a network of friendly people to survive school.

Jason had heard that other kids in St. George were trying to organize Gay–Straight Alliance clubs and he decided to do the same. He was taking on a challenge. Just a few years earlier, when a group of Salt Lake City high school students had tried to start the state's first Gay–Straight Alliance, the Utah legislature had reacted by trying to ban all clubs—yes, all clubs on all campuses across the state. That measure failed, but the legislature had passed a law that required parental permission to be in a club and gave schools the right to ban any clubs they thought could harm the "psychological or moral well-being of students and faculty."

When kids in St. George started organizing GSAs in 2009, high school administrators had said they thought GSAs were potentially "immoral."[3]

"And shoving queer kids into lockers is *perfectly moral*," Jason said at lunch in Delsy's room, rolling his eyes.

Across town at Dixie High School, to organize a GSA, a girl named Bethany Coyle—who was straight—had to get a petition signed by thirty students, unanimous approval from the student council and the principal, and a majority vote from the faculty, which had been no simple matter in St. George. Plus, the club officers had had to sign a form promising not to advocate sex.[4]

Jason had faced similar hurdles at Snow Canyon. But he had not been discouraged. Instead of just getting thirty student signatures, Jason got sixty in one lunch period. He spent a week going class-

3. Erik Eckholm, "An Isolated Utah City, New Clubs for Gay Students," *New York Times,* January 1, 2011, http://www.nytimes.com/2011/01/02/us/02utah.html?ref=us.

4. Rosemary Winters, "Four St. George High Schools Allow Gay Clubs," *Salt Lake Tribune,* April 26, 2010, http://archive.sltrib.com/printfriendly.php?id=14963088&itype=ngpsid.

room to classroom, winning teachers over one by one. Delsy Nielson agreed to be the club's advisor. She was the third teacher Jason
asked. The first two had wanted to help but had been afraid of the
repercussions. Delsy said yes without hesitation.

Over at Desert Hills High School, a girl named Sala was ex-
pelled for passing out flyers and trying to organize students for their
Gay–Straight Alliance club. That's when one of the club organizers
contacted the ACLU. The ACLU got in touch with the school district in St. George, sued the principal of Desert Hills, and demanded
that GSA clubs only be required to file the same basic forms that all
other student clubs had to file.[5]

All across town, students were fighting to form GSAs. Snow
Canyon students were very lucky to have Delsy. There was a courage and sense of conviction deep inside her, forged by growing up
in a very conservative Mormon family in Salt Lake City. She later
told me that when she was six or seven years old she had crept half-
way down the stairs in her home to peek in on a large meeting her
parents had convened: the John Birch Society, an extremely conservative anti-Communist group. She saw something in her neighbors'
eyes—a fear, and from it, a hatefulness—that made a permanent
impression on her. She knew right away she wanted no part of it.

While growing up, Delsy saw how that fear and rigidity extended
to gay people. Her mother had a friend—a friend from high school
she loved so much she had asked the woman to be in her wedding
party. After the wedding, when the woman married and moved to
the other side of Salt Lake Valley, they lost touch for a few years. One
day, the best friend appeared on the doorstep, holding her young son's
hand, just for a visit. She was dressed as a man—a transgender person,
as he would now be called. But back then, Delsy's mom just told her
friend not to visit her again and she shut the door.

---

5. Eckholm, "An Isolated Utah City," http://www.nytimes.com/2011/01/02/us/02utah.
html?ref=us; Editorial, "Gay Teens," *Salt Lake Tribune,* May 2, 2010, http://archive.sltrib.com/
printfriendly.php?id=14994493&itype=ngpsid; and Winters, "Four St. George High Schools,"
http://archive.sltrib.com/printfriendly.php?id=14963088&itype=ngpsid.

When Delsy was in college, she worked at a local modeling agency in Salt Lake City, where almost all of her coworkers were gay. The most handsome of them all was dating another man in the office but asked Delsy to be his girlfriend for family events. Delsy also had a long-term boyfriend who she truly loved, and he loved her; they had a profound connection. But there was a secret he could not bear to tell, even her. Still, she found out one day, when her boyfriend had been house-sitting her apartment and she came home from a road trip early to find him and another man kissing in her apartment.

"We are a culture full of secrets," Delsy once told me. "A town full of secrets. We like to bury things."

Delsy was someone who had decided to live another way, to be the one who could hear terrible secrets without fear or judgment and just hold them in her outstretched hands. She was the one with enough courage to be the GSA advisor at Snow Canyon High School. I grew to admire her greatly. And I would need her help. Sitting with Jason, as much as I thrilled in his courage and his story, I realized how lost I felt. I had a long way to go before I could be open about who I was.

"We finally got approved last April . . . just in time for you to arrive and join." Jason smiled.

There was no way, absolutely no way I could get the permission to stay after school for a Gay–Straight Alliance. Even word that I was hanging out with someone like Jason might cause the Siales to pull me out of school.

I leaned forward in my desk and gave him the warmest smile I could. "I would love to, but I can't," I told him. "And not because I don't want to. I just really . . . can't."

Jason kept smiling—his expression did not change.

With or without the Gay–Straight Alliance, I knew I had strong and loyal allies in Jason Osmanski and Delsy Nielson.

HANGING OUT WITH JASON helped me feel so much less alone, and it changed the way I saw my situation. I had been convinced that the

Siales' house was far on the outskirts of town. One day at lunch in Delsy's room, Jason used Google Maps to show me that I was much closer to town than I'd thought. He also helped me get a new sense of how to navigate my social environment. He was out and so were at least a few other kids in the GSA.

One day, in foods class, sitting on the counter, I realized it was safe for him to know my story. More than that, I *needed* him to know.

"Jason, I need to talk to you about something." I took a deep breath. "I'm gay. I have a girlfriend."

Once the words started, they just tumbled out. "My parents sent me to St. George when I told them about my girlfriend. I'm in this house right now, and it sucks. They say they are trying to fix me. They make me go to group treatment sessions and I had to wear a backpack full of rocks. And I'm not the only one—there are other kids in there too."

Jason's face stayed calm and neutral.

"I wasn't going to ask for help. I need help, Jason. But please don't call the child welfare people because the Siales know every-one, and they'll believe the Siales, and I'll have to stay there and I won't be allowed to go to school anymore."

Immediately, Jason jumped in. "Alex. We're going to get you out of there. First, I have a car. I have a 1993 maroon Plymouth Ac-claim. Her name is Akasha, queen vampire bitch of the damned."

"Okay," I said, smiling.

"And I have a lawyer."

"What?"

"My story was in the *New York Times,* and this lawyer in Salt Lake City emailed me and said if I ever needed anything, he could help me for free. I think we should call him."

I paused to think about it. I thought of the lawyers I had watched on television when I was a little girl, how brave and brilliant they were, how they stood up for the voiceless. I had wanted to be a lawyer once. Could someone now stand up for me?

"And Delsy, of course. We need to tell Delsy. Today."

"Jason, I don't think I can."

As MUCH AS I WANTED to trust Delsy, I was terrified to tell her my story. But two days later I found myself in her room at lunchtime, with Jason by my side.

We huddled around the desk at the front of the room, the three of us. At the other end of the room, one of Jason's best friends, Talia, was eating her lunch at a desk. Talia was a member of the debate team too. She wore her dark hair short and swept forward around her face, and she was wearing a striped T-shirt. I smile now knowing that lesbians loving to wear stripes is something of an inside joke in LGBT culture.

"Delsy," he said, "Alex was sent to St. George for gay conversion therapy. She's not living with her family. The people she's living with didn't let her go to school for months, and I don't think she's safe there at all."

Delsy nodded. She did not seem shocked. It was like she had heard stories like mine before. In fact, she had. Over the course of thirteen years of teaching at Snow Canyon, she had become the trusted confidante of many kids who were hurting.

"I think we should call Paul," Jason offered.

Paul Burke was the lawyer who had reached out to Jason after the *New York Times* profile in January of that year. He worked for a very powerful Salt Lake City law firm with deep ties to the LDS Church and Utah's conservative political establishment—a firm with a proud tradition of community service, but senior partners from the firm had taken leading public roles in the campaigns against gay rights in Utah, including Utah's ban on adoption by same-sex couples and the effort to shut down Gay–Straight Alliances in Utah high schools. Paul was not LDS himself but had grown up in Salt Lake City and understood how to work well with LDS people. He had put in years of hard work at the firm, moved up through the ranks from clerk to associate to partner and general counsel. At the time I placed my first call to him, most of his colleagues did not know Paul was gay.

Back in the 1990s, when senior partners in the firm had been fighting school Gay–Straight Alliances, Paul was just a young law clerk. He had wanted to do something, especially since the controversy focused on a club at East High School in Salt Lake City, a school in the neighborhood where he'd grown up. But he'd realized he needed to wait until he was in a better position to help. Now, finally, he was.

Jason took out his cell phone. The sight of it terrified me. Still, I knew I needed help, and having a lawyer on my side—someone to stand up for me and help me find justice, like one of the lawyers in the courtroom television dramas I'd loved to watch as a little girl— seemed like a good idea. Jason scrolled through his contacts to find Paul and pushed the button to call him.

While the phone was dialing, a girl named Shelly entered Delsy's classroom. Shelly had been Talia's girlfriend for three years, and she slipped into the desk next to Talia and quietly gave her a kiss on the cheek. Something about seeing Shelly kiss Talia on the cheek—the sweetness of it, the simplicity of it—made me feel less afraid.

"Hi, Paul. It's Jason, and I'm with this girl named Alex. I think she needs your help." Jason handed me the phone.

"Hi. This is Alex."

"Alex, this is Paul Burke. I am an attorney in Salt Lake City. Tell me what's happening. How can I help?"

I stood there in St. George with Jason and Delsy by my side and I told Paul my story. I told even though I was terrified, even though I was convinced it would bring me great trouble. In Jason's friendship, in Delsy's classroom, I had the first glimpses of what a safe space might feel like. But making that safe space a reality in my life seemed almost impossible.

I did not know but would later learn what a miracle it was that we had reached Paul at that moment. He had just been heading out the door when the call from Jason came.

I told Paul everything about coming out to my parents and being sent to the Siales, about my efforts to escape, the heavy backpack and the time at the wall, and the suicide attempt. He said little, but I could tell he was listening intently.

"Alex," he finally said, "I would like to offer to be your lawyer, *pro bono*."

I wasn't sure what *pro bono* meant until Paul explained it. When I realized he was offering to help me for free, I immediately accepted.

"If you would like, I can try to help you with the custody issues and getting the Siales prosecuted."

"Okay," I said. "Thank you."

"Alex, I need you to be very clear with me: Are you in imminent danger at the Siales'?"

I thought it through carefully. I considered Johnny's violent streak and the risk that if I were found out I could go back on the wall at any time. For the moment, though, everything seemed to be in a stable place. If Paul needed time to do his homework and get ready to help me, I could hang in there.

"No," I said. "I am okay for now."

"If you are in imminent peril, we will not leave you there." Paul was very focused and very clear.

"No, really, things are stable."

"Then I am going to use the next day to contact a few other people who might be able to help us. Alex, I need you to stick it out," he said. "We will figure out how to get you out of there."

With Jason's help, Paul and I made a plan to talk again the next day, at lunchtime.

Then Jason let me use his phone to call Yvette as well. She started crying as soon as I told her it was me. "Ashley hasn't given up. She is still looking for you, and she calls me and keeps me updated."

"Have the police contacted you?"

"Not yet," she said. "I'm scared, Alex."

Hearing her voice, I could not deny that things had changed between us. How could it not feel different after having been apart so many months and after I had gone through so much, all without her. Still, I tried to connect, to imagine the phone pressed into the side of her cheek, her tears.

"Me too," I said. "Me too."

Riding the bus home after school that day, I felt more terrified than I had before. What if the Siales found out? Someone from our Mormon congregation was in every one of my classes. What if someone detected my friendship with Jason or saw me spending all my lunch periods in Delsy's classroom? One word to the Siales and I would be in deep trouble—out of school, on the wall, or worse. When I got back to the Siales', I silently put away my backpack.

"Alexie!" Johnny yelled from his spot on the couch, "you need to mop the kitchen floor."

LATER, JASON WOULD TELL me that what had made him so anxious to get me out were the stories he had heard from other gay people who had been to reparative therapy in Utah. In every single one of their stories the "treatment" tactics had escalated until the kids finally ran or quit, or even worse. At a booth at the Pride Festival in Salt Lake City, he had heard stories from survivors who had been put in "treatment" by Evergreen, a conversion therapy group supported by the church. At Brigham Young University there were even psychologists who had run electroshock therapy experiments on gay students in the 1970s.[6] Other "therapists" had gay people look at pornographic pictures and then hurt themselves or make

---

6. Max Ford McBride, "Effects of Visual Stimuli in Electric Aversion Therapy" (Ph.D. diss., Brigham Young University, 1976), https://drive.google.com/file/d/0B1u3K43P-3JoY2 Q5NDY3ZjYtNWUyMi00YWJiLWFhM2EtYTE4MjViNWVjOGEz/view?num=50&sort =name&layout=list&pli=1.

themselves throw up, thinking this would create a mental association between being gay and being sick.

Those were especially bad years for gay people in Mormon
Utah. The LDS Church's prophet Spencer Kimball wrote a book
called *The Miracle of Forgiveness* that described homosexuality as a
"vile . . . crime against nature," one step away from "bestiality,"
and "curable" with proper treatment.[7] Jason told me that one of the
top-ranked leaders in the church had even celebrated the fact that a
young male Mormon missionary had knocked out his companion
when his companion revealed that he was gay. "Somebody had to
do it," Elder Boyd K. Packer said, speaking over the pulpit at General Conference, broadcast to Mormons around the world.[8]

Over the decades, Mormon leaders had slowly been changing
elements of the way they talked about homosexuality. No one ad-
vocated physical violence against gay people anymore, and no one
compared homosexuality to bestiality—not from the pulpit at General Conference, at least. But the underlying message was the same:
Homosexuality was a choice, a terrible sin, a sign of deep spiritual
problems, and it could be changed. In fact, it had to be changed in
order for gay people to fit into the plan of salvation and maintain
any hope of having families of their own, being with their families
in the eternities, or being with God in heaven.

Mormon religious leaders, such as bishops, routinely counseled
gay people to pray and read the scriptures until they stopped feeling
same-sex attraction, and some suggested marriage to straight people
as the best cure of all. To this day, some still do. To this day, there
is still no support within the Mormon Church for a gay person who
wants to fall in love, be married, and have a family.

This is the bigger picture that might help explain why families
kick out kids when they come out of the closet or why families send
their kids for counseling to change them, even why these families

7. Spencer W. Kimball, *The Miracle of Forgiveness* (Salt Lake City: Bookcraft, 1969).

8. Boyd K. Packer, "To Young Men Only," LDS Church General Conference Priesthood
Session, October 2, 1976, http://www.lds-mormon.com/only.shtml.

believe homosexuality is something that can be cured. Jason came to see this bigger picture very clearly during his own coming out, as he talked with other gay Utahns, Mormons especially. He understood what I was just beginning to see: I was not alone. I was not the only one. Thousands of gay Mormon kids had been through something like what I was going through.

Eventually, I would really come to understand that. But as I mopped the kitchen floor and watched the Siale kids file in from school, the only thing on my mind was staying quiet and blending into the background. For me, the most important thing was to give the Siales every impression that their "treatment" was working so that I could continue to go to school.

For Jason, the most important thing was getting me out. He had met enough people who had been through what I was going through to know that many never made it out whole. Many ended up killing themselves, even after they got free. Every day I stayed put my life in greater danger.

CHAPTER 14

Can't Take Another Day

I COULDN'T SEE IT AT the time, but as soon as I told Jason about my situation at the Siales', a whole network of people started working to get me out.

Every day in foods class or after school at debate, Jason started teaching me what he called "Gay 101," helping me to understand what it meant to be gay in Utah and to see potential allies and safe spaces that had been invisible.

"There are gay people in St. George," he explained to me. "There are PFLAG meetings on Tuesdays once a month. You can come with me."

I wrinkled my nose at him. The Siales would never let that happen.

"There are also gay kids at Snow Canyon. Me, Talia, Shelly . . ." Jason counted the first three names off on his fingers, then he raised a fourth finger, leaned in with a mischievous smile, and whispered, *"You."*

He continued rattling off names of gay kids, bisexual kids, questioning kids. "You know Allen? The one with the emo hair? Also gay." Soon he was holding up all the fingers on both hands. I connected names with faces I had seen in the halls—kids who wore tight, tight pants, wore their backpacks all the time, or let their hair hang down in their faces. In the world of Snow Canyon High School, a world that seemed to be full of identical, clean-cut Mormons like Spencer, these kids were definitely the minority. But they quietly looked out for one another.

Jason began to tell just a few of the other gay kids about me, ones he felt sure he could trust, like Talia. He also made sure that I got to Delsy's room every lunch period so I could call Paul and check in.

From that very first phone call, Paul felt a deep commitment to my case. As a gay man who had grown up in Utah, he understood the ideas and beliefs about homosexuality that contributed to my situation, and he also felt moved to help create better conditions for LGBT teenagers everywhere.

Paul's commitment to help me was personal in another way. Little did I know then that at the time he took my case, he had recently lost his brother Matt, a surgeon and a decorated army officer. Paul and Matt had been very close: they had been born just two years apart and had gone to the same small college, and Matt was the first person in their family Paul had come out to. After completing an honorable tour of duty in Iraq, Matt came home and he and his wife became parents to a baby girl. Then he was killed in the line of duty during physical training when a driver slammed into a group of bicyclists Matt was riding with—a senseless and violent crash. When my call came in, Paul had just been returning to work after attending Matt's interment at Arlington National Cemetery.

His first stop after he got off the phone with me after our first call was the office of one of the more conservative senior partners in his law firm. Paul had already made his mind up to help me, no matter what and no matter how long it took, but he wanted to gauge whether someone in the firm might object. As he readied himself to talk to his senior colleague, he rehearsed the question in his mind: *Are we the kind of law firm that helps a child who is being tortured?* he would ask. *Or are we the kind that refers her on?* Thankfully, he encountered no open resistance, and he even received support from this senior partner.

Paul then reached out to national child welfare and gay rights organizations. He knew my case would be a complicated one, involving custody issues and maybe even criminal charges against the Siales. He wanted advice and perspective from the experts. And everyone he spoke with had the same reaction when they heard my story: they were shocked, and they were deeply worried for my survival.

One of the people Paul connected with right away was Kate Kendell, executive director of the National Center for Lesbian Rights. Kate immediately promised to help with my case by connecting Paul with legal experts who had expertise with situations like mine. Shannon Minter, NCLR's legal director, had done research on LGBT kids and mental health, and he stressed to Paul how great the risk of suicide was in my case. If I had attempted it once, chances were I would try again. It was crucial that Paul encourage me not to lose hope while we worked on a solution.

Shannon had also worked with gay kids whose families had sent them to residential treatment centers in Utah. The treatment centers would hold seminars in cities like Los Angeles, trying to draw in desperate parents, even coaching them on how to get state money to pay for the costs. But in case after case, treatment had only made matters worse. Even when families really wanted to help, sending their kids away to these centers seemed to break a basic bond. The kids only felt more abandoned and estranged. Being sent away deepened their sense of failure. Many ran away from treatment. Some became homeless. Some attempted suicide. Some succeeded.

His talking to Shannon changed the way Paul saw my situation. He came to realize that it was a matter of life or death. Everyone he talked to emphasized that every day I stayed in that house the chances of my attempting suicide again grew. Child welfare and gay rights experts across the country urged Paul to find a way to get me out as soon as possible, and to get me out of Utah as well. One told him that he just needed to get me on the next bus to California, where I might stand a chance in the legal system. Almost no one believed that a child welfare or legal case like mine could get a positive outcome in the Utah courts. All of this weighed on Paul very heavily.

The second time we spoke, Paul brought in his colleague Brett Tolman, who as a U.S. attorney had worked on the kidnapping case of Elizabeth Smart. Elizabeth's story was different from mine in many respects, but like Elizabeth, I was being held by people who used religion to justify emotional and physical abuse. Brett even observed that the man who had held Elizabeth captive and the Siales used similar control tactics and techniques.

Brett and Paul made calls to contacts who knew the child welfare and legal systems in southern Utah, trying to determine who in the system had a record of being LGBT friendly and might be willing to help.

"Can't we go to the media?" I begged Paul. Maybe if the news cameras came to the Siales' house I could get out sooner.

But Paul knew that a story like mine could be explosive, that lots of publicity could make things harder and more complicated rather than easier for me, and that for things to turn out the right way in the Utah court system, and with my family in the long run, we would have to think clearly, work together, prepare, and be careful. Still, he was prepared to go to the media if we had to—if things got so bad that only the national media could save the day. Thankfully, that day never came.

And then there was Delsy. She racked her brain to come up with ways to help me. Convinced that we needed evidence on the Siales, she spent one of our lunchtimes together checking out secret cameras and microphones on the Internet. She also urged me to bring my journal to school, to stash in her file cabinet for safekeeping.

Her most generous offer to me came just a few days after my first phone call with Paul.

"Alex," she said, taking my hand, "I've talked to Gordon. We want you to live with us."

We got on the phone with Paul and told him our plan, and he reminded us that custody would have to go through the court system.

"That's a very generous offer," he said. "We will look into it. For now, just be good, Alex. We will find a way to get you out soon."

SOON COULDN'T COME SOON enough, as far as I was concerned. It was all I could do to hang on day after day. My new network of friends and allies at Snow Canyon High School helped me imagine for the first time since arriving in Utah a world outside the Siale house, a world where I could be seen and heard. But it did not change the reality of my life inside the house, or the deep sense of sadness and loss that months of wearing the backpack or standing at the wall had carved out in me. It did not fix my relationship with my parents, and it did not stop thoughts of ending it all by killing myself from surfacing in my mind.

Still, I knew that my survival pretty much depended on finding the strength to keep going through the motions—group talk sessions, church, chores, cooking for the family, attending school— without complaint and without a word about Jason, Delsy, or Paul.

One little mistake could bring my whole new fragile world down.

That's what happened. One little mistake. Two minutes too long on the telephone in Delsy's room at lunchtime. A few words too many between me and Paul, planning the next step in our strategy to get me out of the Siale household.

It was a Wednesday, just after Easter. I was so engrossed in my conversation with Paul that no one, not even Delsy, noticed the time until the bell rang to signal the end of lunch.

"Oh, Alex!" Delsy said.

"Paul, I'm going to be late for class!" I hung up the phone, grabbed my backpack, and ran across campus to my animal science class. By the time I slipped into my seat, I was tardy by four minutes.

Little did I know that Johnny and Tiana would receive an automated weekly update call from school reporting my tardiness. But when they asked the whole family—me and Sifa too—to sit down with them at the kitchen table after I washed the dinner dishes that following Saturday night, I knew I was in trouble.

Johnny started, interlacing his fingers and resting his hands on the table in front of him. "You know we know everyone in this town. If something happens, people let us know." He fixed his gaze on each of us sitting around the table, one by one.

"You can't keep anything from us," Tiana chimed in.

"Now," Johnny said, beginning to drum his fingers on the tabletop, "does anyone have anything they want to tell us?"

The Siale kids squirmed uncomfortably in their seats. Sifa and Calvin hung their heads and kept their eyes on the table. After the betrayals of February, never for a moment did we consider trusting one another to keep our secrets.

I didn't dare breathe a word. My stomach hurt. I thought about Jason, Delsy, and Paul—what might happen to Jason and Delsy, especially if the wrong people found out they were helping me.

Johnny let us all sit in silence for a couple of minutes, minutes that seemed like hours.

Finally, he broke the silence. "Alex."

My pulse spiked and my stomach dropped.

"We got a call from school about you."

They did not say it was about being tardy. They did this—Johnny especially—withholding information, giving it out selectively, so that they could stay in control and maximize our fear.

Not a word. Not a word. Not a word.

"It's clear we can't trust you to attend school properly," Tiana said. "As of Monday, we are pulling you out of school."

"And as of tonight, you will go back on the wall," Johnny said. "With the backpack."

The minute I slipped those black nylon straps onto my shoulders, all the old pains in my neck and shoulders returned. So did the black feelings of hopelessness. I spent Sunday at the wall, recounting the months of doing everything I could to earn the tiniest moments of freedom—all of that effort lost now. I regretted talking to Jason and Delsy. I even regretted starting back at school. Once again, I had ruined everything.

Who knows how long I will be here now. Months? Years? Monday my hours at the wall were flooded with panic as I faced the uncertainty of what would come next. That night the local Mormon missionaries came for Family Home Evening and dinner—yet another set of missionaries who saw me at the wall and didn't say a word about it. I was once again invisible, and no one would come to help me.

By Tuesday morning, when I woke up and put on the backpack, I was focused on finding a way out. It would probably take suicide, I concluded. *How to go about it this time?* As I contemplated my options, I remembered what Jason had told me about his own suicide attempt, how he had been ready to cut his wrists but stopped because he didn't want his mother to find him that way. Thinking about him, about his mischievous eyes and the motherly way he had looked after me those last few weeks at Snow Canyon, it made me smile. I despaired thinking I would not be able see him or Delsy again.

But maybe I could . . .

The last time I had been at the wall, I realized, even if I had tried to get out, I'd had nowhere and no one to run to. Everyone I had reached out to for help—from strangers at the grocery store to the Mormon missionaries and congregation members who visited the Siales' house when I was standing at the wall—refused to see me, or they took the Siales' side. But this time, I realized, this time was different.

If I could just make it to school.

This time I had Jason, Paul, and Delsy. If made it to school, they would help me. Maybe I could figure a way out. Maybe it would be okay.

I made it through the afternoon at the wall, counting numbers to keep myself from losing consciousness and thinking through how I could make my break and run. There was no way I could cross the living room and make it out through the garage. Johnny would hear me in a moment. The front door made too much noise and would wake Johnny as well. Blinds covered the sliding glass door from the kitchen to the side yard. The blinds would rattle, but maybe if I was careful, I could keep the noise down.

The Siale kids came home from school. None of them said a word to me as they settled into their homework and video games.

At dinnertime, I ate at the wall, stepped away to do the dishes, then returned. The kids filed off for bed, and Johnny filled his mug with kava, then sat down to play video games on the couch. He played for what felt like hours, filling the living room with sounds of gunfire as he clutched the controls, setting them down only to refill his cup.

Eventually, the sounds of the game wound down and I heard Johnny's steady breathing rise from the living room couch. I glanced back over my shoulder. The microwave clock read 4:30 A.M.

This is it, I thought. *I can't take another day. This is the moment I've been waiting for.* I set down the backpack and stepped away from the wall. Crossing the kitchen, with Johnny sleeping just a few yards away, and reaching for the handle on that kitchen slider was the scariest thing I had ever done.

My flip-flops were next to the sliding door. I grabbed them in my hands but did not put them on. I could not afford the sounds of flip-flops slapping on the rocky walk that led from the house to the street.

The handle felt cold in my hand. I gripped it tightly, closed my eyes, held my breath, flipped the latch, and pulled the door open six inches. It moved soundlessly in its tracks.

I walked slowly across the rocks, placing each foot carefully, praying that I would not make a sound. Somehow I made it through the side yard and onto the street. I did not look back. I was too scared to look back. Instead, I focused all my energy on getting as far as I could from the house and as close as I could to Snow Canyon High School.

My bare feet slapped on the black asphalt as I ran past the houses of the Siales' neighbors and all the people we went to church with on Sunday. I ran past lit porch lights and well-tended gardens, but I could never stop. I knew I could not ask for help. I was sure they all were on Johnny and Tiana's side.

I came up to the school bus stop, paused for a moment. I figured that would be one of the first places Johnny and Tiana would look. No chance. I kept running.

Every time a car came down the road, I paused and started to walk slowly, or I hid myself in the bushes of a neighborhood yard.

Finally, I made it to the public bus stop, slipped my flip-flops onto my feet, and squatted down in the sagebrush, trying to make myself as small as possible. It was still early; the bus wasn't scheduled to come for a while. The bus stop was on the bank of a dry riverbed lined with a row of scrubby cottonwoods. Cold air came up from the riverbed and made me shiver in my cardigan sweater. No more than fifteen yards away stood a beautiful white house, roses around the front steps, porch lights burning bright in the early morning hours. I was so cold. I wanted to go inside so badly. But I couldn't. Instead, I crouched in the sagebrush.

My stomach hurt with anxiety and my mind raced, trying to come up with a plan: What would I do if the Siales found me? What would I tell them? How would I get out of it? I racked my brain and came up with nothing. I was out of options. I had to get to school. It had to work this time.

I watched the color of the sky begin to change over the eastern edge of the desert, then heard the sound of a large engine rumbling toward me.

For a moment, terror gripped my stomach. If the Siales found me, I had nowhere else to go. I prepared myself to run.

Just then, the lights of the morning's first city bus crested the hill. I stepped out of the shadows and to the edge of the curb.

When the door opened in front of me, I stood in the circle of light at the foot of the steps but didn't climb in. "I don't have any money but I really need to get out of here."

Tears ran down my face and dropped into the red dirt at my feet. The light from the bus shone against the back of the driver's head. I could see her steel-gray hair pulled back into a ponytail. I could not see her face, but her voice was warm and reassuring. "Do you want me to call the police, honey?"

"No, I just need to get to school."

"Okay," she said. "It's going to be okay. Come on in."

There was no one else on the bus besides the driver and me. It was the first run of the day, and the heater had not been on long enough to chase out the chill. I took a seat a few rows back from the driver. When I sat down I realized I could not feel my toes. All I had on were jeans, a tank top, a cardigan, and flip-flops, not enough for the early morning desert air. I shivered, from cold and from fear as well.

I watched the red-rock desert and lava fields go by outside the windows. We were getting closer to Snow Canyon, and the closer I got, the more I felt my courage grow.

I saw the row of cypress trees that stood at the west edge of campus and then the lights of campus itself as the bus crested a hill.

"We're here now," the bus driver said, her voice soft. "You going to be okay, honey?"

"Yes," I said, though my voice shook and my body shivered. "And thank you."

My mind flashed back to all the times I had reached out to strangers in town for help—in the grocery store, at the football game. I thought about all the people at church who had seen me in desperate moments—the missionaries who had come by and seen me facing the wall, the bishop who I had opened up to. In the end, help came not from them but from a bus driver just driving her early morning route in a desert town in southern Utah. What would have happened to me had she not allowed me to board without paying? I was overwhelmed by a sense of relief and deep gratitude.

I stepped off the bus. The doors closed behind me, and the bus drove away.

I crossed the front lawn, heading for the first door I could see. It was locked. I turned right and circled around the side of the building. Trembling, my hands turned every handle. Every one of them was locked.

I must have tried a dozen doors before I made it to the back of the building. The football stadium—where I had tried to escape months earlier—stood a hundred yards away.

Anxiously, I watched for headlights on the road leading to the school. I expected to see the Siales' blue TrailBlazer appear at any moment.

I found a gap between a wall and the school building. I wedged my body into the gap, figuring I would hide myself from view until the janitors arrived and opened the building.

Feeling the cold cinder-block wall against my back and my knees, I watched the light shift as the sun came up over the desert.

It's going to be okay. I repeated the words over and over in my head. *I'm going to make it out this time.*

I heard the first of the janitors' trucks pull into the parking lot, the sound of boots on the asphalt, keys jangling on a ring. Still, I stayed hidden a few minutes longer. Just to be sure.

It must have been about seven A.M. when I finally slipped out of my hiding place between the walls and made it through the back doors of the school building.

Delsy usually arrived at about seven thirty to get ready for the school day. I went straight to her room.

"Alex!" Delsy had come in early to prep her lessons. My arrival had startled her, as did the panic in my voice.

"I'm not going back," I blurted out, tears coming to my eyes. "Not one more day. We have to do this now."

"Okay, Alex," she said, rising from her desk and crossing the room to put her hands on my shoulders. "You're freezing!"

"I ran. I ran last night, then hid behind the bus stop until the sun came up. They put me back on the wall and I just couldn't. So I ran."

"Well, you made it, Alex," she said. "And I won't let them take you back. But we're going to have to call the police and the Division of Child and Family Services. We really don't have a choice. Can you come to the office with me?" Delsy's hands felt warm on my shoulders, and her voice was gentle.

"There's a lady who works in the front office—she's in the Siales' ward. She's going to tell them I'm here. She's going to get me sent back, I know it."

"I won't let that happen, Alex." Delsy put her arm around my shoulder and walked me out of her classroom and down the long, tiled hallway to the front office. Students were just beginning to arrive for school.

We walked through the front office doors, and Delsy squared her shoulders and cleared her throat. "This girl is in trouble," she told the entire office staff. "If you notify the Siales that she is here, you will go to jail."

There she stood, all of five feet five inches in her sundress and sandals, but her voice projected a tone of unmistakably firm identity—like she had taken all the skills she taught the debate club and put them to use in this moment. I had forgotten what it was like to have someone be firm on my behalf. Hearing Delsy talk like that gave me fresh courage.

It's going to be okay. I repeated the words over and over in my head. *I'm going to make it out this time. People are going to help me. I have Delsy, Jason, and Paul.*

Delsy escorted me to a little conference room in the back of the school office, then left for a few minutes to get her classes covered for the day.

"Oh no," she said on her way out the door, "I'm not leaving you alone until we get this figured out."

Within fifteen minutes, Jason appeared and sat down with me in the conference room. He looked as scared as I felt, but he put on a brave face for me. "I'm so glad you came back, Alex," he said, taking my hands in his across the table. "I called the Division of Child and Family Services to report your case."

"You did?"

"Oh, I would have come to find you anyway, Alex." Jason laughed his mischievous laugh. "I would have rammed my car through the Siales' garage door to get you out."

CHAPTER 15

Safe

"I**F THEY WANT TO** argue with me, let them try—I'm the debate teacher," Delsy said, smiling. "If they want to fire me, they can fire me."

My favorite English teacher had positioned herself as a barricade between the little conference room where I was holed up and the outside world. "If the Siales are out looking for you," she insisted, "the safest place is here, until we can get you somewhere safer."

Safe. What did it mean to be safe? Where could I go in a town like St. George, where the Siales knew local church leaders and police officers well enough to enlist them in bringing back kids who ran from their house, a town where almost everyone felt the same way about gay kids—or so I'd thought in my terrified state.

I knew I had Delsy, Paul, and Jason on my side. But there was so much I didn't know. Who else would believe my story? What were the next steps to get me out of the Siale house forever? How would I get back home? What was home to me now?

That's why I didn't feel relieved when a caseworker from the Utah Division of Child and Family Services arrived, along with an officer from the local police department. Would they believe me? Could they help me? I wasn't entirely sure.

The DCFS caseworker's name was Brook. She was young and blond, with a sweet, high-pitched voice. I was pretty sure she was Mormon. I hate to say it, but over the months at the Siales', especially when I was trying to figure out who I could trust and who might help me get out, I quietly assessed who was Mormon and who was not. I could often tell by the way people talked or dressed. With her pretty look and sweet voice, Brook seemed to fit the mold, and I worried she might see things the way the Siales did and be more sympathetic to them than she was to me.

The police detective, Choli, was tall, skinny, and pretty and wore her brown hair pulled back in a ponytail. She had a stern look and seemed disconnected, but I knew that was just part of her job. Was she Mormon? I couldn't tell for sure, but she certainly didn't fit the mold the same way the DCFS caseworker did.

"Alex," Detective Choli started, "we need you to tell us what has happened to you."

"You're not in trouble," the blond caseworker assured me. "Nothing you say will get you in trouble."

"Is it okay with you if we record your story, to help us get the details right, in case we need them later?" the detective asked.

I nodded. She set a small recording device on the table. I took a breath and began to speak.

I told them my story. I told them about coming out to my parents and getting taken to St. George to live with the Siales to straighten me out. I described what the Siales called "treatment": group sessions where I was told that God didn't want gay people in heaven, long stretches of time standing and facing the wall, and wearing a backpack full of rocks to represent the burden of my homosexuality. I told them the Siales had not allowed me to

attend school for months, that they had told me there was no place
in God's plan for me because I was gay and that my family didn't
want me anymore. I told them I had tried to escape at least twice
and that Johnny had beaten me. I told them about the night I took
the prescription pills, trying to escape from it all for good. Both
the detective and the caseworker hunched over their notebooks,
writing quickly.

I stopped for a moment and scrutinized their faces, looking
for any kind of a reaction. Recognition? Judgment? Compassion?
Pity? It was so hard to tell what they were thinking, whether or not
they believed me or believed that what I had been through was bad
enough to warrant getting me out of there.

"Do I have to go back there?"

The detective and the caseworker looked up from their notebooks.

"Please don't make me go back," I begged.

Before Detective Choli or Brook could answer me, Delsy stuck
her head into the room. "Alex, do you need your journal?"

I had stashed my journal in Delsy's room for safekeeping.

I looked to the caseworker. She nodded. She and the detective
continued writing for a minute or two more.

The caseworker was the first to speak: "I think what we have
here is a mild case of abuse."

I could see Detective Choli stiffen. "This is not a *mild* case of
abuse," she said. Her tone was firm and certain.

From there, things started to move more quickly.

Delsy had to go back to her late-morning and afternoon classes.
She sent Jason to the office with the journal. On his way, Jason must
have hurried to photocopy all the pages in order to fax them to Paul
in Salt Lake City, using the school fax machine. Detective Choli left
campus to go to the elementary school where the Siales' daughter
Olivia was a student. She tried to get Olivia to verify my story, but
Olivia told the detective that her family had told her not to discuss

family business with strangers. She denied that anyone ever had to face the wall.

Brook stayed behind at Snow Canyon High, stepping out of the conference room to make telephone calls. Through the window in the door, I could see a larger stream of students passing in and out of the school office. Was it lunchtime already? I hadn't eaten since dinner the night before, but I had no appetite.

Brook returned with a piece of paper and a pen in her hands. "Alex," she said, "we need you to write down everything you have told the detective and me."

She passed the paper across the table, and I began to write.

September 7th of 2010, I, Alexandra Cooper, was brought to live with the Siale family.

I wrote down everything I had been through, everything I could recall of the last few months, even as my hands were shaking. Sentences piled up on the page in front of me. I had to write enough to convince the DCFS officer not to send me back. This was my chance. I needed help. I concluded the statement by asking for it as plainly as I could:

I am currently very afraid for my state of being and my sanity. I feel if I don't get out soon I'll go crazy. Suicidal thoughts often pop into my head. It seems like an easy way out. I just hope and pray someone will be able to help.

As I finished writing, Detective Choli came back with a school telephone. She and Brook spoke outside the conference room for a moment, then returned to talk to me.

"If you want to be able to leave the Siale house," Detective Choli told me, "I need you to call them on the phone, Alex, and tell them where you are. I need you to tell them you are at school."

My reply came hard and fast. "No way." I was terrified by the thought of any contact with them. Even by phone. What if something I said or something the Siales said could be used to send me back there? I must have argued with Detective Choli for thirty or forty-five minutes. I argued like my life depended on it, but she was just as firm.

"You have to tell them where you are, Alex," she insisted. "If you want us to be able to remove you permanently."

I relented and allowed the detective to dial the number. As the detective and the caseworker listened in over the speakerphone, Tiana answered.

"Tiana, this is Alex," I said. "I am calling you from school."

"I told you you weren't allowed to go to school anymore!" she said, sounding groggy and confused, like she had just woken up. In the background, Johnny was yelling. "Start walking back to the house, Alex," she said.

"No," Johnny yelled. "I'll go pick her up. Don't let her walk anywhere."

"Okay?" I turned to the detective and the caseworker.

"Yes," Detective Choli said. "Thank you, Alex. You can hang up now. Let's take you downtown."

My eyes adjusted to the late afternoon light, I pulled my cardigan close around me, and I hugged my journal to my chest as we walked through the parking lot toward her squad car. The terror of escaping the Siale house, the feel of cold asphalt under my feet as I ran, the smell of the sagebrush I hid in behind the bus stop, the sound of the bus's brakes and the door drawing open—was it really just a few hours ago that I'd run? It felt like years. Settling into the back of the squad car, I felt for the first time the depth of my exhaustion. I wished that Jason or Delsy had been there for a goodbye hug.

Detective Choli started the engine and drove the squad car out of the school parking lot, through the lava fields, along the red-rock canyon road, toward town. I counted every mile we put between us and the Siale house. *It's going to be okay now,* I told myself over and over. Still, I was gripped by a fear that something would happen, that the Siales would come and get me, and there would be nothing I could do to stop them.

The squad car pulled into the parking lot of the Youth Crisis Center in downtown St. George, nestled up against a wall of red-rock hills on the north side of town. The building was beige with turquoise trim, set back in among a cluster of city buildings.

Detective Choli walked me in through the front door. We were greeted at the front desk by a blond older woman with a warm smile who introduced herself as Sandra. When she stood to greet us, she was tall—very tall. She reached out to shake my hand. Hers were warm and plump. I found everything about her comforting.

"This is Alex Cooper," the detective said. "I think you can take it from here?"

"Thank you, Officer." Sandra smiled, and Detective Choli left the building.

"Now, Alex, let's start your intake forms," she said, sitting back down at the desk. "You don't have to tell me why you're here, but I want you to know that I know it is not your fault."

Something in her smile and in the careful way she spoke to me reminded me of Delsy.

Sandra asked me a series of questions about where I was born, where I lived, where I attended school. Then she paused, and she lifted her eyes to meet mine. "Alex, are you hurt? Is there anything that hurts?"

I mentally scanned my body, trying to feel something beyond exhaustion and fear. I realized then that, yes, I was in physical pain. My back hurt. In fact, my back had been hurting for months, ever since my first stint wearing the backpack and facing the wall. I had just gotten used to the day-to-day pain. It had become a part of me, not even something I thought worth mentioning to Jason or Delsy. Maybe I could get help for it now. The idea seemed a revelation.

"Yes," I said, "my back hurts."

"Okay," she said and made a note on my forms.

After we finished the intake forms, she apologetically gave me a pat down, then walked me back into a lounge area adjacent to a kitchen. There was a couch, board games, and a television.

"Can I make you some dinner?"

"You want to make me dinner?"

"Sure, honey. Just decide what you want."

After making dinner for the Siale family every night for months, the idea that someone would make dinner for me seemed incredibly kind.

I can't remember now what it was that Sandra cooked for me. But I remember sitting with her in the kitchen while she stood at the stove, watching the afternoon light change to evening, and talking. Every few minutes I found myself glancing out toward the front door, still terrified that the Siales could just walk in and take me.

"Sandra," I asked, "what are the chances they can take me back?"

"No chance as long as you're here, Alex."

"Please don't let them take me back."

She smiled. "It's okay, Alex. You're safe here."

Safe. I tried to let the word sink in as I finished my dinner. I took a shower and changed into a new pair of pajamas Sandra had laid on my bunk in the crisis center dormitory. My bed was a wood-frame twin topped with a hand-tied pink, white, and yellow quilt. Relieved to be the only one in the dormitory that night, I put my journal under the bed, climbed in, and pulled up the covers.

Safe. I was exhausted down to my bones, relieved, but still so terrified that at any minute the Siales would come to get me. What if they just showed up at the crisis center? What if they walked into my dorm room? The idea seems far-fetched now, but that night it was all I could think about. What could I do? Where could I go? As kind as Sandra was, I had no idea what my next steps would be. I was out of options.

But at least for the moment I could sleep.

THE NEXT MORNING, I slept in late, then took another shower and picked out something to wear from a big closet full of secondhand clothes that belonged to the shelter. They weren't my clothes, but at least they weren't the castoffs the Siales had forced me to wear either. I nervously poked at the plate of breakfast that Brittni, the desk worker for the day, had cooked for me. I was too nervous to eat, mostly because I hadn't yet talked to Paul. Paul was the only one I believed could help me negotiate the next steps—whatever they might be. And he *was* trying to help me, right at that very moment, even though we hadn't yet been able to speak by phone. Jason had called Paul that first morning I had run from the Siales', and that day Paul had made contact on my behalf with the police, the DCFS, and the attorney general's office. Even as I wondered how to get in touch with him, Paul was hard at work trying to get a call to me.

After breakfast, another caseworker from the DCFS arrived to take me to a pediatrician's office downtown. A knot of panic formed in my belly when I recognized the name on the doctor's office door: she was a woman from the ward of my grandparents and the Siales. I felt my guard go up instantly.

"You've been staying with the Siales?" she asked me in the exam room as she started my physical. "I heard they were really good people."

My pulse quickened, and the knot in my belly tightened.

"I don't want to talk about it." Those were the only words I could manage. I could feel the anger rising inside me as the doctor checked my pulse and blood pressure, looked in my eyes and ears. She reviewed my intake forms from the shelter, then ran her hands down along both sides of my spine.

"When did the pain start?" she asked.

"When the Siales started having me wear a backpack full of rocks."

"We'll need to send you for an X ray and a CT scan," she said, her brows slightly furrowed.

When I returned to the crisis center, the bags with my belong-ings had arrived from the Siales' house. Brittni helped me carry them into my dorm room. When I opened them and began to lay my belongings out on my bunk, I found that someone had cut my clothes with scissors.

I heard Brittni draw in a quick breath. "Okay," she said. "Well, you're welcome to anything in our closet. I promise we'll make sure you have what you need."

That afternoon, Brittni walked me to the downtown library and helped me get a library card. I had no address of my own to put on the forms, so she let me use hers. On the new arrivals shelf, Brittni found a book titled *It Gets Better,* a collection of personal stories about growing up, coming out, and facing the challenges of being gay.[9] I checked it out, along with a novel or two.

For dinner, Brittni took me to a café on Main Street that was famous for its cupcakes. The walls were painted a light tur-quoise blue and hung with brightly colored art that featured lots of images of birds. Empty birdcages hung from the ceiling as chandeliers. I settled into a big comfortable booth and listened to Brittni talk while I tucked into a plate of pasta and finished with a strawberry shortcake cupcake for dessert. *It gets better.* Both Jason and Delsy had tried to tell me that, but it still seemed so far away.

I STARTED TO BREATHE a little easier on my third day, when I finally got a call from Paul on the crisis center house line.

"How did you find me here?" I asked him.

"I have my ways," he gently joked.

In fact, Paul had already faced down some challenges just get-ting me on the phone. The attorney general's office, he explained, did not believe that someone my age and in my situation had the

---

9. Dan Savage and Terry Miller, eds., *It Gets Better* (New York: Dutton, 2011).

right to choose her own attorney; a *guardian ad litem* had already been appointed by the juvenile court to represent my "best interests." When Paul had insisted that I did have the right to retain my own lawyer, the attorney general's office had pushed back and even implied that they could press to have Paul disciplined and his license to practice law revoked if he continued to press my case. Still, Paul had persisted, citing a provision in the Utah state constitution that guaranteed *everyone* the right to choose his or her own lawyer, and after several days of negotiation, he had managed to get permission from the *guardian ad litem* to call me at the crisis center.

By phone, Paul carefully explained the next steps in the process. I would soon meet my *guardian ad litem*. On Tuesday, the courts would make a plan for my immediate future, whether that would mean staying at the crisis center, being placed with a foster family, or even going to my grandparents' for a few days while the courts continued to deliberate who should take legal custody of me. And even though the state had appointed a *guardian ad litem,* Paul promised he would stand by me and represent my wishes for as long as I wanted.

The deepest part of me hungered for home, but I was also frightened by the thought that my parents might try to send me away again or put me in another kind of "treatment" like that I had faced at the Siales'. I knew for sure that I could not go back to the Siales, the wall, the backpack, or any other kind of "treatment." And I knew I trusted Paul, even though he was still at that point just a voice on the other end of the line. I hadn't yet seen his face, but there was something about his voice—the calm, measured way he spoke, the gentle sense of humor that occasionally broke through—that made me feel things might actually get better.

"You're not going back to the Siales no matter what," Paul assured me. "I am working on every possible option to get you to a safer place. We'll make it so you won't have to go back. Don't worry."

ON MONDAY, I WENT downtown to the courthouse to meet my *guardian ad litem*. The courthouse was an imposing three-story building built from blocks of quarried red sandstone, with tall white Roman columns out front, and topped by a rotunda. To get to the *guardian ad litem*'s office, I had to pass through security. The lobby was cold and tiled with marble, and the walls were covered with rich wood paneling and murals of Utah pioneers.

I stepped into the *guardian ad litem*'s office.

"You must be Alex," said the receptionist, a sweet older woman with short brown hair. "I'll let Matt know you are here."

The *guardian ad litem* greeted me at the door of his office with a handshake. He was tall and skinny with dark hair and a beard.

"Alex," he said, gesturing toward a seat at the table, "why don't you sit here?"

He explained his role in the process was to represent my best interests and that he would continue to do so until the courts determined the best outcome for my case. He told me that on Tuesday we'd meet in court with the Siales and possibly my parents, to resolve the question of who should have custody of me and where I should live.

Then Matt shifted uncomfortably in his seat. "I know you've retained outside counsel," he said, clearing his throat. "An attorney named Paul Burke."

"Yes." I watched his face for a reaction.

"I've worked with other lawyers before, and I've found that sometimes we don't agree, and it may not make sense to work together." He paused, and I continued to watch him. "I hope we can find a way to work directly together, you and I," he said.

There was no way I was giving up Paul, no matter what the *guardian ad litem* said, no matter what he thought was best for me. Plenty of adults had thought they knew what was best for me. Only Delsy and Paul had listened to my story and trusted that I could make choices for myself.

"Can he stop us from working together?" I asked Paul later that day during our phone call.

"No," Paul said. "He can't. I'll make sure of it."

THE NEXT DAY I returned to the courthouse for my first custody hearing. At the crisis center, I had carefully chosen a black skirt and pink sweater, anxious to look my best. Everything seemed so fraught and fragile and uncertain. What if the Siales lied and no one believed me? What if my parents did not come? What if I said something wrong and made things worse? Before the hearing started, in the *guardian ad litem*'s office, I told Matt that I wanted to be in the courtroom for a bit, but I didn't want to be left alone with anyone. He explained that I only needed to be present for a short portion of the hearing, and he reassured me that I would never be left alone.

When it came time for me to join the hearing, I climbed the stairs with Matt to the second-floor courtroom, my legs feeling a bit shaky beneath me. We pushed through the double wood doors, and I took my place at a table on the left. I could hear Paul's voice coming through to the courtroom on a speakerphone, pressing the issue with the judge and the *guardian ad litem* that I should have the right to my own representation in the hearing. I tried to keep my eyes down. I was too nervous to look at anyone. Still, I could see the staff lawyer from the attorney general's office sitting at a table at the far right. Then I heard my mother crying—sobbing, really. She and my father, their attorney—a gruff, heavyset, gray-haired man—and Tiana were all seated at the center, directly in front of the judge. It was terrible, hearing my mother sob, hearing the pain in her voice, but I also felt a surge of anger rise into my chest and throat, like a form of self-protection. I had to look out for myself. Especially as long as she seemed not to accept me for who I was and there was the slightest chance she would send me away again or try to change me. I had to ignore her pain and focus on keeping myself safe.

From my seat in the courtroom, I fixed my eyes on the judge.

Judge Karla Staheli had auburn hair and a no-nonsense way about her. I would later learn that she herself had worked as *guardian ad litem* and adopted two foster children. She was a respected judge and it was clear the courtroom belonged to her. I tried my best to follow the complicated legal proceedings, watching Judge Staheli carefully, trying to read her intentions. After about fifteen minutes, though, Matt suggested I be excused, and Judge Staheli agreed. Again, as I exited the courtroom, I avoided looking at Tiana and my parents.

In an hour, Matt met me back at his office to give me his report. The Siales' custody of me had been revoked, but even though my parents were moving to Utah, I wouldn't be going home with them any time soon.

"Your parents are characterizing you as an 'ungovernable child,'" Matt explained. "That means they can't keep you from making harmful choices or running away. They're not sure it's a good idea for you to go home with them right now."

I sat silently with the weight of his words.

"But there is also some question about how much your parents understood about the circumstances you were in and whether they are responsible in sending you there," he continued. "The judge wants you to stay in the crisis center while we sort this out."

MY NEXT HEARING WAS scheduled for late May, which meant three more weeks in the crisis center. It wasn't always the easiest place to be. Just a few days after I arrived, I realized that the center director was actually a friend of the Siales, someone I had seen them socializing with at the Snow Canyon High School football game. I shared my panicked realization with Sandra, voicing my fear that he would send me back. She promised me over and over again that she wouldn't let him know I had been with the Siales, and she kept true to her word. Still, every time I saw him, I was afraid.

It was also difficult to be at the crisis center because I saw a lot of kids my age come and go. They'd arrive for a night—loud and angry, fighting, being awful to their parents—and be gone the next day, with the police or back home. I was never sure exactly what happened to them. It was painful watching the constant turnover, reflecting on the times I'd caused my own parents trouble or worry, sorting out my feelings about my family, wondering if we would ever find a way to be together again. Yes, I had given them cause for worry, but was I really "ungovernable"? Did they really not think they could raise me? Did they really not know what was happening at the Siales'? Did they really not hear me or believe me when I'd told them about the backpack and the wall?

My *guardian ad litem* had encouraged me to write my parents a letter, to try to put what I wanted into words, even if I never sent it to them. I turned words and phrases over in my head as I moved through the crisis center daily routine. Finally, one quiet afternoon, I sat down at the kitchen table and gave it a try:

I'm sure you're surprised about what's happened and I think it will be easier for me to tell you through writing than anyway else. I feel like I've been living a double life. I feel like I'm going to split right down the middle. The bottom line is I like girls. I'm sorry but that's just the way it is. I've tried not to, I've repented, I've asked for help. But I don't need help. It's not a disease or a sickness, and I'm not going to try to change it anymore. I'm tired of hearing I'm wrong and I'm going to hell, because I'm not. And I'm not going to surround myself with people who tell me I am.

I looked at the paper in front of me. It was surprising how quickly and forcefully the words came. What I had to say was not easy, but I knew there was no turning back. I took a deep breath and continued:

I want to be treated like I'm normal. I want to go out on dates and have fun during the last part of my teenage years. And I don't want to be locked away in the house. I won't let that happen. That's why I'm requesting and fighting for a foster home. So I don't have to pretend I'm something I'm not, and I don't have to be punished for my opinions. I love you guys so much and this really does suck, but I'm going to make sure I'm not miserable anymore. I'm going to be happy.

I'm supposed to be happy. I'm sorry. I really am and I love you guys so much.

A foster home—there it was, the words right in front of me. If I could not be myself, if there was a chance my parents would send me back to the Siales, or anywhere like it, I could not go home with them.

At a time when I was so uncertain about my future with my own family, the staff at the crisis center became a kind of family to me. They always made sure I got to talk to Paul every day, and even when the *guardian ad litem* was not cooperating, the crisis center staff made sure Paul was informed about my situation. The staff also made sure I had plenty of books; someone would walk me to the library just about every day. Most days, I would lie on my bunk or sit on the couch in the lounge and polish off a book. I lost myself in *The Hunger Games* series for hours on end.

Sandra confided in me that she used to be a makeup artist. One afternoon, she took me to the makeup counter at the local department store and used all the samples to do my face. Brittni took me to Target and bought me nail polish—something I hadn't been allowed at the Siales'. At night, Brittni and I would stay up late watching movies. She'd bring in *peperoncini* and ranch dressing, and we'd dip the peppers in the dressing and snack on them while we watched. To be sure, living in a crisis center without my parents was not normal teenage life. But it was way better than the Siales'. Being free from the day-to-day fears of abuse and enjoying small pleasures like quiet reading time and sparkly nail polish reminded me of how good it was to be alive.

Every day, Sandra brought updates from home of some baby horses that had been born just that spring and lived on the lot next door to her house in a small town called Hurricane. "Why don't we go see those horses?" she asked me one warm May afternoon.

We got into her car and drove about twenty minutes up the highway, north out of St. George, toward the red-rock canyons of Zion National Park. I rolled down the windows and felt the spring air on my face.

Hurricane was a typical Utah small town. Just like St. George, it was all laid out on a grid of numbered streets, organized neatly by the Mormon pioneers who'd been sent there by Brigham Young in the nineteenth century to grow cotton and peaches. Sandra lived in a little wood-frame house, and her bedroom window overlooked the horses grazing in a penned-in field.

We pulled into Sandra's driveway, parked, walked over to the pen, and leaned up against the metal railing.

There were four foals—three of them brown with white legs, one spotted white. They gamboled about on their skinny legs, playing, and nosing one another.

"Alex, I know you've been through a lot," Sandra spoke carefully, tentatively. "A lot of it because you came out as a lesbian."

I looked at her and nodded.

Sandra returned my gaze and added her warmest smile. "I just want you to know that not all Mormons are like that—like the Siales, like all the people who thought it was okay, the way they treated you. We don't all think that way."

I took a deep breath and felt the warmth of the sun start to melt into my shoulders and down my spine, moving through all the knotted muscles and vertebrae.

"It's totally fine to be gay, Alex," Sandra offered gently. "I think so, and I am certain God thinks so as well."

Looking back, I realize that this was the first moment someone had spoken up as a member of my religion to tell me that they were on my side, and that God loved me just as I was.

Even with all the strain my time at the Siales' had put on my faith, even with all the reason I had to be angry with the LDS people who'd stood by and said nothing when I was hurting, it was so important to hear Sandra say *as a Mormon* that I didn't deserve to be treated that way.

It's hard to describe even now how much it meant to me. It really matters that there are people in conservative and religious communities who speak up for a loving and accepting God, even when others don't.

CHAPTER 16

Going Home

THREE WEEKS AFTER I ran from the Siales, I finally met Paul Burke face-to-face. His voice had been my lifeline during that last difficult month, but I had not been able to picture him. I pictured instead the lawyers I had watched in my favorite courtroom dramas when I was a kid. I had always loved their fierce intelligence and their loyalty to their clients. Little did I know back then that I would someday need that kind of help.

Paul and I met in a law office in downtown St. George. There he stood in the foyer, medium height, with light brown hair. He wore a navy suit and a red tie. His face was calm and kind; his voice was clear and even. Only a glint in his blue eyes gave away the fact that he was a top-notch lawyer with an incredible legal mind and a willingness to fight—although not loudly, like the lawyers in the television shows, as I would learn, but with civility and persistence.

Together, we sat down in the law office conference room to

plan our approach to my case. Paul took out a yellow legal pad and placed it on the table.

"Alex," he asked. "What do you want?"

He stopped. I waited. I waited for a complicated legal conversation. But that was it—his question was direct and simple.

What did I want?

My days at the Siales' and at the crisis center had given me plenty of time to consider the question, and I wanted to be able to give Paul a clear answer. But it all felt very complex. I knew my options were running out. I had been at the crisis center too long, and the foster agency was finding it difficult to place me. The *guardian ad litem* wanted to send me back to my parents. In my heart, I did want to be reunited with them. But what if they tried to send me back to the Siales or change me or prevent me from living a normal teenage life?

I took a deep breath. "I want to go home," I told Paul. "And I want to date girls."

He took every word down on his yellow legal pad, just as I had said them.

Then he stopped. "Okay." That was it. He had heard me.

"I want to go to school." Paul's pen started moving again. It gave me courage. "Maybe we could do some therapy—me and my parents. And there is this group I heard about from Jason—it's called PFLAG: Parents and Friends of Lesbians and Gays. It's a support group, and there's one in St. George. Maybe they could go there?"

"Okay."

"I just don't want them to try to change me. I don't want to talk with them about being gay unless it's in family therapy. Can we do that?" I asked him.

"We can certainly work for that if that's what you want."

YES, I WANTED TO go home, but what it really meant to go home was a complicated problem. I wanted to be in a familiar place with the people I loved, but I also wanted them to see me and accept me as I was. Above all, I wanted them to promise not to try to cure me. I wanted them to make that promise in court. Without it, home would not truly be home.

The court set May 24 as the date for my hearing. But just the day before, on May 23, the attorney general's office convened a mediation with the *guardian ad litem* and my parents. Without me or my lawyer in the room, they decided that rather than look into how the Siales had treated me they would pin the trouble on me and my "ungovernability." Together, they resolved to ask the court to send me home, right away, with no conditions on my parents, no guarantee that they wouldn't try to send me away again. I was furious.

"I won't," I told Paul when he called me at the crisis center the morning of the hearing. "I won't go back on those terms."

I could feel anger stiffening my back and my jaws.

"The *guardian ad litem* is recommending that you go back. He has the attorney general, the Division of Child and Family Services, and your parents on his side." Paul had spoken calmly, deliberately, offering a clear-eyed assessment of the situation. "The deck is stacked against us. There are no guarantees that if we challenge them we will win. If you do fight them and lose, it could make going home even more difficult."

He paused.

My feet and legs tingled beneath me as I stood, eyes closed, clutching the phone in the crisis center office. "I won't," I told him. "I won't go home if they won't hear my voice. Let's fight."

"Okay, Alex," Paul responded in measured tones. "Let's fight it."

A member of the crisis center staff drove me down to the courthouse. Before the hearing started, the *guardian ad litem* pulled me aside for a brief meeting in a tiny conference room.

"Alex," he said, "sooner or later the courts are going to return custody to your parents."

I looked down at the table, trying not to say a word.

"How do you feel about going back to your folks?"

"Someday, yes." I raised my eyes to meet his. "I do want to go home. But right now, I just don't feel that they are on my side. If there is any chance of them sending me back to the Siales or any other kind of 'treatment,' I can't go back."

I chose to wait in the *guardian ad litem*'s office while the assistant attorney general, my parents, their attorney, the DCFS worker, the judge, and Paul (who phoned in that day from Salt Lake City) convened in a courtroom on the second floor. I was too agitated to make it through the hearing. But I learned about it all later from Paul.

The very first thing the Utah Office of the Attorney General did was to try to get Paul dismissed from the hearing and as my lawyer altogether. Paul worried, with good reason, that in a conservative place like southern Utah the *guardian ad litem*'s or juvenile court's view of my "best interests" might not line up with my own sense of what I needed as a gay teenager. What if the *guardian ad litem* and the State of Utah agreed with my parents and wanted to take the side of all the parents who might want to send their kids away to "treatment" or want to change their kids' sexuality even when the kids objected? They had already negotiated an agreement with my parents the day before about sending me home with no guarantee that my parents wouldn't try to change me.

During the hearing, Paul pushed back and pointed out that the "agreement" had been made without my input, my voice, my participation. The judge had questions about the agreement too, asking why it put all the pressure on me and had no conditions on my parents. That's when the assistant attorney general blamed me, saying that I was an "ungovernable child," which is a legal term the system uses to characterize young people who are so out of control that there is no option but for the state to take custody of them. Because I was "ungovernable," according to the assistant attorney general, the whole court order should focus on requiring me to obey my parents.

Thank goodness Paul was there. He asked whether it was really my fault that I had ended up with the Siales and then in state custody. Or did the fault belong to my parents, who had shown poor judgment in handing custody to the Siales, whom they barely knew and whose treatment methods, Paul argued, were actually a form of torture? Paul challenged the court to recognize that the reason I had been sent away was to try to change my sexuality, to change a very basic part of who I am.

Standing before the judge, my dad defended their decision to send me away and denied that it had anything to do with me being gay. He denied that I ever told them about the backpack or the wall.

Paul pushed back again, arguing that my parents were misrepresenting their motives, that the Siales themselves had told me their job was to change me from being gay, and that being gay was a basic part of my identity, not something I should have to defend against my own family.

Judge Staheli was listening. She agreed that in order for me to go home, there would have to be some rules for my parents too. They would have to go to family counseling, take parenting classes, maybe even attend PFLAG, and they could not seek to change my sexual orientation.

This set off all kinds of alarms for the assistant attorney general and for my parents and their attorney. The attorney general's office again tried to get Paul kicked off the case and said that I was using him as a weapon against my parents. My parents' lawyer actually implied that I was making up stories about the backpack and the rocks and the wall. But clearly the big issue was that the court seemed to be telling my parents they had to let their gay child be. This was untested territory in Utah, a state where, as I knew from growing up Mormon myself, it was practically an article of faith that being gay was something that could and should be changed. In fact, the assistant attorney general argued that protections for religious freedom and the constitutional right of parents to raise a child in the religion of their choice also gave them the right to choose the child's sexual orientation, and the court had no authority to try to stop them.

The judge watched all of this blow up in her courtroom, and she sent everyone away for the day without arriving at a final decision of where I should be. My *guardian ad litem* had no clear plan when he returned to the office where I was waiting. But I felt so relieved— relieved that the agreement the attorney general's office, the *guardian ad litem*, and my parents had made without me would not hold, re- lieved that I wasn't being forced back home without any protection, and relieved that, through Paul, my voice had been heard.

MY NEXT HEARING WAS scheduled for May 31, and I was determined to be there myself.

Before the hearing started, I met with the *guardian ad litem* in his office. "Alex," he asked me, "if you change the way you relate to your parents, if your parents change the way they interact with you, if you all work on your relationship in counseling and therapy, would you want your family to be back together again?"

I took a deep breath. "Yes," I said. "I don't know if that's pos- sible. But yes. I want to go home."

"Let's get you home then."

Paul and I also had a brief phone conversation before I stepped into the courtroom. "Let me be clear," he said in his measured, careful way. "You want to go home, but with protections in place that will keep this from happening ever again."

"Yes," I said. I took another deep breath and felt good about my decision.

There was a pause on the other end of the line. "Okay," he fi- nally said. "I'm with you."

I walked into the courtroom and took a seat on the right with the *guardian ad litem*. My mother and father had traveled from Cali- fornia to be present for the hearing, but once again we did not look at one another. That did not help my nervousness one bit. My parents and their lawyer sat directly in front of the judge. The assistant attorney general sat on the left side of the courtroom. Paul was again there by phone.

"I spoke with Alex this morning," the *guardian ad litem* told the judge. "She misses her mom and dad and asked that I ask the court for her to be allowed to go home today."

Paul intervened and addressed the court. "Let's talk about some of the ground rules for that relationship so that it can be a positive one. It's important for there to be an understanding that the parents are not going to change who Alex is, change her sexual orientation. We talked before about attending counseling or PFLAG. Alex also wants to be able to belong to her school's Gay–Straight Alliance."

"I object to Mr. Burke's presence in this case," the lawyer for my parents forcefully interjected. "I think he's interfered with their rights to raise this child."

"She has the right to have her own lawyer in matters that affect her," Paul countered.

I could feel the tension in the courtroom build. Who would get to decide what was best for me? What if what my parents wanted conflicted with what I wanted? Would I have a voice in the process?

"You can still set rules in the home like curfews and schooling," the judge responded. "But we need to give her a chance legally, to let her voice be heard."

"My client wants to go home," Paul continued. "She wants to be in a relationship with her parents where she's respected and where they don't subject her to what they have subjected her to in the past, but it is her desire to go home."

"I'm putting on hold any sexual-orientation issues," the judge explained. "I would hope that the parents would do the same thing. Just put that on hold and deal with building your relationship with her."

And that is what it said in the first custody order the judge issued:

May 31, 2011

IN THE FIFTH DISTRICT JUVENILE COURT

IN AND FOR WASHINGTON COUNTY, STATE OF

UTAH

STATE OF UTAH, in the interest of

ALEXANDRA COOPER

A child under 18 years of age

The Court makes the following:

FINDINGS & ORDER

The child expressed her desire to be reunited with her parents.

The guardian ad litem would like a slower transition to home.

The parents are willing to do what is necessary for the child.

The above-named child is hereby returned to the custody of the parents, subject to protective supervision services provided by DCFS.

The child shall contact the guardian ad litem and report weekly to him.

The Court ordered the termination of Mr. Burke's representation of Alexandra Cooper in this proceeding.

The child is a mature minor and is competent to have retained Paul C. Burke to provide her with legal representation.

The guardian ad litem also consents to allow the child to contact Mr. Burke.

The Court rescinds its order for the parents to attend PFLAG.

The parents are not to discuss sexual orientation with Alexandra except in therapy.

Signed,

Karla Staheli

Fifth District Juvenile Court Judge

It wasn't a perfect order, especially because the judge dismissed Paul as my legal representative. The judge affirmed that Paul had been a help to me up to that point, but she wanted his involvement in the child welfare proceedings to end. Paul promised that we would appeal so he could continue to represent me. Knowing that Paul would still be fighting for me, I felt I could go home.

I was so relieved a few days later when I saw my dad's car pull up. Even when he greeted me without a smile or a hug, even when he refused to make eye contact and just silently put my bags into the car. Even when he didn't say a word for the entire thirty-minute drive to my grandparents' house in St. George. Not a single word between us.

IT WAS A SUMMER of long silences and fierce but unspoken battles. My dad and I lived at my grandparents' house while my mom was back in California working. I talked to her on the phone every few days, but most of the conversations ground down to silence or wound up to angry tears. It was rough going. Tensions were incredibly high. Everyone in my grandparents' house kept an incredibly close watch on me. It was like being super grounded. There was no school, no work, no outside life. I had no phone, no access to Jason or Delsy or anyone I had met in my few months at Snow Canyon. I did get to call Ashley and Brianna. I had missed them so much.

"We tried so hard to find you," Ashley said. "I called every treatment center in St. George looking for you."

I told them about everything that had happened at the Siales'. Then we just cried together, all three of us, on the telephone.

Most days I stayed in my room, reading, just as I had done in the crisis center. Once in a while, my dad took me to downtown St. George and bought me patterns and fabric, and since all of my clothes had come back to me at the crisis center cut into ribbons, I started to sew myself a new wardrobe. I had learned to sew years before from my mother, and my grandmother had a machine I could use. As I planned my fall wardrobe for my return to school—with the court proceedings still under way, I would be staying in Utah and going to Snow Canyon—and cut pieces of new outfits from bright lengths of fabric, I tried not to think about the fact that my grandparents' house was just a few blocks from the Siales'. I tried not to think about how physically close they were, how little distance actually stood between me and them.

My grandparents, parents, and I said very few words to one another about my coming out and everything that had followed. I could feel every day my grandparents' deep discomfort with me, with the fact that in court my parents had been described as irresponsible parents, that what happened at the Siales' had been characterized as torture. At the same time, they did everything they could to maintain their relationship with the Siales, greeting them warmly at church every Sunday, even inviting them over to the house from time to time. They did not want me to pursue a legal case against the Siales, even though we both knew that in order to see justice done I very well could. Maybe it was because they wanted to keep the peace in their Mormon neighborhood, the community that profoundly shaped their day-to-day lives. Maybe it was because they still believed deep down inside that everything that had happened was really my fault, that had I gone along with it, that this trouble could've been far behind us. Very few words passed about these matters. My parents did not bring up my coming out and I did not bring up the Siales. I played by the unspoken rules and quieted my voice. Just like how all the people coming and going from the Siale house had refused to see me standing at the wall, my own family still refused to see me. If this was the way it had to be, could I ever really live at home with my parents?

In order to be seen and heard for who I was, I realized I would have to talk to my parents through the court system, through the long process of appeals and mediations that would set the terms for the final custody order. And I knew I would need Paul's help. It was Paul's voice that had guided me. It was Paul who had asked me what it was I wanted, and listened—actually listened. In Paul, I knew I had an advocate who had only my interests at heart. I needed that. I knew I needed someone, an adult, who was firmly on my side. Thank goodness, he called me every day.

But Paul seemed to make everyone deeply nervous. He was pretty much the only non-Mormon person involved in the case, and the fact that he was from Salt Lake, not St. George, compounded his outsider status. The lawyer from the attorney general's office had tried to get him disqualified as my attorney and kicked out of the hearing, and the orders issued by the court supported him. My parents and their lawyer seemed to believe that he and some larger group of LGBT activists were trying to manipulate me into part of some larger gay rights plot, part of the movement for LGBT equality that was transforming the country. In fact, Paul did reach out for advice to the National Center for Lesbian Rights, but they and other legal and civil rights experts had agreed it was best to stay in the background to keep the case focused on getting me to a safe place.

In June, Paul came down to St. George again to help me get ready for another custody hearing. My father drove me to meet him at a legal office downtown. When they met in the office lobby, Paul offered his hand, but my father refused to take it.

"I need to have a word with my daughter before she goes in," my father said. "Be truthful in all that you do," he told me, with Paul standing within earshot. "In your heart know that you are being 100 percent honest."

I looked into his eyes. I could tell he did not believe my account of what had happened at the Siales'. He didn't believe me even though I had given a written statement of what had happened to me and even though there was evidence that would come out in court if the Siales went on trial. It hurt not to be believed. But I held up my end of the family rules and did not say anything.

"You okay?" Paul asked when we sat down in the conference room.

"Sure," I said.

Paul smiled a wry, knowing smile. "Good, because we have a lot of work to do." Paul was usually pretty unflappable. But today there was no mistaking his concern. "The orders from May 31 that the court is ready to finalize—Alex, we have several problems.

"First, the court is continuing to try to disqualify me as your lawyer. If that represents your wishes, you may let me know," he said, pausing to make sure I could answer thoughtfully and fully. "You can fire me whenever you want." He smiled, trying to lighten the mood a little.

"No," I said. "I need your help, and I want your help."

"Okay. Second," he continued, placing a page of the orders in front of me and directing my attention to one of the numbered findings, "in this paragraph, the court characterizes you as 'repeatedly running from her parents' home, drinking alcohol, abusing illicit drugs, and being sexually promiscuous.' They're making it sound like you're in state custody not because you were abused but because you were out of control. The court calls it 'ungovernable.'"

There was that word again. Ungovernable? Yes, I had a fierce streak of independence. I had lived some wild times with Ashley and Brianna, and I had caused my parents more than their fair share of worry. But were Ashley, Brianna, and all the other kids at my high school who had done the same kinds of things given up by their parents? There was a reason I had been hauled across the desert and Ashley and Brianna had not been. The Siales themselves had told me that I was there because I was gay and that ridding me of the "burden" of my homosexuality was their job.

"Alex," Paul continued, "when the court order says that you are 'ungovernable,' it's basically calling you a slut."

He was exaggerating, of course, but I got the point, and I felt a surge of anger rise inside me. The courts were about to blame me for everything that had happened. They were about to erase the real story of why I had been given up by my parents, a story about abuse and torture, about the costs of coming out as a gay kid in a conservative community.

I would later learn that being characterized as "ungovernable" is an issue for LGBT kids across the nation, especially in families where the parents do want to accept that their child is gay. One study found that nine out of ten LGBT kids entering the legal system had been characterized as "ungovernable."[10] In many cases, calling a gay kid "ungovernable" was basically a way of blaming and criminalizing gay kids for being themselves and for pushing back when their families told them they shouldn't be. Paul was right: I couldn't let the court orders do this to me without a fight. I had to speak up, for myself and for all the others who weren't lucky enough to have a lawyer as dedicated as Paul or a judge as fair-minded as Judge Staheli. I would have to become an advocate for justice, like the lawyers I had admired on television.

"We have a third problem, Alex," Paul continued. "The court is treating your sexuality the way your parents and the Siales did—as an idea that's in your head. Read this." Paul pointed to another paragraph in the court orders. *"The court finds that the child says she is a lesbian."*

I read the words, then looked up at Paul for an explanation.

"Alex, just about everyone in that courtroom looks at your sexual orientation not as a fact but as something you've been led to believe, something you've been fooled or manipulated into by Yvette, or as the result of your own misguided choices. Is this how you see yourself?"

No, it wasn't. If those long hours at the wall in the Siales' house had given me something, it was time to reflect on my feelings and experience. How I felt about Yvette was connected to how I had felt about Samantha back in seventh grade, and even more fundamentally, to who I was—my difference, my independence.

---

10. Katayoon Majd, Jody Marksamer, and Carolyn Reyes, *Hidden Injustice: Lesbian, Gay, Bisexual, and Transgender Youth in Juvenile Courts* (San Francisco and Washington, DC: Legal Services for Children, National Juvenile Defender Center, and National Center for Lesbian Rights, 2009), http://www.equityproject.org/wp-content/uploads/2014/08/hidden_injustice.pdf.

"If this is their assumption, that your sexuality is not a basic part of who you are but just a bad idea that's been planted in your head, the attorney general's office will continue to assert the rights of parents to influence or change the sexual orientation of their children."

Here was another important reason to fight back—not just for all the other LGBT kids who ended up in the system but for all the other LGBT kids growing up in Utah. If the state attorney general believed that it was okay for parents to send their kids away as I had been sent away, to try to change them by whatever means necessary, none of them were safe at home.

My dad had urged me to be truthful, to be 100 percent honest about what had happened. It was time to honor his advice.

"Paul," I said, "I need to speak up. For myself and for everyone else who has been or could be in my situation. I want the court to know that I want you as my lawyer, and I want the record to show what really happened." I could feel my old fighting spirit rise—the same spirit that had propelled me into all those battles with my parents, the same spirit that had kept me on my feet hour after hour at the wall. Now my determination pushed me in a new way: to name who I was, to the world, to the courts, in a way that would help all the gay teenagers who had been sent away from home or told that they needed to be fixed, that being gay was something to be cured.

That day, with Paul's help, I produced a sworn statement, an affidavit, that the court, the assistant attorney general, and my parents would have to acknowledge:

AFFIDAVIT OF ALEXANDRA COOPER
Case No. 1051684
Judge Karla Staheli
Alexandra Cooper, being duly sworn, deposes and states as follows:
I am now more than sixteen and a half years old.
I am a lesbian. Last fall, I came out to my parents. When I told

them that I am a lesbian, my parents flipped out.

My parents sent me from our home in California to St. George, Utah, and placed me in the custody of Tiana and Wesley Siale. This couple tortured and abused me because they wanted to change my sexual orientation.

In late April 2011, I contacted Paul C. Burke of the law firm of Ray Quinney & Nebeker P.C. Mr. Burke and his law firm offered to represent me on a *pro bono* basis.

I accepted Mr. Burke's offer and retained Mr. Burke and the law firm of Ray Quinney & Nebeker to represent my legal interests. This retention occurred shortly before the Utah Division of Child and Family Services was contacted about my circumstances.

Sometime after I was taken into custody by the State of Utah, I understand that a *guardian ad litem* was appointed for me.

I have been told that it is the job of the *guardian ad litem* to determine for himself what would be in my best interests.

My *guardian ad litem* and I have not always agreed on the best course of action for me.

I prefer to receive legal advice from an attorney whose loyalties and professional judgment are owed only to me.

I understand that this court has terminated the representation of Paul C. Burke and his law firm in this juvenile court proceeding. I object to this order because I wish to continue to be represented by counsel loyal to me.

I think I have the right to be represented by an attorney of my choosing. I wish to be represented by Paul C. Burke and the law firm of Ray Quinney & Nebeker P.C. in the juvenile court case that bears my name.

DATED this 20th day of June, 2011

When court convened the next day, it was clear that a sworn affidavit was only the first step in claiming my voice and telling my story. There was a long road ahead, and I would have to fight every step of the way—even with my own parents.

The air between my father and I was thick with tension that morning as we moved about the house, getting ready for court, and then drove from my grandparents' house to the courthouse downtown.

Not until he stood before the judge did my father actually speak his mind. "Alex's words have been taken as gospel," he complained to Judge Staheli.

"Somehow I get the impression that you don't believe her," the judge observed.

"No, no, no," my father countered. "I care for my daughter deeply and for her protection."

Judge Staheli took a breath and then turned to address me. "The truth has to be told. And people believe kids. We would have to find some reason that you would put yourself through this to make you uncredible. So tell the truth and things will be fine."

Before the hearing ended, the lawyer for my parents once again tried to get Paul dismissed. He questioned how Paul was being paid—when, in fact, Paul was working *pro bono*—and he alleged that "someone" was helping me prepare paperwork to be emancipated and leave home altogether, which couldn't have been further from the truth. It was clear to me how nervous my parents were about Paul—and how resistant they were to hearing my voice and my story.

BACK AND FORTH WE went all summer as the courts tried to arrive at a final version of the custody order but with the right kind of protections in place for me. And we were starting to make some progress. The court agreed that my parents should not try to change my sexuality if I went home:

> **The parents shall fully comply with the service plan prepared by the Division of Child and Family Services, including**

Family therapy.

PFLAG for 30 days.

Parenting classes.

> The child shall attend individual and family therapy. The child
> shall attend public school. She shall not use drugs or alcohol,
> and she shall not run away from her placement. She shall have
> no contact with Yvette Espinosa, Tiana, and Wesley Siale.
> The child shall obey all rules of her home and her parents.
> The parents shall not seek change of child's sexual orientation.

That was it—that was the promise I had been looking for, the promise that my parents would not try to cure me. It seemed like we were making progress, until just two days later, when in the final version of the orders, the judge once again terminated Paul's ability to represent me in the child welfare case.

There are three hundred miles between Salt Lake City, where Paul works, and St. George, where I was living. All through the months of July and August, Paul and I burned up those miles with emails, phone calls, and visits, working furiously to keep Paul as my advocate—my voice in the courtroom.

On July 26, Paul came down to St. George, and together we prepared our best appeal:

> These appeals of Ms. Cooper should be sustained so that a
> teenage girl, who entered Utah's child welfare system after
> suffering alleged abuse as the result of misguided efforts to
> change her sexual orientation, may protect her own interests,
> dignity, and identity. Ms. Cooper's voice should be heard by the
> courts of the State of Utah.

Yes, it was a matter of voice, having my voice heard at home and having the voices of other LGBT kids in my situation heard and acknowledged by the State of Utah. I felt a sense of pride and courage as I inked my thumb, pressed it into the notary's book, and signed my name to the appeal, just below Paul's.

Not surprisingly, the State of Utah pushed back on us, and hard, in an August 1st response to our appeal. "Children are not afforded the same constitutional protections as adults," the state argued. Young people could not, according to its argument, choose their own lawyers or know what was best for them. State-appointed lawyers and parents always knew best, especially when it came to matters like sexuality. Preventing parents from trying to cure their own gay children, Utah argued, would "interfere with the parent–child relationship." As if the struggle over my homosexuality hadn't interfered with our relationship enough already.

Paul volleyed with six new filings and again challenged the State of Utah's efforts to deprive me of a voice in court and to characterize me as the source of trouble rather than as a torture survivor. He also reached out to high-level contacts in the Utah Office of the Attorney General, asking them if the State of Utah was really prepared to make a stand in defense of the idea that parents should have the right to determine a child's sexuality. A new *guardian ad litem* named Martha Pierce joined the case and took my side, agreeing that the Siales' unlicensed "treatment" of my homosexuality was abusive.

My parents filed their own challenge to my appeal and lined up with the State of Utah to get rid of Paul. They also restated their view that my homosexuality was a "choice," not a fact of who I was but an idea I had come up with after hanging out with Yvette, or retaining Paul to represent me. That hurt. The air between us that August was heavy not only with southern Utah desert heat but with all that went unsaid as the courts argued the future of our relationship. Only the lawyers talked. Only the lawyers spoke the huge feelings that both my parents and I were struggling with—their feelings of being accused and misunderstood, and my feelings of wanting to be seen and heard as who I was.

One time, when my parents' lawyer came to the house, he seemed so angry with me. I summoned my courage and told him that I didn't want to have a war with my parents.

"'War,'" he snapped at me. "That's a good word for it."

I didn't want a war. I didn't want to cause any more trouble for my parents or to get them in trouble for anything they'd done. I wanted a voice. I wanted to live at home, as myself, peacefully. Did I really have to fight the State of Utah for the right to live at home with my own family as a gay teenager?

Finally, the fight turned our way when the Utah Court of Appeals issued a ruling and an emergency order that Paul could act as my lawyer in the child welfare case. It was a really big deal for the Court of Appeals to side with us, especially because we knew that the State of Utah was not eager for a teenage lesbian to claim the right to date girls and challenge the entire *guardian ad litem* system to do it.

Just a few weeks later, we convened a final mediation at the courthouse in downtown St. George. Everyone was there: my parents, their lawyer, Paul, the new *guardian ad litem,* two state attorneys general, a representative of the Division of Child and Family Services, and a highly respected mediator from the Utah state courts, who had volunteered her time to help. I watched the mediator and Paul go from room to room, trying to figure out how to get everyone to a place where we could stop fighting.

When they came into my room, Paul had just one question for me, the same question he'd had when our legal battles began. "Alex, what do you want?" he asked.

This time, finally, the *guardian ad litem* and the state-appointed mediator were there to witness what I said and to try to make it happen. "I want my parents not to feel threatened or get in trouble. I don't want the courts to blame them for everything that has hap-

pened. I do want the Siales held accountable. But for me, I want to
be home. I just want to finish growing up, with my parents. I want
them to see me for who I am, but if they can't do that, I won't try to
change them. I won't try to change them as long as they won't try
to change me. I want to graduate from high school. I want to work
and save money. I want to date girls. That's what I want."

Paul's pen scratched across the legal pad, then stopped. He
looked up and smiled. Although it was her job to stay neutral, I
think the mediator had a smile in her eyes as well. The air in the
room seemed to lose its heaviness. It was like everyone exhaled.

"Alex," Paul said, "we're going to go talk to your parents and
their lawyer, and then we'll talk with DCFS and the lawyers from
the attorney general's office."

He and the mediator stepped out of the room, leaving me with
my own thoughts.

I won't try to change them as long as they won't try to change me.

Maybe this was as good as it got for families like ours and kids
like me. If my parents could not accept my homosexuality and I
could not change it, we could both choose to let each other be.

It was not the plan of salvation I had learned growing up at
church. It was not an ironclad promise that my family and I would
all go to heaven. It was not the kind of bargain that promised if I was
good enough, if I sacrificed enough—deep parts of myself, or even
my own children—we might get to be together forever someday.

It was a plan for being together now, a plan for the family we
actually were: broken, complicated, struggling, anxious, and, yes,
some of us queer. Though there would still be painful silences and
things left unsaid, we could be together while we had one another
on this earth, and that was certainly good enough for me.

By the end of the day, Paul and the mediator had hammered out
a settlement that worked just well enough for everyone. For the first
time, the court findings acknowledged that the Siales' treatment
was "abusive and neglectful," that I had been made to wear a back-

pack of rocks and face the wall. The court finally stopped blaming what had happened at the Siales' on me and my behavior, and it allowed me to keep Paul as my attorney. I would have to hold up my end of the bargain, attending school, not using drugs or alcohol, not running away, following the house rules, all of which I was happy to do. The court also placed specific demands on my parents:

The parents shall fully comply with the service plan prepared by DCFS including:

- **Family therapy.**
- **Parenting classes.**
- **The parents shall not discuss Alexandra's sexual orientation with her except with her consent or in therapy.**
- **The parents shall allow and will promptly provide any consents required so that Alexandra may join her school's Gay–Straight Alliance and participate in all of its activities. The parents shall also permit Alexandra to attend meetings and activities of PFLAG and other organizations that provide support for gays and lesbians.**
- **The parents shall allow Alexandra to participate in normal teenager activities, including dating and attending dances.**
- **The parents shall permit Alexandra to date females.**

There it was, in writing: I could go back to my parents and live as myself. As a gay teenager, in the State of Utah, where just a few weeks before the whole legal system had stood behind the idea that parents should have the right to try to change their gay children.

I'd had to fight for myself, and I'd had to fight the State of Utah to make it happen. But now, here it was, with the stamp of the court and the force of law: *I could go home. And live as myself, an openly gay teenager.*

If my fight made the State of Utah recognize the human rights of gay teenagers for the very first time—and I believe it did—then it was worth it. Every difficult step.

THAT FALL I WENT back to Snow Canyon High School. I settled into the hard work of making up for my lost junior year while at the same time starting a full load of senior-level courses. Jason had transferred out of Snow Canyon to another high school, where he would graduate, and I missed him terribly. It helped to join the debate club and to get to spend after-school hours with Delsy and her irrepressible spirit and the brainy, artsy, independent-minded kids who circled around her.

At my grandparents' house, there were still a lot of silences and tough spots my father and I stepped tenderly around as each of us tried to follow the court's orders.

One night he came back from a PFLAG meeting and called my mom, who was still living and working in California.

"I met a woman who is going through the same thing we are. I got her number," I overheard him tell her.

Things were easing up a bit between me and my mom. On the phone, she told me how much she wanted to visit and see me. "We'll go out to dinner," she promised, "and eat dessert first."

But as far as I could tell my parents never went back after their first PFLAG meeting. I was so hopeful it might work for them, that they might find the support they needed and deserved.

Certainly some remarkable sources of support had lined up for me. I'll never forget the day I clicked open my email to find a message from Kate Kendell, the executive director of the National Center for Lesbian Rights:

From: Kate Kendell
Date: Wed, Sep 7, 2011, at 2:23 P.M.
Subject: You are an inspiration

Dear Alex:

You don't know me, but we here at the National Center for Lesbian Rights know of you. Paul has been in touch with us about your situation and we have helped him where we can. He is an amazing lawyer and is very committed to making sure that you are safe and that you have the support you need and deserve. It has been so distressing to hear of the harassment and mistreatment you have endured just because you want to live a true and authentic life. The fact that you did not give in or give up, but fought back, has inspired all of us at NCLR. I am from Utah and grew up Mormon. I do not believe I would have possessed the strength and courage to do what you have done.

You are on the path to a spectacular and fulfilling life. Living honestly is the most important thing we can do as human beings. I know that being true to yourself will bring you much joy and confidence. I hope so much to meet you one day. Please stay strong and know that you have many friends whom you have never met, who are pulling for you, and we are all here to do whatever we can to help you live your dreams.

Take care,

Kate

Kate Kendell, Esq.

Executive Director

National Center for Lesbian Rights

I swallowed hard. An inspiration? I fought back. I stayed stubborn. I ran when I had to. I held on. I knew it had been important to use my voice, to stand up not just for myself but for others in the same situation.

I wrote back:

Dear Kate,

I'm so happy to hear that my story is an inspiration to anyone. I strongly believe in happiness, and I feel to truly achieve being happy you must first start by living a truthful life. I am not going to hide who I am or try to change who I am. I hope to one day share my story with young girls like myself, that have been or are being tortured or pressured into changing something they have no control over. I know that not all girls in my situation or similar situations can fight or speak out, so I'd like to do it for them. I'm so happy to hear that I have a strong group of people behind me. Thank you for all you've done.

Alex

CHAPTER 17

Standing Strong

I would rely on Kate's encouragement and Paul's support many times in the weeks ahead. Even though I was living with my family again, I needed to take one more step to put what had happened behind me. I had to face the Siales, really face them, in court, so that they would be held accountable for what they had done.

This would not be easy. In the neighborhood, in the local ward, the Siales were still respected members of the community. As I had seen in St. George, sometimes the bond between Mormons and the hunger to fit in and not ruffle any feathers is so strong that families turn their backs on the feelings of their own children. Especially children who are perceived to be wrong or troublesome. The drive to be accepted, to be able to stand with everyone else in the community and say, "We are okay, we are safe, we are on the right path" is very intense. The feelings of those of us who do not fit the mold just don't matter as much as keeping the peace.

Still, Paul and I met with the county district attorney to discuss filing charges against the Siales and possibly even pursuing a hate crimes prosecution. The deputy county attorney seemed nervous to take my case.

To prepare for the Siales' depositions, Paul subpoenaed every kind of document you can imagine from treatment centers in St. George where Johnny and Tiana had worked, requesting copies of their employee manuals, policies, and training materials. Her employer suspended Tiana, and one treatment center in St. George signaled that it would try to resist the subpoena. Residential treatment centers are a big business in southern Utah, and the people who run them are deeply connected—to the church, to politics, to one another. Paul knew that the whole subject of reparative therapy made the residential treatment centers nervous. If the evidence showed that they provided reparative therapy, the centers would be in trouble. If the evidence showed that they did not provide reparative therapy, Tiana would be in trouble for failing to follow her employers' rules. Either way, there would be trouble. Still, Paul managed to complete preparation for the deposition.

When I woke up the morning of the deposition, on October 28, I could barely find the courage to get out of bed. I certainly had no appetite to eat. Somehow I showered, then dressed for court in my black skirt, a pink cardigan sweater, and heels.

When I walked out of my room that morning, my mom eyed me carefully. She was still living and working in California, but she had come to town and volunteered to be with me during the deposition.

"Are you okay, honey?"

"Yeah," I said.

I'm sure we both knew I was lying.

We drove to the law offices downtown where the deposition would be held. I left my mom waiting in the reception area to let Paul know I was there. When I returned, I found the lawyer for the Siales interrogating her.

"Did you send her away because she was gay?" he asked.

My mom was about to answer, when I intervened. "Mom! What are you doing?" I turned to face the lawyer. "You shouldn't be talking to her out here."

I was so tired of not having my parents on my side. I took a deep breath and headed into the deposition.

"I'll be right here, okay?" she said, sounding apologetic.

I would have loved to have her sitting by me in the deposition for support. But it was enough that she had come so far to be with me, even if it just meant sitting in the lobby.

In the conference room, I took my seat next to Paul at the big table. To our left sat the court reporter, at the end of the table, the lawyer representing the Division of Child and Family Services, and across from us, the Siales' lawyer.

Then Johnny and Tiana walked in, and their youngest daughter Grace was with them.

I felt a wave of panic flood my body. Seeing them again brought back so many memories of pain, cold, loneliness, and isolation, memories rooted deep in my body: pain in my back and shoulders, the feeling of a spoon being forced down my throat, the sound of Calvin whimpering from the garage. My reaction to the Siales was instinctual. Everything inside me wanted to run.

"Grace really wants to hug you," Tiana said to me as she took her seat at the table. "Can she hug you?"

"No," I said. I dropped my eyes to the table and kept them there, though I could feel Tiana's eyes on me. I could feel Johnny's eyes on me too as he wordlessly took his place with Grace in a row of seats behind Tiana. Every time I looked up, he would look at me and shake his head, as if to say, "No, you better not" or "No one will believe you."

Paul began the deposition by rehearsing the basic facts: that I had been sent to St. George by my parents so the Siales could "help" me, that my parents had arranged my stay with the Siales through my grandparents, that Tiana had worked in residential treatment centers but had no formal training in youth counseling and was unlicensed to do the treatment from her home.

Just as the assistant attorney general had, Tiana tried to make it sound like the reason my parents sent me was drugs, not the fact that I had just come out to them as gay.

"Did you ever talk with Alex about the fact that she is gay?" Paul asked.

"I don't recall," Tiana said.

"Did you ever talk with Alex about homosexuality?"

"Not sure. I don't know."

"Did Alex ever talk with you about her being gay?"

"Yes."

"What did you say?"

"I don't recall exactly."

Every time Tiana said "I don't recall," I could feel my blood pressure rising. I started writing notes to Paul on a yellow legal pad, noting her lies.

"What do you recall?"

"I do recall asking her if she felt that was a right choice."

"Were you supportive of Alex having an intimate relationship with a female?"

"No, I wasn't."

"And why were you not supportive of that?"

"I don't believe in that kind of behavior."

"Do you have religious beliefs about homosexuality?"

"That it's wrong, that men and women were created to not have relationships between the same sex. That it is against God's commandments."

"Do you believe that people are born gay?"

"No. Because it's a learned behavior, I feel."

"Do you believe that people who say that they're gay, do you believe that they can change and not be gay?"

"I don't know."

"Do you think a person's sexual orientation is a core part of their identity?"

Tiana's lawyer objected to the question as "an irrelevant fishing expedition."

I knew from the look in his eyes that Paul had no plans of giving up. He asked Tiana about the time I tried to call for help from McDonald's, the time I had begged a stranger to help me run away at the football game, the times Johnny had hit me. She denied that she or Johnny had ever laid a hand on me.

"Did you ever require Alex to wear a backpack?" Paul asked.

"I did at one point, yes."

"And was that only on one occasion?"

"Yes."

"What caused you to raise the subject of wearing the backpack?"

"The older boys that were living with us told me that she was planning on running away."

My pulse started to race. This was not how I remembered it. Tiana had come home from work that autumn day and started the backpack regime because their "cure" for my homosexuality wasn't working yet. She did it to break me.

"What did the backpack represent?"

"Well, I put little rocks in there because at the time she was dishonest about— It was a lot of things. . . . It was a bunch of things that accumulated and the dishonesty that kept going on and on, and we sat around as a family and talked about solutions and situations, and just teaching Alex with love, and she knows this. She knows that, you know, everything I ever did and tried to do for her, it was just out of my pure love. . . . The rocks represented things that she was holding on to and each time she was being honest and was able to let things go, that's when I took her off the backpack."

"When did you put her on the backpack?"

"Third week in December. It was just—she wore it for—she wore it for like four hours—and then the next day I took her off."

"Was this the only time Alex was required to wear the back-pack?"

"Yes."

"So this all happened in one day?"

"And then the next day."

I could barely believe what I was hearing. I was honestly sur-prised that Tiana would lie so much—that they had put the back-pack on me because I was trying to run away, that it had only been one day, that the rocks inside had been little. Here was someone who had spent eight months talking to me about God, morality, and heaven, and she was lying in court. If she was proud of her beliefs, proud of her methods, if she believed in everything she said she did, why did she feel she had to lie about it all? I could feel the hair on my arms stand on end. I was just so angry.

The time came to break for lunch, and without looking at Tiana and Johnny, I stepped into the office lobby, where my mom was waiting expectantly. Did she know how hard this was for me and how afraid I was of the Siales still?

She stood up and brushed the hair from my eyes. "Let's get some lunch," she said.

We were silent on the drive down to the lunch place. Maybe in the silence she could feel how tired I was, tired of having to stand up for my story and tired especially of feeling I had to do it without her on my side. I needed my mom, no matter what she felt about my liking girls or how badly I had disappointed her. Families are forever—that's what I had learned both from my parents and at church. I needed a family that would stand by me now.

"Sometimes it's okay to order dessert first," my mom said as we sat down to eat, offering a gentle smile.

I remembered the times we had spent together on the couch at home, hiding out under the blue-and-white blanket, watching reruns and eating donuts. I wanted to be there now.

We ate the rest of our meal, starting with dessert, silently.

After lunch, Paul focused his questions on Tiana's methods. Tiana revealed that she had first seen weighted backpacks used in a residential treatment center in Nevada and that one of the treatment centers she had worked with in Utah used backpacks full of sand as a method to help kids change. Still, she denied that she wanted to change me from being gay and that there was anything excessive about the way she had treated me.

Paul removed from his briefcase a large stack of training manuals he had subpoenaed from the residential treatment centers where she had worked and set them on the table.

"Have you received training regarding acceptable methods of discipline for teenagers?" he asked.

"Yes."

"And you know a lot about the difference between discipline and abuse."

"Yes."

"And you've received training about that difference, right?"

"Yeah."

"So your testimony today is Alex was required to wear the backpack on one occasion for four hours?"

"Yes. If it changes, I will review it. When I do get to review it."

"What do you mean by that?" Paul asked.

"I think I was just talking out loud to myself," Tiana said. "Do I have a chance to review this after?"

Her story was beginning to fray at the edges.

Paul pressed on. "Can you explain what the wall was?"

"It was to get Alex away from the situation she was in. Every day she would play and not really focus on why she was there. I asked her to go there and be away from everyone and just think about her past actions and stuff like that."

"Did she have a choice?"

"I did— She had a choice in everything."

I lifted my eyes to meet Tiana's, to confront her in the lies she was telling. As soon as my eyes met hers, she dropped her gaze to the table.

"Is it your testimony today that Alex volunteered to stand against the wall for long periods of time?"

"I'm sure she didn't like it, but she did go to the wall. She was obedient and she went to the wall."

"So was standing against the wall to help her?"

"I'd like to think that, yes."

"So you thought it was therapeutic to have Alex stand against the wall for hours?"

"It was not hours."

I looked Tiana straight in the eyes, or tried to. She quickly turned her head to face Johnny.

"Do you recall telling the St. George police that the longest period of time that Alex was required to stand against the wall was five hours?"

"No. It was five hour increments of those times I just told you."

"So what you're saying is that on those four or five occasions they collectively added up to five hours standing against the wall?" Paul asked.

"To about five hours."

I felt my heart beat hard in my chest. I could barely contain my feelings. But I knew I could trust Paul to lead the deposition.

Calvin had told the St. George police about wearing the backpack and facing the wall when they had come to the house back in April, looking for evidence to substantiate my report.

Paul asked Tiana, "Was Calvin required to stand against the wall while earing his backpack?"

"No."

"So when Calvin told the St. George police that he had worn the backpack and had to face the wall he was lying?"

Tiana's lawyer objected.

"I don't recall."

Paul asked her how long Calvin had to face the wall.

"I don't recall," Tiana said.

He asked whether Calvin had to stand for the same amount of time I did.

"I don't recall," she said.

He asked how long Dante had to face the wall.

"I don't recall. It's been since last year. I don't recall exactly."

"Do you think it can be a proper form of discipline to require a child to stand against a wall?" Paul continued.

"I feel it is a proper form of discipline. It's better standing at the wall than getting beat."

"If that's the choice?" Paul asked.

Tiana paused, took a deep breath, and spoke. "Yeah, she did stand at the wall. Yeah, she did wear the backpack. Yes, she did. She did go through that, but in the end, she learned something. In the end, she became more honest. She had a better relationship with her parents."

Tiana talked about how she had helped me and how with her help I was able to go back to regular school.

"We did everything in our care—and she knows this—to show her love and compassion in a family-oriented environment."

I looked Tiana straight in the face as Paul pressed deeper into his line of questioning.

"Is requiring a resident to stand against a wall a form of discipline approved by your employer?" Paul asked, putting his hand on the stack of training manuals.

"Of course not."

"Would it be abusive of the residential treatment center to require a student or resident to stand against the wall?"

"I would say so."

"And the standards of abuse at work are the same as at your home."

"Yes."

"So it was abusive to require Alex to stand against the wall at your home?"

Tiana had talked herself into a corner, and there was no getting out. If the backpack and wall would have been abusive at her work, as she herself admitted, were they not also abusive at home? I kept my eyes on Tiana's face. I wanted to hear her answer.

Her lawyer objected, forcibly. More than that, he became visibly angry and rose to his feet. "Don't answer that," he sharply instructed Tiana. "Those are Fifth Amendment rights."

"You can invoke the Fifth Amendment. I'm fine with that," Paul coolly replied.

In the days leading up to the deposition, as we had prepared, Paul had explained to me that in a civil case, if a witness took the Fifth, the judge and jury were allowed to see it as a problem, a sign that the whole truth was not being told or that there was something to hide.

"She is not answering your question, period." Tiana's lawyer raised his voice at Paul. "Move on or we got to go."

"Is the witness invoking her Fifth Amendment privileges?" Paul was unflappable.

"Yes, I am," said Tiana.

"No, no, no, no," her lawyer interrupted. "Don't answer that question. She is not answering your question, period."

If Tiana took the Fifth, it was pretty much like admitting she knew she had been abusive in her home. It was like admitting she knew what had happened to me was wrong.

"Let's call the judge," Paul said. Tiana's lawyer agreed.

It was late on a Friday afternoon. Paul called Judge Staheli on her cell phone.

"This is Karla," she answered.

Paul quickly explained the situation and asked the judge whether Tiana could just duck the question or whether she had to invoke the Fifth Amendment.

"They either answer or they invoke the privilege," Judge Staheli said.

Everything in the room seemed to stop. Tiana looked to Johnny, then her lawyer.

"We invoke her Fifth Amendment right to not incriminate," the lawyer said.

Johnny looked at me, as menacing as ever, unbowed by the fact that Tiana's answer helped to substantiate our charges of abuse.

I could see the weight of the answer rest on Tiana, as she kept her eyes on the table. I knew it was Tiana who always had to figure out how to get the family out of difficult situations. I remembered all the times, even when I was at the wall, that she had confided in me, pulled me into her, like I was not just a member of the family but a trusted friend. Maybe she felt like she was being abused and held captive too, captive by a million circumstances that made her life difficult.

Finally, she raised her gaze from the table to look me in the face.

I felt everything in the room stop again. I noticed how the light had changed, how late in the day it had become. For hours my body had been flooded with adrenaline, my shoulders tight, my stomach nauseated, anger burning in my brain.

I wanted it all to be over. Was Tiana ready for it to be over too?

Finally, she spoke to me, in a tone hard and cold. "Why are you lying, Alex? I don't know why you're lying about all of this."

What happened next is sort of a blur. My mind went blank. I stood up from the table. A torrent of hot anger came pouring out in my words. I think I yelled at Tiana. I know I cursed at her. I hadn't said a word all day, but now I couldn't stop.

Next thing I remember, Paul was dragging me out of the deposition room by my arm.

"Oh, Alex," he said, his voice still calm. "You have to stop. You can't do this."

He pulled me through the law office lobby, past my mother, into a smaller conference room.

"Take a breath," he said. "Calm down. Everything is okay. You're safe."

It was like all those times at the wall when I felt my mind and my heart leave my body. In that moment, I did not know how to put myself back together.

"Don't you see she's lashing out at you because we've won?" Paul asked. "When she took the Fifth Amendment, she essentially confessed that she abused you, and in front of a judge. That was one of our big goals. To get her to acknowledge that what you went through was abuse."

I tried to find my breath. All I could hear was my heart pounding in my head and, over the sound of my heart pounding, Paul's gentle but firm explanation.

The next words out of my mouth surprised me. "I can't. I can't. I can't do it."

Paul looked at me intently.

"It's too hard. I can't."

"Okay," he said. "We'll stop now."

Paul went back into the big conference room to close the deposition for the day.

I stepped back into the office lobby, just in time to catch Johnny and Tiana lecturing my mom. "Your daughter cursed at me in there," she said to my mom, accusingly, standing over her.

My eyes locked in on my mom. I realized I didn't know just how she would react. For months she had believed the Siales, gone along with their plan, because she had believed it would make everything better. She had believed them, handed me over to them, given them custody of me. Even when I had begged to come home with her, she had believed the Siales over me. She had taken their side.

Who would she side with now?

I watched her shift in her seat. She stood up and picked up her purse. She looked past Tiana to where I was standing. My mother's eyes met mine.

"Alex," she said, "it's time to take you home."

We didn't say much on the drive home, my mom and I. I guess that was always the way it was between my parents and me. Maybe we had never learned to really talk about difficult things. Maybe that's why it had meant so much to them—everything the church taught about following the plan of salvation, that if you just stick to the plan, everything will turn out all right, even difficult things you barely have the ability to name and talk about.

My mom drove out of downtown St. George, along the line of red-rock cliffs, on the road that led back to my grandparents'.

"What would you like for dinner, Alex?"

She seemed tired, and also changed somehow. Something inside her had shifted during those long hours in the law firm lobby. At the end of the day, when Tiana had come out and confronted her, my mom had not just silently agreed and gone along with her. She was willing to stand by my side, even if it meant standing out in a community that valued quiet conformity, even if it meant standing up to Tiana and Johnny.

A familiar arc of pain formed across my shoulder blades and radiated down my spinal column, through my vertebrae, ignited by the incredible stress of the day.

I had faced another wall and stood strong. I had gotten the Siales to plead the Fifth—a huge concession. I had gotten my mom to stand with me.

I really couldn't ask for any more than that.

I just wanted to go home.

CHAPTER 18

Moving On

W HEN I SLIPPED OUT a side door in the middle of the night, ran as far as I could, and then hid myself in sagebrush until the busses started running, all I knew was that I wanted to put as many miles as I could between myself and the house where I had been held and abused for eight months because I was gay.

When I sat with DCFS workers, police officers, therapists, doctors, and court-appointed lawyers, telling my story time and time again, all I wanted was to make sure I would never have to go back and see the Siales again.

But during my month in the crisis center, I realized not only that I wanted to go home and go on with my life but that I wanted the Siales held accountable for what they'd done. As a little girl I had loved watching the lawyers on *Law & Order* stand up for fairness and fight wrongdoing. Once I had even dreamed of moving to New York City and being a lawyer myself. Justice—I wanted justice then, and I wanted it now too. I wanted the Siales to stop making promises that they could cure people like me. More than that, I wanted to stop anyone who promised to cure gay kids with beatings, backpacks, lectures, curses, and chores. Maybe if the Siales were held accountable, I could help stop them all, or even help end the idea that kids like me need to be cured.

But to do that, I had to face them.

I had never anticipated how terrifying and difficult that would be.

After the deposition, Paul was very clear about what it would be like to go forward. "If you want the Siales prosecuted," he told me on the phone, "you will have to give your testimony."

I thought about going back into a room with the Siales and their lawyer for hours and hours, sitting across the table from Johnny and Tiana while I tried to hold it together. I had barely survived Tiana's deposition. I had lost my temper. All of the fear and rage that had built up in me over those months was still there, in my nerves, under my skin, along my spinal column, in my bones. If I couldn't make it through Tiana's deposition, how would I make it through my own?

"I want you to be prepared," Paul said. "They will make you a target. They will challenge every detail of your story."

I had worked hard to recall all the excruciatingly painful details, to find the strength to say them out loud, to believe that someone would hear me and help me. I had worked hard for my story. I wanted to keep it and protect it and make sure that when I told it, good would come of it.

"A criminal trial on child abuse charges would be public," he explained. "You might have to testify in open court with the media present. It could take weeks or even months."

I reflected on Paul's advice for a few days as I attended my school classes and worked shifts at my new hostessing job at a restaurant. I wanted to see it through. I wanted to be brave for myself, for Paul, and for all the other kids who had been or might go through what I had. But who knew how long the case against the Siales would take.

It could eat up all the energy I needed to catch up in my classes, finish high school, make and save money, and plan for my life ahead. In addition to eating up my energy, it was already eating at my soul. Every time I saw the Siales, or thought about them, I felt dark waves of anger surge up in me. I felt hateful. I did not want to feel or give more energy or expose more of myself to those hateful feelings.

"I'm sorry," I wrote Paul in an email one night. "I just can't."

I took a deep breath and pressed SEND. I had fought hard, and I realized it was time to stop fighting. It was time to live my life, to focus on moving forward, not on what was behind me. Not surprisingly, Paul was incredibly gracious and understanding. I need not have worried about disappointing him.

That fall, I stayed really busy, doing schoolwork, taking shifts at the restaurant where I held a part-time job, and even traveling with the debate team. With Delsy as my coach and champion, it felt amazing to learn to use my voice and be heard. I also started cosmetology school, thinking that after graduation I'd need to find a job that would make me more money so I could save enough to move away from St. George. I kept myself focused on the future. I knew there were things I needed not to cure but to improve and heal in myself. I needed space and quiet to heal from the trauma of my time with the Siales. I needed to reflect, on my own time and my own terms, on what a healthy life would look like for me as a young gay person. I needed to get ready to live on my own.

But I also managed to have fun. I made friends with as many of the gay-friendly kids at Snow Canyon as I could. Acceptance of LGBT kids was like a great invisible dividing line at our school. We all hung out together, all of us queer kids and our allies, the smart and artistic ones, the different ones, the flawed ones. There were the debate team kids, like Allen, and there was Gabby, not a debater but the most outrageously spirited girl I had ever met. She had curly red hair and she seemed to be afraid of nothing. When I wasn't working or studying, we would drive around St. George, blare the radio, hike into the canyons, and plot ways to escape from town for good, just like kids in any other small town in America.

Some good things were happening that fall for gay kids in St. George. Lots of campuses were organizing GSAs, and the struggle brought us all closer together. Even though Jason no longer attended Snow Canyon, we stayed close. I remember one night going with him to a PFLAG meeting at a woman named Claudia's house. She had been the PFLAG leader in St. George for a long time, and she always opened her home to the community. So many high schoolers were there, including straight kids, and lots of older people too. It made me so happy to see everyone.

On campuses, it was a bit more tense. As more and more kids came out and started organizing GSAs at their high schools in St. George, some people, including principals, pushed back. Kids tore down our GSA signs. Principals at some southern Utah high schools tried to prevent the clubs from forming. The ACLU held a briefing with all the high school principals in the area, telling them that if they tried to shut down the GSAs, they would have to shut down all the nonacademic clubs on their campuses, including sports.

Right before homecoming, staff from the ACLU met with the Snow Canyon GSA and gave each of us a Know Your Rights card. They filled us in on all the legal rights of same-sex couples at school events and parties. I had asked another GSA member named Karen to go to a dance with me. She was a sophomore at the time—short, with cropped dark hair. She was Mormon. Her dad was even the bishop, but her whole family was very accepting and supportive.

The night of the dance, I dressed in a strapless navy-blue dress. When I drove to her house to pick her up, Karen's whole family, including her three younger siblings, were waiting to celebrate. Karen was wearing trousers and a pressed shirt. Her mom made us pose up against the fireplace and took lots of pictures. Her parents were just awesome.

The dance was held inside the Snow Canyon gym. Karen and I

walked up to the door and presented our tickets to the staff members working the door.

One older, gray-haired woman took a hard look at me and Karen. "Are you guys just friends?" she asked.

"No," I said. "We're going to homecoming together."

"We can't do this," said another staff member, her arms folded across her chest.

"If you come back with a real date, you can come in," the gray-haired woman told us.

Thank goodness we were prepared.

"So," I said, pulling my cell phone out of my purse. "Should I call the ACLU or my lawyer first?"

The staff gathered in a circle for a minute to talk, then relented, took our tickets, and waved us in.

Inside the gym, the dance committee had assembled a giant white tent, and there were fairy lights everywhere and swings suspended from the ceiling. We danced all night, and truthfully, none of the Snow Canyon kids said a negative word to us. There was absolutely no conflict and no uncomfortable moments after we got inside. We danced, we took pictures, and we left. After the dance, Karen and I drove out into the red-rock canyons, with the windows rolled down and the radio turned up high. I felt such an amazing sense of freedom, like this was how it ought to be—like things were going to be okay. Karen and I parked for a bit and kissed before I took her home. The next day was Sunday and I skipped church and slept late. I really can't say that I missed going to church. There were too many hard feelings there too, and it just felt good to be free, to have a quiet Sunday morning to myself.

As alive as I felt on nights like homecoming, sometimes I realized how far I had to go before I was really free from the Siales, physically, mentally, and emotionally.

I remember one day pulling into a gas station at the same time as Johnny pulled up to the pump in his blue TrailBlazer. I was alone, and so was he, and seeing him out in the real world without anyone else at my side was utterly terrifying. I froze in my seat. My mind went blank. Next thing I knew, I was pressing into the horn on the steering wheel. I can't tell you whether he looked at me or saw me. I just don't remember. But I must have held down the horn for two minutes before I collected my senses. For a moment, I imagined stepping on the gas pedal and ramming my car into his, but I took a deep breath, gripped the steering wheel, and let that thought leave me.

Right after Thanksgiving, I was shopping at a church-owned thrift store with my friend Allen when I saw Tiana working there. I knew she had been suspended from her job at the treatment center because of the inquiries Paul had made in connection with my case. I knew she was under a lot of pressure to provide for her family. Still, I lost it, just as I had at the deposition. My mind went blank. My legs went numb underneath me. I could hear myself yelling at her, but I don't remember what I said. I do remember Allen pulling me from the store and taking me home.

In December, I found myself driving by the Siales' house every day on my way back from work. I would let my car idle in the street in front as I watched for shadows moving across the windows, looked for any sign that there were new kids in the house. I fantasize about crashing into the garage and freeing anyone who might be trapped inside. For a while, I drove by several times a day, driving really slowly.

Then I started dating a new girl named Lina, a quiet, dark-haired, artistic girl whose family was not Mormon and was totally accepting. One night Lina was in the car with me.

"I want to egg their house," I told her impulsively. "I want to slash their tires."

I could feel this black weight on me, this heaviness that I had to push back against with anger. Or so I thought.

"Alex," Lina said, taking my hand off the steering wheel and holding it in her own. "We're not going to do this. Take a deep breath. You are safe now."

When the memories of those eight months grabbed me and held me under, my friends helped bring me back to the life I wanted, the life that was ahead of me.

I also helped myself. I realized that even after the court case ended I had been spending too many hours reading the journal I had kept at the Siales'. Every time I opened the pages I felt so angry—angry with the Siales but also angry with myself. I tortured myself with thoughts of all the things I could have done differently. Even though I was out of their house, as long as I stuck myself in those pages, I felt terrible. I could not be free until I freed myself. I wanted that part of my story to be finished, and in that sense my journal was doing me no good. One December night, I took the journal out in back of my grandparents' house, set it in a planter box, and lit it on fire with a cigarette lighter. I stood under the stars with my bare feet on the red clay of my grandparents' backyard, and I watched the painful pages I'd made during those months dissolve into ashes.

One of the great lessons I was learning was that none of us are as alone as we feel. If you try to help yourself, people who can help you will come into your life in the most unexpected ways. During my early days at the Siales', I never could have imagined that anyone in town would help me or believe me. And it's true that there were people who saw me standing at the wall and people I asked for help—from the bishop to strangers in the grocery store— who did not help me. But there were also people like Jason, Delsy, Paul, Sandra, and the bus driver who allowed me to board even though I couldn't pay the fare; people like Brett Tolman and John Mackay, colleagues of Paul's who contributed time and expertise on my behalf; and people like Kate Kendell and Shannon Minter of the National Center for Lesbian Rights, gay rights leaders who rooted for me from afar.

After I burned my journal, I got this message from Kate:

From: Kate Kendell
Date: Wed, Dec 14, 2011, at 4:09 P.M.
Subject: You are destined to do great things . . .
Dear Alex:
I am very relieved for you that the nightmare of the past months is now
over. I hope you know that your courage and standing up has been
an inspiration to us. You have made a big difference in how the entire
child welfare system operates in Utah, and no other young woman or
man will have to endure what you did because you chose to fight back.
I hope now you can move on with your life. Graduating from high
school and moving on to college will prepare you for a meaningful and
powerful future. There is no doubt in my mind that you are meant to
do some great things. You are so smart and you are braver than almost
any adult I know. There is something you are meant to do and I can't
wait to see it.

I hope you can also surround yourself with people who love and
support you. If you need any contacts in Salt Lake, please let me
know. You have been through so much and you now deserve to take
care of yourself and rebuild the relationships that matter most to you
and that will sustain you. I hope we meet someday, but until then
know that you have a large community of folks who are on your side
and are here if you need us. Please stay in touch if you like and let us
know how things are going from time to time.
I hope you have a great holiday, Alex.
Warm wishes,
Kate
Kate Kendell, Esq.
Executive Director
National Center for Lesbian Rights

CHAPTER 19

Sharing My Story

My STORY HAS BEEN a difficult one to tell, but it has a positive ending. It is very important to me that everyone knows that stories like mine can have positive endings! The media tells many stories about gay teenagers who take their own lives or face other tragic circumstances. The pain and suffering they face are terribly real. But we need more stories about how strong and resilient we can be, even when we face extreme pressures to change who we are.

So let me share with you where I am today. I did take Kate Kendell's advice and worked hard to build a new life. I graduated from Snow Canyon High School in June 2012 and earned my cosmetology license. Lina worked too, and we saved enough money to move to Portland, Oregon, where I live now, in a little apartment downtown. I walk the wet and leafy streets, smell the amazing aromas from the food trucks, browse the shelves at bookstores, hold hands with my girlfriend, and feel a kind of freedom I never could have imagined while facing the wall at the Siales'.

In Portland, I work as a fundraiser for a global fund that helps make sure impoverished children can get a basic education. Right now one hundred million school-aged kids in the world are not attending primary school. Just two years of primary school education can make the difference between being trapped in poverty and having enough basic literacy to create a way out. It makes an incredible difference for girls especially. With just two years of education, a girl is far more likely to delay childbearing and have a voice in determining the size of her family. And just two years of education significantly reduces the likelihood that she will end up in the world of human trafficking. One Saturday the team I supervise reached our goal to get sponsors for ninety-five girls in the Philippines, where it's estimated that a hundred thousand children have been forced into prostitution, making it the fourth most dangerous country in the world for sex trafficking. I've signed up to sponsor four girls myself: two in Colombia and two in Sierra Leone. It can be a bit wet and chilly standing on street corners in the rain, asking people to become sponsors. Standing all day long tends to make my back ache as well, inflaming the old injuries I sustained while standing at the wall wearing a backpack full of rocks at the Siales'. But the pain is manageable, really—especially because I've strengthened my back with exercise. And I love the work that I am doing. I love it because I'm doing what I've always wanted to do: stand up against injustice, use my voice for those who don't have a voice, and make it possible for them to have a brighter future.

I am also planning to continue my own education. And day by day I'm quietly processing and sorting through the emotional and spiritual aftermath of my time at the Siales'. Even the process of writing this book brought back painful memories I wanted to put far behind me. The memories bring with them surges of fear, anxiety, sadness, and pain. I manage most days, but there are still overwhelming and difficult moments. As for faith, even though my religion played a huge role in my family and my upbringing, and it helped me through some of the hardest times at the Siales', my feelings are conflicted and I try not to think too much about it on a day-to-day basis. That feels like the healthiest path forward for me.

Paul comes to visit me in Portland when work brings him to town. I cook him dinner at my apartment, or we visit our favorite Portland diner. Even in the difficult times when he was dealing with his brother's death, he really has been a remarkable advocate for me, working for some measure of justice to be done. In addition to working for me *pro bono*, he kept at it despite powerful forces inside Utah's legal system threatening him with repercussions just for insisting that a gay teenager deserved her own voice in court. He still has his job at a high-powered law firm in downtown Salt Lake City, and he has been a leading public advocate for the huge changes that have taken place for LGBT people in Utah. It's hard to believe that just a few years ago, when my life was on the line, the State of Utah went on record arguing that parents should have the right to try to change their gay children, to cure them, even through abusive forms of so-called "treatment." In December 2013, Utah became the seventeenth state to legalize same-sex marriage. Paul himself officiated at the first lesbian wedding in Utah. He also led a team of lawyers at his firm to file an amicus brief with the U.S. Supreme Court on behalf of a coalition of LGBT rights organizations in rural southern and western states to ask the court to overturn California's Proposition 8 and the Defense of Marriage Act. In recognition of his work, Paul was awarded the Pro Bono Lawyer of the Year award from the Utah State Bar association, and in June 2015 he was honored with the Utah Hero award at the Utah Pride Festival.

Yvette still lives in Arizona. I hear from her once in a while. Last time she called, she had finished putting herself through college and was getting ready to start medical school. She has channeled her independent spirit and her resourcefulness into education and a career helping other people. I wish her well.

Jason is in St. George, finishing his training for a career in massage therapy. He continues to live a true and authentic life. I am grateful to him for seeing me even when I couldn't speak my own truth, for winning my trust, and for connecting me with Paul and Delsy. With his courage and commitment, Jason has made a major impact in the lives of gay teenagers in Utah, but I'm trying to convince him to move to Oregon. Hopefully, he will do it soon.

As for Delsy, every morning when the sun comes up over the red-rock foothills, you can count on her being in her classroom, getting ready to teach the books she loves, books about bravery and courage, and making a beautiful, safe space for the high school kids who absolutely continue to need it.

LGBT kids are still vulnerable, especially in conservative religious communities and in conservative and rural parts of the country. We are more vulnerable to physical, emotional, and sexual abuse at home and more likely to end up in the criminal justice system than kids who are straight. LGBT kids are also more likely to experience emotional health issues and to use or abuse drugs and alcohol, especially when their families reject them. In places like Utah, it's estimated that five thousand youth experience homelessness every year—at least 40 percent identify as LGBT, and the majority are from Mormon homes and families.

I want my story to help those kids. I want them and anyone else who feels trapped in an impossible situation to know that it does get better. During our frantic lunchtime conversations on Jason's cell phone, when I was still being held at the Siales', Paul would tell me that it gets better, and I didn't believe him. I could not believe it at all. But it does. My story shows that there is reason for hope, even in difficult circumstances, even in places where you believe no one will help you, that you are the only one. If you are brave, if you stand up for yourself, if you can open your mouth and tell your truth—no matter how impossible that seems or hopeless you feel— people will help you. People like Jason, who trusted his instincts and knew he could make a difference just by befriending the quiet new girl in class; people like Sandra at the crisis center, who treated me so gently and reminded me that not everyone in my faith feels the same about gay people; people like Delsy, who took huge risks at her job to make sure I would be safe; people like Paul, who worked for free to make sure I would be safe and have a voice; even people working for the system like Judge Staheli, who was willing to listen to my side of the story.

I want my story to encourage and celebrate people like Jason, Delsy, Paul, and Sandra, the thousands upon thousands of good-hearted people who go out of their way to reach out to help young LGBT people.

But I also want my story to help parents and families like mine, families for whom faith and tradition feel familiar and safe and the reality of having LGBT kids feels terrifyingly foreign.

By silent agreement, my parents and I never talk about what happened at the Siales'. I tried one time—early one Saturday morning, when my dad was teaching me to drive on the streets of downtown St. George. We were sitting at a red light at the corner of Bluff Street and St. George Boulevard. I sat behind the steering wheel. The morning was clear and bright, and it was just the two of us. I took a deep breath.

"Dad," I asked, "why did you leave me there?"

He paused. "So they actually had you stand at a wall with rocks on your back for hours upon hours a day?" His eyes did not meet mine. He looked straight ahead at the red-rock hills above Bluff Street. "That's impossible. You wouldn't have been able to do it."

The light changed. I pushed down on the gas pedal and let the subject change.

It hurt that he did not believe me, even with the police records, court records, and medical records. Even when I can still feel the damage in my back every day, with one shoulder blade out of alignment, higher than the other. But I can understand how difficult it must be to accept that I was abused—tortured, really—for being gay, and that they put me in the place where that happened.

Still, I know they love me. My dad took days off work to drive with me to Portland and help me move into my new apartment, and I saw the tears in my mom's eyes when we left. And just in the last few months, they have made remarkable steps toward accepting me as a gay person. My mom and I talk regularly by phone, and she keeps telling me how much she wants grandkids. And my dad teases me about marriage—something that would have been unthinkable just a few years ago, before the laws on gay marriage changed across the country.

"When do I get to walk you down the aisle?" he asks with a laugh in his voice. "You're the last one in the family to have kids."

I tease him back. I tell him that I'm not sure about having children yet, that I'm not quite ready to settle down. It feels amazing to come to a place where we can joke and smile together.

I know that what I've been through has been rough on my parents as well. Being a parent of an LGBT kid can be challenging. Especially when you have a child as spirited as I've been—as I've had to be to survive my circumstances. When you believe there is no place in God's plan for gay people and that God's plan is the only way to keep your family together, for your own child to come out as a lesbian must turn the whole world upside down. I know they believed that they had to change me to save me, to save our whole family's chances of being together in heaven. It is incredible that any family, any child, should be under so much pressure. It is awful that there are people who take advantage of that fear and pressure to sell parents on the idea that sending their kids away to live with strangers in boot camps and treatment centers will somehow help. I have never felt more terrified, more lost, than when my parents turned me over to total strangers and drove away. It made me want to die, and the statistics show that I'm not the only one.

Kids who go to residential treatment centers often end up in more pain and are more likely to hurt themselves. If you are a parent who feels like you and your child are in an impossible situation, let me be the one to put my arms around you and tell *you* what you deserve to hear as well: *It gets better.* It gets better for parents and families as well. You don't have to send your child away. Only you are capable of giving your child what he or she wants most: your love, your strength, your reassurance. Even when you feel you don't have the answers, even when the choices your child makes terrify you, there are people who will help you become a stronger and more informed parent, and without sacrificing your beliefs. In conservative and religious communities too, like the one I grew up in, there are more and more avenues of support and resources for families. (I've included a list of resources for families at the end of this book.)

Today, more parents are standing up with their LGBT sons and daughters. Just in the last few years there has emerged a group of Mormon mothers of LGBT kids who call themselves Mama Dragons, and they are standing up to defend and protect their children from abuse and misunderstanding. I hope my story encourages all the Mama and Papa Dragons across the country—Mormon or not—to stand strong.

LGBT teenagers and our families have an important story to tell the world. We know that when the traditional plan falls apart or does not seem to have room for us, we have to find a way of making our own home in this world. We have to expand our definition of family to make space for all the differences of belief and levels of discomfort that still come with the terrain of being gay. Family means simply choosing one another every day: choosing to see one another and acknowledging that what each of us feels is absolutely real. Even when the plan falls apart, we can take a deep breath, stand still, and be with one another. And things will get better for all of us—parents and children—as my story shows.

I'm not sure I know what Kate Kendell had in mind when she told me I was "meant to do some great things." I know that it feels wonderful to finally be free—free to live a full life as my authentic self. That's my first message to anyone in a situation like mine: Yes, it will get better. It takes time, work, and courage, but it will get better.

I know too how important it is that I was able to find and use my voice—not only in my own defense but for the good of others. It has been difficult, even painful, to tell my story. But I know that being willing to stand up for myself in court made the State of Utah recognize the human and legal rights of gay teenagers. In Utah, and across the country, LGBT teenagers deserve to live full and safe lives under the protection of the law. We deserve to have a voice. We deserve to be protected from dangerous experimental "treatments" that promise to "cure" us. We deserve schools that are safe from bullying and harassment. We deserve a legal system that helps us when we need it.

Today, laws have changed and are changing for LGBT people around the country—even in places like Utah. Look at the huge strides this country has made in recognizing that marriage is a human right all committed couples should be able to enjoy. Marriage equality is a major achievement. But there is more work to do. I look forward to the day when equality is a fact of life for LGBT people of all ages, when there are no more LGBT teens sleeping on the streets or being bullied in schools, when no one looks at someone like me and imagines that she needs to be fixed or cured. Many state legislatures are now considering laws to end these "therapies" that claim to "cure" homosexuality. Maybe my story will help make these protections a reality.

I am sharing my story in the additional hope that no more LGBT teenagers will find themselves up against a wall—physically, emotionally, or spiritually.

And I am sharing my story in the hope everyone can know that what makes us different makes us strong.

Left to right: Jason Osmanski, Alex Cooper, and Paul Burke
in Portland, 2015.

ACKNOWLEDGMENTS

IT WAS A CHALLENGE telling the story of this extremely difficult period in my life. This book reflects my best effort to put together the pieces from my own memory, my journals, and court records in a way that stays true to the heart of the story. I have changed the names and identifying details of the people I grew up with in Victorville and the people I lived with in St. George to protect their privacy.

I want to thank Paul Burke, Brett Tolman, and everyone at Ray Quinney & Nebeker and in the legal community who helped with my case, and Paul especially, for helping me grow into my independence with advice on matters big and small; Kate Kendell and everyone at the National Center for Lesbian Rights, for reaching out to me when it really mattered; Joanna Brooks, for being more than a ghostwriter, but a friend as well; Jason Osmanski, for helping me tell my truth and learn to trust other people; Delsy Nielson, who risked her job for me, because she felt it was the right thing to do—you are a hero; Sandra, who was there not only for me but for every kid in need who came through the shelter; Ivey and Alex, who have been like family to me and Lina in Portland; Lina, for letting me love you; and finally, my parents—I am so grateful that we have come to the point where I can share my life with you and you are supportive.

RESOURCES FOR FAMILIES

I F YOU ARE A parent of an LGBT teenager, please visit the Family Acceptance Project at http://familyproject.sfsu.edu to find resources that support families who want their LGBT children to live safer, healthier lives. The site includes information in English, Spanish, and Chinese as well as materials specifically designed to support families of faith (like Mormon, or LDS, families) who find themselves in a difficult position between the doctrines of their church and the needs of their child. Family Acceptance Project staff have also published research on best practices for working with LGBT youth in the child welfare and criminal justice systems.

To join the nationwide movement to end misguided and dangerous efforts to "cure" or change gay young people, please support the National Center for Lesbian Rights' #BornPerfect campaign. Does your state protect gay teenagers? You can find out at the NCLR #BornPerfect website: http://www.nclrights.org/our-work/bornperfect/.

If you are an LGBT teenager who needs help, please visit The Trevor Project at http://www.thetrevorproject.org or call 1-866-488-7386. Trained volunteer counselors are available to text, chat, or talk twenty-four hours a day, seven days a week. The Trevor Project also offers resources for adults who work with LGBT youth at http://www.thetrevorproject.org/section/education-training-for-adults.